THE APOTHEOSIS
OF JANAAB' PAKAL

THE APOTHEOSIS OF JANAAB' PAKAL

SCIENCE, HISTORY, AND RELIGION AT CLASSIC MAYA PALENQUE

GERARDO ALDANA

UNIVERSITY PRESS *of* COLORADO

Gulf of Mexico

MEXICO

Kalak'mul

Tortuguero

Piedras Negras

.Waxaktun

Palenque

Yaxchilan   Tikal

BELIZE

Caribbean
Sea

Dos Pilas

Quirigua

HONDURAS

GUATEMALA

Copán

EL SALVADOR

0   100   200 km

Pacific Ocean

15370506

Published by the University Press of Colorado
5589 Arapahoe Avenue, Suite 206C
Boulder, Colorado 80303

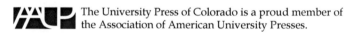 The University Press of Colorado is a proud member of
the Association of American University Presses.

The University Press of Colorado is a cooperative publishing enterprise supported, in part,
by Adams State College, Colorado State University, Fort Lewis College, Mesa State College,
Metropolitan State College of Denver, University of Colorado, University of Northern
Colorado, and Western State College of Colorado.

∞ The paper used in this publication meets the minimum requirements of the American
National Standard for Information Sciences — Permanence of Paper for Printed Library
Materials. ANSI Z39.48-1992

Library of Congress Cataloging-in-Publication Data

Aldana y Villalobos, Gerardo.
    The apotheosis of Janaab' Pakal : science, history, and religion at classic Maya Palenque /
Gerardo Aldana y Villalobos.
        p. cm. — (Mesoamerican worlds)
    Includes bibliographical references and index.
    ISBN 978-0-87081-866-0 (hardcover : alk. paper) — ISBN 978-1-60732-071-5 (pbk. : alk.
paper) — ISBN 978-1-60732-072-2 (e-book) 1. Palenque Site (Mexico) 2. Maya astronomy —
Mexico — Palenque (Chiapas) 3. Maya cosmology — Mexico — Palenque (Chiapas) 4. Mayan
languages — Writing. I. Title.
    F1435.3.C14A54 2007
    972'.75 — dc22

                                                                                              2007007082

Design by Daniel Pratt

20 19 18, 17 16 15 14 13 12 11   10 9 8 7 6 5 4 3 2 1

CONTENTS

FIGURES

FOREWORD

The study of Mesoamerican worlds has been enormously
enriched by breakthroughs in decipherment of Maya
writing during the last thirty years. As our understanding
of Maya writing has advanced, giving us insight into the
imaginations and rituals of Maya scribes and priests,
public and published debates about glyphs, gods, myth
and history, political order and social hierarchy, and
culture and ecology have spread with precision and
intensity. Maya studies has become a site for cooperation,
opposition, dialogue, and disputation. Gerardo Aldana's
*The Apotheosis of Janaab' Pakal: Science, History, and Religion
at Classic Maya Palenque* is an impressive example of these
interpretive styles.

   Working from the borderlands of the disciplines of

Chicana/o studies and indigenous studies, which supply him with a strong sense of accountability to the communities being studied and a deep concern for honoring the agency of indigenous cultures, Aldana interacts critically and cooperatively with the works of Linda Schele, Nikolai Grube, Simon Martin, Anthony Aveni, David Friedel, among many others. Central to his approach is a strong critique of what he considers to be a highly influential but thinly contextualized "scientific" approach to Maya religion, ritual, calendars, and politics. Maya astronomy and calendars can indeed be studied as scientific practices but always in relation to the social processes and political struggles that supported astronomical practices and shaped their usages. According to Aldana, adequate attention has not been paid to the ways Maya social realities and religious imaginations shaped and reflected calendrical patterns and innovative ritual practices. Aldana uses what he considers to be a new contextual method (in Maya studies at least) to reveal a new awareness of the "historically contextualized human agency" of Maya kings as well as a "more sophisticated job description" for Maya astronomers than has heretofore been realized in Maya studies. Aldana also calls for a more rigorous standard in the use of *our* science to understand *their* science, a practice that has concerned Anthony Aveni, among others, for a number of years. The results of this new rigor and social contextualization, Aldana hopes, will be something akin to a new revelation of the "intellectual history" of Maya people, incorporating a deeper sense of what their specific intellectual agendas were as practiced in kingship, interpolity relationships, genealogical world views, and esoteric calendrical visions.

The specific Maya site for this study is Palenque, and Aldana focuses on the ritual and political life of Janaab' Pakal and especially his son Kan B'ahlam, who, according to the author, used his scientific patronage as a ritual strategy to carry out his royal agenda of controlling local and international politics in pressured historical circumstances.

Aldana has used this social contextualization and astronumerology to discover a "specific creative spurt underlying some of the thematic coherence of the architecture and iconography of Late Classic Palenque." From there, he suggests that the 819-day count was part of a ritual language created to ensure that the ruling elite remained in power. Aldana argues that he has uncovered in the Classic period what others have found in the Postclassic—namely, a secret language utilized by the nobility to "restrict the size of the community with access to the throne."

There is much to admire in this inventive addition to our Mesoamerican Worlds series, which aims to lead us in a "journey into modern interdisciplinary research." Some years ago Paul Wheatley cautioned me about new approaches in the study of Mesoamerican cities and religion, stating: "Some scholars believe that by finding new data they are able to overthrow a long-standing theory or approach to society and culture. But the only thing that overthrows a theory is a better theory." It will be up to the readers to determine to what extent Aldana, through his work of cooperation and disputation, has achieved a new theory, or at least a new approach to the study of Maya kingship, calendars, and social history.

DAVÍD CARRASCO
GENERAL EDITOR

PREFACE

Classic Maya culture is best known in popular imagination for its purported "collapse" or for its equally
enigmatic astronomical acumen. Both cases contribute
substantially to modern mythology concerning native
cultures of the Western Hemisphere. Both have also been
significantly revised within scholarly circles over the last
fifty years, even if the revisions have still not made it into
the popular media. In this work, I attempt to contribute
explicitly to the revision of only the latter case, exploring
Maya astronomical knowledge through its historical
context.[1]

The means by which a historical treatment has become
possible is through the (continuing) decipherment of the
Maya hieroglyphic writing system. This decipherment,

maturing during the 1980s and 1990s, immediately generated scholarly and popular histories of the Classic Maya written as short vignettes by epigraphers focused on one or another anthropological problem (e.g., Martin and Grube 1995; Schele and Freidel 1990; Schele and Mathews 1998). Although rich in information and often groundbreaking in the presentation of new perspectives on an ancient people, such studies often leave the reader seeking a fuller treatment of the personalities and events so succinctly presented. In other words, there is a difference between history written by epigraphers and history written by historians — thus far the former has been the most abundant.[2]

This book constitutes an effort to satisfy some of that historical need in the popular and scholarly literature. Readers familiar with Mayanist literature, however, must be wondering why another manuscript on Palenque is warranted. It may seem unwise to generate yet another manuscript devoted to the site with Merle Greene Robertson's four volumes dedicated to Palenque's sculpture (1983, 1985a, 1985b, 1991), Linda Schele and David Freidel's chapter devoted to its dynastic history in the popular *A Forest of Kings* (1990), various parts of a book by Freidel, Schele, and Joy Parker inspired by Palenque inscriptions (1993), yet another chapter in a more recent popularization by Schele and Peter Mathews on Middle Classic Palenque (1998), and the exhaustive chronicle of royalty by Simon Martin and Nikolai Grube (2000).[3]

The majority of these studies, however, can be traced to a single scholar's reading of the hieroglyphic texts, despite the fact that the richness of its hieroglyphic record is perhaps the most distinguishing feature of Palenque. Moreover, although these specific readings were historically and historiographically very significant, the decipherment of the hieroglyphic script has gotten substantially more sophisticated since they were produced. Simply updating the reading of these texts — for example, to incorporate Stephen Houston and David Stuart's epigraphic revision of select passages (1996) — provides new insight into their context and so an incentive for "another" treatment of Palenque. But there is an even more powerful incentive — one coming from a long tradition of investigation into Classic Maya culture.

Herein I have taken up a concerted investigation into the astronomy patronized by Palenque's ancient rulers. Some of this astronomy has already been revealed — in particular by Floyd Lounsbury — over the last decades of the twentieth century. But this book demonstrates a much more extensive and nuanced role for astronomy than has been suspected previously. Specifically, this book recovers a calendrically based language used in the construction of some of Palenque's most important texts. We will find that the astronomical interests of Palenque's ancient rulers added another level of meaning to the hieroglyphic and architectural records—astronomical interests and applications that have only recently come to light (Aldana 2001b, 2004a).

Yet, in this work, I am cautious with the exploration of ancient indigenous astronomy. As spelled out explicitly in Chapter 2, this investigation is guided by the discipline of the history of science. That is, *because* there is an extensive hieroglyphic record for the Classic Maya, there is much more potential for contextualizing intellectual culture through a historical approach. Although there are many problems inherent in the interpretation of historical documents, these documents unequivocally contribute a level of insight significantly beyond that possible through statistical inference. For the Classic Maya case, therefore, I suggest simply that history of science methodologies possess an important potential for building on and challenging insights produced by other means.

The central theme, then, that ties this book together is the heretofore ill-understood Classic Maya calendric construct known as the "819-day count" (Aldana 2001b). By recovering the link between this count and its astronomical utility, I have been able to shed light on the religious and political purposes behind the buildings known collectively as the Cross Group at Palenque. Here, I present this research along with its extension and corroboration by other intellectual feats of Palenque's royal court. Together, they open up a new perspective on otherwise familiar aspects of Palenque and the Classic Maya world as a whole.

A further complication considered in this book is the degree to which recent moves in the social sciences and humanities have brought into focus scholars' need to consider their own subjectivity. Such a caveat is especially warranted in the interpretation of ancient cultures since available data is extremely partial. Indeed, one need not go far to see the concerns of contemporary societies read into ancient contexts (e.g., the potential collapse of civilizations by environmental degradation, by warfare, or by natural disaster). Of course, a recognition of subjectivity does not by itself credit or discredit any given piece of scholarship, but it does raise a pointed concern about method and theory.

The degree, then, to which the following chapters fit into traditional Euro-American–archaeological models for scholarship demonstrates an overlap in methods and tools. The degree to which it differs may be attributed to postprocessual, postcolonial, or poststructural influences, but from my perspective they more accurately reflect the concerns of an indigenous investigation into the past.

Such expressed goals present fantastic challenges. In attempting to address them, I was aided by a geographically and temporally diverse community of support. First, I must recognize the ancient Maya people, who for their own individual and collective reasons chose to maintain a hieroglyphic record. They have made it possible for us to tap into indigenous thoughts intended for indigenous audiences—how we interpret (or misinterpret) these thoughts is, of course, our own responsibility. Equally important are the living Maya and indigenous people of the Western Hemisphere. Their maintenance of identity and our ensuing responsibility to them challenges our work to be relevant on multiple levels. In particular, I must mention my debts to Pedro Pablo Chuc-Pech, Pantaleon García-Ramos, Salome Gutierrez, Juan Gonzalez, Rosalba Solis, their families and the communities of Popolá, Jocotán, Copán Ruinas, Piedra Labrada, Amamaloya, Soteapan, and Oventik. Due to economic, political, and historical factors, however, their knowledge, experiences and understandings remain local without—in part—the academic communities supporting broader dissemination.

As for my own pursuit of academic understanding and dissemination, I have been patiently mentored by my dissertation advisors William L. Fash and Owen Gingerich through and beyond the doctorate. My attempts to repay them have led me to join them in challenging and nourishing the minds of future generations of students. The dissertation itself also benefited greatly from the training and insights provided by John Womack, David Stuart, and A. I. Sabra. While performing much of the research behind this manuscript, I was aided in kind or in spirit by friends and colleagues in and around the Harvard community, especially Shannon Plank, Edward Jones-Imhotep, Robert Brain, Ann Blair, Sarah Jackson, Michael Gordin, Matthew Jones, David Kaiser, Mahalia Gayle, Karla Davis-Salazar, Craig Martin, Alan Maca, Marcelo Canuto, Lucia Henderson, William Saturno, and James Fitzsimmons. For pushing my archaeological engagement with the material and extending my academic friendships into the U.S. Southwest, I owe the Archaeological Research Institute at Arizona State University for the opportunity it afforded me to work with Arleyn Simon, Ian Robertson, George Cowgill, Oralia Cabrera, Joshua Watts, and Barbara Stark. I would be remiss in failing to recognize Stephen Houston and Joel Skidmore for their contributions as well.

Most recently, I have benefited immensely from my arrival at the California central coast and my reception by the various communities here. In its latest stages, my work has profited substantially from conversations with Inés Talamantez, Chela Sandoval, Jonathan X. Inda, Guisela Latorre, Rudy Busto, Stuart Smith, Nathan Henne, Amara Solari, Phoebe Hirsch, Julianne Cordero, Brian Clearwater, Luis Leon, Xuan Santos, Oscar Fierros, and James Matthew Kester.

Over the course of this project, institutional support came first and foremost from the Tozzer Library (and its irreplaceable staff) and from the David Rockefeller Center for Latin American Studies at Harvard University. My work also gained from the feedback generated by its presentation at the IV Mesa Redonda de Palenque, for which I owe thanks to the Instituto Nacional de Antropología y Historia de México. The highest quality images in this book were generously provided by Merle Greene Robertson and Justin Kerr. And, of course, I heartily thank Darrin Pratt for taking a chance on this manuscript and sticking with it to completion, Laura Furney for her meticulous and sensitive editing, and Dan Pratt for his patience and attention to visual design. Obviously, all of the above are to be exonerated of responsibility for any of the inaccuracies or outright errors contained in this book.

Contributing myriad other forms of support that must be mentioned here are the Aldana-Villalobos and the Torres-Lopez extended families. And, finally, the publication of this book gives me the opportunity to recognize, however insufficiently, the support provided by the three people for whom I get out of bed every morning—literally and figuratively—my ux juntanoob: Cita, Lulu, and Seri.

NOTES

1. I do hope, however, that the work will contribute *implicitly* in other ways.

2. Of course there are also limitations on histories written by historians with only some epigraphic training. Each approach offers valuable yet different contributions to the field.

3. Also, all major introductions to Maya culture contain a section on Palenque. Moreover, the Pre-Columbian Art Research Institute maintains an excellent Web site (www.mesoweb.com) devoted to the archaeological site along with other topics of concern to Maya studies.

ORTHOGRAPHY

In this book, I have adopted the orthography standardized by the Academia de Lenguas Mayas de Guatemala (ALMG). For the most part, this orthography has the effect of treating the alphabet as though it were Spanish. Notable distinctions in pronunciation from English, therefore, are listed below:

a — as *a* in *father*
e — as *e* in *set*
h — soft aspiration
i — as *e* in *seen*
j — as *h* in *house*
o — as *o* in *omega*
u — as *oo* in *oops*

A second unfamiliar sound comes from the use of the glottal stop in Mayan languages, indicated by an apostrophe. Vowels may be glottalized as well as the consonants *b, k, p,* and *t*. Also, *ch* and *tz* are considered single "letters," and either of these may be glottalized as well.

NAMES

Most of the contemporary names of Classic Maya cities were given to them by later indigenous inhabitants of the region or by the scholars who have come upon their ruins. In a number of cases, epigraphers have been able to read the original names of these cities. When these readings are secure, I use them rather than the more familiar ones. Both are used in this book, although in distinct contexts. In the main text, I use archaeological site names, but in translations of quoted hieroglyphic passages I retain the original place names. Table N.1 gives the hieroglyphic names of the cities referred to in this book along with their commonly recognized names.

Another note of clarification is required for the treatment of the names of rulers. When they were first

TABLE N.1: List of Maya city names in ancient and modern times

Hieroglyphic Name	Modern Name
B'aakal	Palenque or Tortuguero
Kan	Kalak'mul
Mutul	Tikal or Dos Pilas
Pa'chan	Yaxchilan
Yokib	Piedras Negras

TABLE N.2: List of Maya rulers' names

Name used here[1]	Name(s) used elsewhere
Janaab' Pakal	Pacal, Pakal
Kan B'ahlam	Chan Bahlum
K'an Joy Chitam	Kan Hok' Chitam, Kan Xul
Ahkal Mo' Naab'	Akul Anab, Chacaal
Ix Muwaan Mat	Lady Beastie, Na Mat Muwan
Nuun Ujol Chaak	Nun Bak Chak, Shield Skull
Yax Nuun Ayiin	Curl Nose, Curl Snout
Waxaklajuun Ub'aah K'awiil	18 Rabbit
Jasaw Chan K'awiil	Ah Cacao
Ix Yohl Ik'nal	Ix Kan Ik', Ix K'anal Ik'nal
Aj Ne' Ohl Mat	Ac Kan, Ah Lawal Mat
Ix Tz'aak Ajaw	Na Tz'ak Ajaw
B'alaj Chan K'awiil	Flint Sky God K

1. These follow the spelling conventions of Martin and Grube (2000), who have compiled a tremendous list of Classic Maya royalty.

identified (and before their names were deciphered), rulers were commonly given nicknames. Some that have found their way into the greater literature are 18 Rabbit of Copán and Curl Nose of Tikal. In other cases, the names have been deciphered and scholars have translated the Maya names into English, e.g. Bird Jaguar of Yaxchilan. I avoid both of these practices (should we translate Johnson into Spanish as Hijo de Juan?) and use either the deciphered name or the number of the ruler in its dynastic count. Thus, "18 Rabbit" is here "Waxaklajuun Ub'aah K'awiil" or "Copán Ruler 13," "Curl Nose" is "Yax Nuun Ayiin" or "Tikal Ruler 11," and "Bird Jaguar (IV)" is "Yaxun Balam (IV)" or "Yaxchilan Ruler 13."

CALENDRICS

Contrary to popular belief, the Maya may not have "invented zero." Rather, the Maya borrowed their numeral and calendric systems from the earlier Isthmusian tradition (Epi-Olmec), which left several examples of the basic components. In both cases, Mesoamerican scribes worked with a base-twenty number system comprising zero markers (shells), dots (beans), and bars (sticks). Each dot held a value of one, each bar a value of five dots. Depending on the context, scribes used a strict positional notation or they affixed coefficients (0–19) to the units they represented (see Figure C.1). In the preponderance of cases during the Classic period, Maya scribes used these coefficients for the Long Count.

FIGURE C.1: *A sequence of dates in the Long Count and Calendar Round. 9.9.2.4.8 5 Lamat 1 Mol. Twelve days later, it happened, 4 Ajaw 13 Mol. Zero days, and one winal later [it is] 11 Ajaw 13 Ch'en.*

The Long Count may be conceptualized as an odometer of days. Each day adds a unit to the lowest register, and as each register fills up, the count carries forward into the next higher register. In order to facilitate calendric computations, the Long Count did not follow a strictly vigesimal format (i.e., it is not strictly base twenty). Instead, Maya scribes counted days according to the following units:

1 *bak'tun*	=	20 *k'atun* (= 144,000 days)
1 *k'atun*	=	20 *tun* (= 7,200 days)
1 *tun*	=	18 *winal* (= 360 days)
1 *winal*	=	20 *k'in* (= 20 days)
1 *k'in*	=	1 day

The deviation from a strict vigesimal system is located in the accumulation of winals, which reaches a maximum of seventeen (the eighteenth rolling over into the next register). It may be that this deviation was introduced in order to facilitate astronomical computations since eighteen winal make up an interval precisely between twelve lunar months (355 days) and a solar year (365 days).

The standard notation that modern scholars have developed for writing a Long Count date takes the form *bak'tun.k'atun.tun.winal.k'in*, e.g., 9.9.2.4.8.[1] A few exceptions in the Classic period inscriptions—a couple of which will be discussed in Chapter 3—record the next one or more higher units, for example, *pik'tun* = 20 *bak'tun*; *kalabtun* = 20 *pik'tun*.

The two other principal components of the Maya (and Isthmusian) calendar are the *chol qiij* and the *haab'*.[2] The *chol qiij* (literally, the "ordering of days" in K'iche') consists of the numbers one through thirteen affixed to twenty different day signs, making for a 260-day

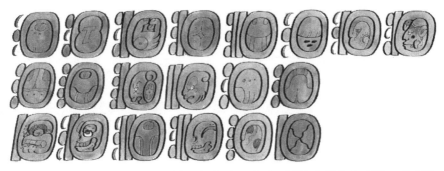

FIGURE C.2: *Daily progression of the* chol qiij: *1 Imix, 2 Ik', 3 Ak'bal, 4 K'an, 5 Chik-chan, 6 Kimi, 7 Manik, 8 Lamat, 9 Muluk, 10 Ok, 11 Chuwen, 12 Eb, 13 Ben, 1 Ix, 2 Men, 3 Kib, 4 Kaban, 5 Etz'nab, 6 Kawak, 7 Ajaw.*

count. The names of the day signs are Imix, Ik', Ak'bal, K'an, Chikchan, Kimi, Manik, Lamat, Muluk, Ok, Chuwen, Eb, Ben, Ix, Men, Kib, Kaban, Etz'nab, Kawak, and Ajaw. A sequence of days in the *chol qiij* would then proceed as in Figure C.2.

The *haab'* was a 365-day approximation to the solar year. It was composed of eighteen 20-day "months" and one 5-day "month." Numbering went from 0 to 19 for each of Pop, Wo, Sip, Zotz', Tzek, Xul, Yaxk'in, Mol, Ch'en, Yax, Sak, Kej, Mak, K'ank'in, Muwaan, Pax, K'ayab, and Kumk'u, and from 0 to 4 for Wayeb (see Figure C.3). Collectively, the *chol qiij* and the *haab'* form the Calendar Round, which repeats every 18,980 days. This dating system (without the Long Count) was common to all of Mesoamerica.

Within a Maya hieroglyphic inscription, Long Count dates with their Calendar Rounds were generally reserved for the opening paragraph. Each ensuing date was listed only as a Calendar Round with a distance number (DN) anchoring it in the Long Count. As an example, we might have "9.9.2.4.8 5 Lamat 1 Mol Janaab' Pakal was seated as king. Then, 12 k'in, 13 winal, 17 tun later, it came to pass, the end of the k'atun, 1 Ajaw 8 K'ayab," where the Long Count 9.10.0.0.0 is omitted but unequivocally the date corresponding to the following Calendar Round.

9.9.2.4.8	5 Lamat 1 Mol
+ 17.13.12	
= 9.10.0.0.0	1 Ajaw 8 K'ayab

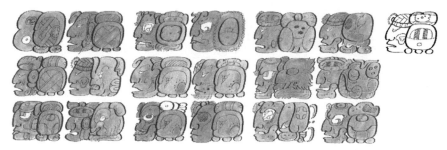

FIGURE C.3: *A sequence of 21-day intervals through the* haab': *0 Pop, 1 Wo, 2 Sip, 3 Zotz', 4 Tzek, 5 Xul, 6 Yaxk'in, 7 Mol, 8 Ch'en, 9 Yax, 10 Sak, 11 Kej, 12 Mak, 13 K'ank'in, 14 Muwaan, 15 Pax, 16 K'ayab, 17 Kumk'u; then after six days, and two days before the beginning of the following year, the last glyph represents 3 Wayeb.*

The Long Count, the Calendar Round, and the distance number were the three most fundamental parts of the Maya calendar, but there were others. Sandwiched between the two parts of the Calendar Round, for example, scribes often included what has come to be known as the "Supplementary Series." The two most widely and frequently utilized components of the Supplementary Series were the Lords of the Night and the Lunar Series (Aveni 2001:155–163; Lounsbury 1978:767). Other components show up only in geographically or temporally restricted zones, such as the "819-day count" — the focus of this book — which is restricted to the south and west of Maya lands and shows up in the Late Classic.

NOTES

1. In the 1930s, John Teeple, however, used the *tun* as the basic unit of the count and so wrote the sequence using dashes rather than periods to separate the three smallest units: *bak'tun.k'atun.tun-winal-k'in.*

2. This treatment follows Teeple's in the sense that the entire construct is considered the Maya calendar, with each element construed as a "count" (1931). Also, I use the term *chol qiij* rather than the more common *tzolkin*, since the former is used by contemporary daykeepers (the K'iche) in Guatemala.

BOX C.1: SERPENT NUMBERS IN THE DRESDEN CODEX

There was no clear consensus on the interpretation of the Serpent Numbers in the Dresden Codex (pages 61–73) while Eric Thompson and Floyd Lounsbury studied them in the 1970s, nor has one developed since then. A number of interesting patterns, however, have been accepted by virtually everyone. These include (1) a strong basis in multiples of 7 and 13; (2) coverage of vast spans of time (over 30,000 years); and (3) a mythical/astronomical/calendric inspiration. Perhaps least controversial is the numerology since the Serpent Numbers sit adjacent to a table of multiples of 91 (= 7 × 13). Moreover, the almanac that follows is based on 7 × 260 (= 7 × 13 × 20 = 5 × 364), which naturally shows up as the fifth entry in the multiplication table. And 364, as we will see, was a handy computational number for Maya computers (Lounsbury 1978:772–773; Thompson 1972:81). Bringing these patterns back to the Serpent Numbers, we find that all of the Ring Number–based Long Counts as written are even multiples of 13 (8.16.15.16.1, 8.16.14.15.4, 8.11.8.7.0, 8.16.3.13.0, 10.13.13.3.2, and 10.8.3.16.4). As for the Serpent Numbers themselves, depending on the method used to "read" them, either five or seven out of eight of them are divisible by 13 with remainders of 7. Of course with the number 13, it may simply be that Maya calendar specialists were looking to preserve the same *chol qiij* coefficient as they moved through immense spaces of time, but given the cosmological associations of 13 and 7, we must leave open the possibility of broader motivations. Either way, the Serpent Numbers, along with the various tables of multiples in the Dresden Codex, serve as explicit evidence for the concerted interest in numerology and calendrics within elite Maya intellectual culture.

FIGURE C.4: *Serpent Numbers from page 61 of the Dresden Codex*

HIEROGLYPHIC SCRIPT

I should also note here certain conventions that have come from the decipherment of the hieroglyphs (glyphs). First of all, Maya scribes generally ordered texts as pairs of columns in which the reading order is top to bottom and left to right. The square elements filling these columns and rows are termed *glyph blocks*. Each glyph block may be composed of up to four types of elements: numerals, calendric units, phonetic glyphs, or logographic glyphs. Phonetic glyphs are composed of consonant-vowel phonemes (e.g., *le, b'i,* and *k'a*) or pure vowel elements (e.g., *a, i,* and *o*). Logographic glyphs are those elements that represent entire words (e.g., *chak, ek',* and *b'ahlam*). When a text is transcribed according to the ALMG orthography, phonetic elements are written in lowercase script and logographs in complete upper case. When a glyph is undeciphered, or at least unknown by me, I transcribe it as a question mark.

In this book, I have used two forms of representation for hieroglyphic texts: published archaeological illustrations showing the text in its iconographic context and my own script illustrations of the text. In most cases, the original texts were carved into stone. Because of erosion or the ambiguity created by the original artist's style, rendering them as line drawings necessarily introduces a degree of interpretation. These drawings, however ambiguously rendered, are historical texts, and this book quotes from them extensively. To make this anchoring clear, I have redrawn numerous passages in my own hieroglyphic hand to editorially treat these quotes as such throughout the book.[1] This approach also serves the purpose of reminding the reader that history is interpretation, and although intimately tied to the scholarship in the field, in the end these readings are my own and may differ from others. Such is the nature of humanities-based inquiry.[2]

This information should provide a sufficient base for the reader unfamiliar with such matters to get through the text. There are now several treatments available that provide much more extensive developments (Coe 1992; Coe and Van Stone 2001; Houston, Chinchilla Mazariegos, and Stuart 2000a; Wichmann 2004).

NOTES

1. Hieroglyphic quotes are referenced by column and row relative to their position in the original inscription, for example, (A1–B4) refers to the glyph blocks in columns A and B, from rows 1 through 4.

2. See also the Introduction, pages 12–13.

INTRODUCTION

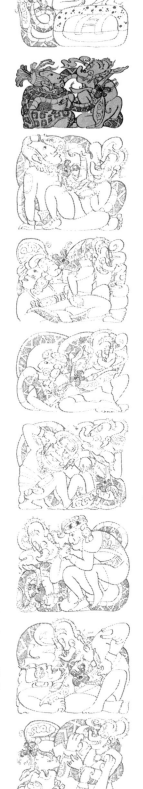

Just before dawn, a Maya king sat ready with his troops, awaiting the sighting of Venus as morning star before consenting to engage his enemy in warfare—or so a number of studies would have us believe. According to conventional interpretations, Chak Ek' (the Maya name for Venus) would have to show his celestial face in order to generate an omen favorable for entering battle. Thus, the astronomer's grave responsibility was to make accurate predictions of Chak Ek's visibility so that his king and the king's army would not have arisen early for nothing.

Such a practice—that of preparing for what recent studies have called the "star war"—represents a type of labor often attributed to the ancient Maya astronomer.

Indeed, numerous studies have attempted to show that ancient Maya kings set their political and ritual events according to celestial periodicities (Aveni and Hotaling 1994; Closs 1994; Dütting 1985; Martin 1996; Schele and Freidel 1990; Tate 1985; against the "star war" interpretation, see Aldana 2001b, 2005a). These studies begin by choosing a correlation between the Christian calendar and the Maya Long Count.[1] They then attempt to reconstruct the night skies observable to the ancient kings on the dates of the recorded ceremonies or events. Although straightforward in approach, these studies produce results that cannot be accepted unequivocally at least until a day-for-day calendar correlation is proven beyond a reasonable doubt. Several competing studies, however, show that the validity of the calendar correlation most often invoked is still in question.[2] At some level, then, we must be wary of the specific findings and eventual interpretations produced by methodologies that are utterly dependent on the accuracy of the calendar correlation utilized.[3]

A different approach to revealing the work of the ancient Maya astronomer avoids the calendar correlation entirely. Popular during the early twentieth century when computers were not available to reproduce hypothetical historical night skies (making the search for correlations between astronomical events and historical records excruciatingly tedious), this method holds the potential for more stable interpretations since the results would not change with a change in calendar correlation. In the 1930s, John Teeple (1931) used this method effectively to show interesting patterns within the lunar records of the Classic period. Almost fifty years later, Floyd Lounsbury (1980) used a similar approach to reveal an astronomical component to hieroglyphic treatments of mythology. Both of these studies (covered in detail in Chapters 2, 3, and 4) suggest a more sophisticated job description for ancient Maya astronomers by revealing their concern with mythology and political rhetoric alongside their purported appointment-making duties. Moreover, Teeple's and Lounsbury's studies will remain relevant regardless of any future calendar correlation revisions.

Despite the value of these studies, they, too, have left out what I consider to be a critical aspect of analysis. Like many others, they rarely refer to specific historical individuals or their social, religious, and political contexts with regard to the theories proposed. At some level, these omissions may result from the relative scarcity of scholars trained both to read the hieroglyphic inscriptions and to understand the ancient practice of astronomy. On another level, however, the oversight has been methodologically intentional, following an effort to create direct associations between hieroglyphic records and natural phenomena. Rhetorically, such an approach might be considered a revelation of the *science* of astronomy, intentionally leaving out the human agents who enacted it, but in this book I take precisely the opposite approach.

In the pages that follow, I argue for a very specific role of astronomy to the reign of K'inich Kan B'ahlam, tenth[4] ruler of a Classic Maya city then known as B'aakal (now known as Palenque). In doing so, I take an approach inspired by recent studies in the history of circum-Mediterranean-derivative (cMd) science.[5] These studies demonstrate that the practice of science and the developments that derive therefrom are best understood by examining the historical context — physical, political, social, religious, and economic — in which they were enmeshed. The point is only accentuated, I argue, because we still are coming to an understanding of the type of sciences under study. That is, the discipline of archaeology has revealed much about the social structure and general development of Maya culture, but we are only just beginning to use hieroglyphic decipherment to understand the intellectual history of these people.

Through a close reading of several hieroglyphic texts from Palenque, I work through the recovery of a calendric and astronomical development to unpack the broader intellectual agenda of a set of historical Classic Maya rulers. This scientific lens allows for the recognition of a consistent message delivered by three specific kings and expressed in architecture, art, and science for their contemporary commoner, noble, and royal audiences. In turn, this focused study reveals two larger themes within Maya civilization. First, examination of this royal agenda reveals the Classic Maya kings' efforts to maintain and exercise power on both local and international levels. Second, the scientific development reveals a secret language utilized by the nobility to restrict the size of the community with access to the throne. Such a language has already been well documented for Postclassic and Postcontact times; this book extends the practice backward at least to the Late Classic—albeit in a newly recognized form that I call K'awiilil Zuyua.[6] In order to begin this treatment of the history of Palenque and the decipherment of the enigmatic 819-day count, we must first address the broader context surrounding such an endeavor.

SOME CLASSIC MAYA HISTORIOGRAPHY

Janaab' Pakal is probably the best-known of the ancient Maya kings.[7] The Mexican archaeologist Alberto Ruz-Lhuiller uncovered his sarcophagus in 1952, setting off a still-active public fascination with the archaeological site in eastern Chiapas, Mexico, known as Palenque (see Figure 0.1). Janaab' Pakal's achievements—and their significance to his successors—form the nucleus of this study. Yet Janaab' Pakal was only one of more than fourteen rulers of this ancient city and one of some hundreds of men and women who directed Maya cities as *ajawtahk* over the more than 600-year Classic period.[8] The difference, however, between what contemporary scholars know about Janaab' Pakal and his peers and what Ruz understood in the 1950s has everything to do with the maturation of Maya hieroglyphic script decipherment during the 1980s and 1990s.

Although few dispute that Ruz and others, notably the U.S. archaeologist Gordon Willey, transformed our appreciation of Classic Maya culture by turning their attention to non-royal lives, the decipherment of Maya hieroglyphic writing has provided the most transformative window into ancient Mesoamerican society. The texts produced by ancient Maya scribes for the ruling elite have given us access to indigenous thoughts recorded for indigenous audiences. On the most practical level, this information allows epigraphers to recover Classic Maya political structures and records of the events that maintained them. Indeed, scholars have trained their attention on this material since the 1980s, some of which will be reviewed in this chapter.[9] Yet the decipherment also allows for a substantially more subtle investigation into Classic Maya thought and expression. Herein lies the value of the historical endeavor. Through the subtlety and detail of a focused historical case study, we gain a vista into the political and religious world of the ancient Maya as they intended to preserve it.

FIGURE 0.1: *Site map of Palenque*

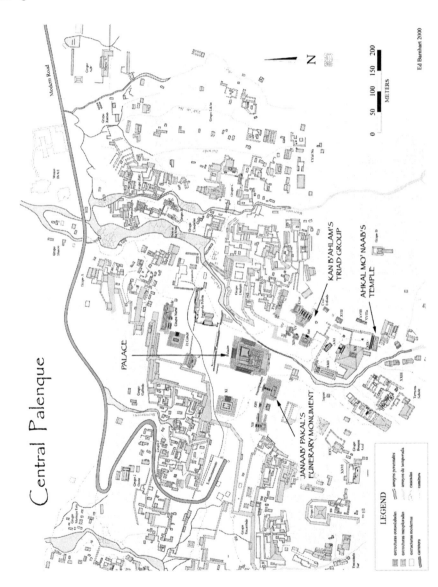

As a cultural body, the Classic Maya thrived from about A.D. 250 to 900 in the region of Mesoamerica that has now been split up into the Mexican states of Yucatán, Campeche, Quintana Roo, and Chiapas and the countries of Belize, Guatemala, and parts of Honduras and El Salvador (see Frontispiece). As a subgroup of larger Mesoamerica, the Classic Maya maintained one of only two phonetically based writing systems upon which the Maya elite relied for political, economic, and religious legitimation.[10]

Key in deciphering this hieroglyphic script was Heinrich Berlin's (1958) recognition of a glyphic compound that had a structure and site distribution, suggesting it served as an identifier of Classic Maya cities. Uncomfortable with calling this glyphic compound the "name" of a given city, Berlin instead referred to it as an *Emblem Glyph*[11] (see Figure 0.1). Historiographically, the acceptance of the Emblem Glyphs' significance forced a shift in the basic interpretation of Maya hieroglyphic writing—namely, that their content did at some level reflect mundane, political interests.[12]

Since Berlin's work in the 1950s, epigraphers have been able to separate the Emblem Glyph compound into its three basic elements.[13] The main sign indeed may be considered the name of the polity, but the framing elements are read *k'ujul* ("holy"[14]) and *ajaw* ("ruler"), such that the Emblem Glyph for Palenque would have been read as "K'ujul B'aakal Ajaw," or "holy lord of Palenque." The implications arising from this reading are at least twofold. For one, in Classic Maya cities, politics and religion were not separated. Also, we now recognize that the carved human figures that accompanied the hieroglyphic inscriptions, especially on public monuments, are portraits of precisely the *ajawtahk* for those particular cities (see Figure 0.2).

Beyond representing the protagonists of the iconography and inscriptions, the content of the texts tells us that more often than not these *ajawtahk* were genealogically related. Most frequently, the throne was passed from father to son, although brothers sometimes succeeded brothers and nobles (including women) not within the immediate ruling family occasionally came to power in the forging of alliances, both local and international (Ardren 2002; McAnany 1995:24–26).[15] In each case, accession to power was recorded as *chumwan ti ajawlel* ("becomes seated into rulership"), *k'alaw ju'un tu b'aah* ("s/he ties the headband

FIGURE 0.2: *Copán Stela H bearing an image of Waxaklajuun Ub'aah K'awiil dressed as the Maize God*

FIGURE 0.3: Various aspects of accession for Maya *ajawtahk*: (a) *k'aljiiy sak ju'un*; (b) *chumlaj ta ajawlel*; and (c) *ch'am k'awiil*

on oneself"), or *ch'amaw k'awiil* ("s/he receives k'awiil") (see Figure 0.3). Any one of these phrases signified the ruler's new place within the royal dynasty.

As elaborated thus far, Classic Maya political organization does not appear radically different from what we understand of Renaissance European or pre-Imperial Chinese political organization—kings ruling various lands tied together within dynasties. The parallel remains strong as we consider both intra- and inter-polity relationships. Namely, dynasties were part of larger noble classes forming the elite society of ancient Maya cities. Here again, the hieroglyphic texts are indispensable in giving us the names of various titles held by the non-ruling elite. Marc Zender's recent dissertation (2004) has shed substantial light on these titles, but common readings in the literature include, for example, *sajal* ("feared") as a title for a military leader (Schele and Mathews 1998:339n44). *Aj k'ujuun, aj tz'iib,* and *itz'aat,* on the other hand, are titles that refer to learned ones and artists (Coe and Kerr 1998:89–101; Jackson and Stuart 2001). In martial or artistic cases, the titles reflected membership in a royal court, which recently has been the subject of serious investigation both archaeologically and epigraphically (Inomata and Houston 2001; Martin and Grube 1995).

Inter-polity relationships are a second major theme of the hieroglyphic texts. Here the reader confronts connections characterized by three terms: *yajaw, yichnal,* and *u kab'ijiiy.* The first is simply the possessed form of the term for "ruler," *y-ajaw* ("the ruler belonging to"). This title signifies that the nobleman using it, the *yajaw,* is subject to another hierarchically superior political agent. Smaller cities, for example, were often led by "rulers" who were the *yajawtahk* of larger, more powerful cities (Martin and Grube 1995). The two other terms reflect similar relationships but in more oblique fashion. *Yichnal,* for instance, translates as "in the presence of." Such a record might give prestige or recognition to either party and does not necessarily reflect a hierarchical relationship. The last phrase, *u kab'ijiiy* ("under the auspices of"), does carry with it a relative ranking. Here, the secondary polity acts *u kab'ijiiy* a larger polity — often in matters of war (Martin and Grube 1995).

Although not preserved within the inscriptions recovered thus far, trade tied the cities to each other and maintained connections throughout larger Mesoamerica. Elite goods, such as quetzal feathers, jade, and obsidian, were traded over large distances. Many of these trade relationships remained friendly, others undoubtedly induced conflict, and one is truly enigmatic. The connections between the great city of Teotihuacan and the Classic Maya have fascinated scholars for decades and have again come to the forefront of Mesoamerican research.[16] The historical record within hieroglyphic texts has already radically transformed our understanding of this relationship (Aldana 2003b; Braswell 2003; Harrison 1999:82–91; Stuart 2000a), and the next set of archaeological findings will further elucidate precisely what types of social linkages existed between these two distinct cultural groups.

There is no question that trade was a particularly important factor in the development of Palenque. At the western entrance to the Maya region and just off the Usumacinta River — a major trade route — Palenque held a powerful geographic position throughout the Classic period. We will see that such a position was also very likely the cause of conflict with their Usumacinta neighbors, such as Piedras Negras and Yaxchilan. We will also see that the influence of Teotihuacan reached even into the affairs of Late Classic Palenque.

Finally, and for this manuscript of great import, the hieroglyphic inscriptions record many of the rituals conducted by Classic Maya *ajawtahk* in the maintenance of their authority. The most common of these rituals (recoverable from the surviving record) derived from Classic Maya calendrics and formed the basis of Classic Maya monumental culture (Justeson and Mathews 1983). After *ajawtahk* were seated, for example, their tenures were validated through the performance of a *k'altun* ("stone binding") or *chumtun* ("stone seating") at the next major period end, either the end of a thirteenth *tun* or the end of a *k'atun*[17] (Schele and Mathews 1991). We will see some of these records explicitly in Chapter 4 and how they characterize "normalcy" in Classic Maya society. Although Palenque *ajawtahk* were anomalous in not erecting stelae for each major period end, hieroglyphic records in other forms at the site make it clear that the rituals were still performed.

Not entirely dissociated from these *k'altuns,* hieroglyphic inscriptions also record rituals of the maintenance of each Maya polity's cosmos. For the Maya, the cosmos consisted of three realms.[18] The region below the surface of the earth was the Underworld. The region above the reach of the highest trees constituted the Upperworld. And the region in between was, appropriately, the Middleworld. All three levels of the cosmos were inhabited by different communities. Most members of these communities made a single realm their permanent home, but some members had the ability to move between realms or at least communicate across their borders (Aldana 2005b).

One such border was breached upon death. A person's dead body was placed below the surface of the earth such that a part of that person entered the community of the Underworld. Through the enacting of certain rituals, members of the Middleworld (the living) were able to communicate with their deceased ancestors (Klein et al. 2002; McAnany 1995:29; Schele and Miller 1986:175–185). As explicated by Patricia McAnany, elite state religion was, then, a vast elaboration on a more ancient domestic spirituality (1995:53). Namely, monumental pyramids were conceptualized as mountains, extending this cosmological realm such that deceased rulers placed therein were entering a ritually controlled region of the Underworld. Moreover, the temples atop these pyramids functioned as caves, allowing for communication with deceased rulers and other members of the Underworld community (Houston 1996).

A portal provided the means by which this communication occurred, allowing access to the "center/heart" of a ritual space; often hieroglyphic inscriptions use the phrase *tan yohl ch'en* ("at/in front of the center of the cave") to describe the location of the ritual. Such usage directly parallels Evon Vogt's ethnographic research with Tzotzil Maya during the 1960s. Vogt (1976:6) describes Christian crosses as "doorways" that allow for communication as the performer kneels "in front" of the portal — *tan yohl witz* ("in front of the heart of the mountain").[19] Formalized communication through this portal, and thus between cosmological communities, constituted a fundamental aspect of Maya royal ritual.

To complicate cosmographical matters, it appears that the Maya saw the night sky as a reflection of the Underworld. When full, the moon took the character of the Jaguar God of the Underworld — the ruling celestial body, twin of the Sun. Also, God L, one of the highest ranking lords of the Underworld, usually possessed a numbered *chan* ("sky") glyph in his headdress.[20] Additionally, the Milky Way was seen as a great starry caiman, twin reflection of the crocodile forming the earth's back (Aldana 2001b; Stuart 1995a, 2003). Through this cosmic relationship, the Maya gained insight into the activities occurring within the Underworld by increasing their understanding of the inhabitants of the night sky — a strong impetus for developing an interest in astronomy.[21]

THEORETICAL CONSIDERATIONS

So the hieroglyphic record has already done much to illuminate the lives of the ancient Maya, and the epigraphic recovery of this information is both important and exciting. Yet there is even more that can be learned from this record. As noted by Stephen Houston as early as 1993, there is a simple matter of disciplinary expertise that holds potential for providing further insight into Classic Maya history.

Namely, it is one endeavor to linguistically and sociologically extract information from a set of hieroglyphic records; it is another to treat them historically. This observation is not trivial. Especially when taking into account recent theoretical work on the social maintenance of language (Bourdieu 1977; Latour 1987; Lyotard 1993; Mignolo 2003; Sandoval 2000), the hieroglyphic texts allow for a wide range of intellectual inquiry into ancient Maya experiences. Moreover, although several anthropologists (often epigraphers) have developed an interest in Maya history (see Grube 1996; Houston 1993; Martin 1996; Martin and Grube 1995, 2000; Stuart 2000a) and although historians have appealed to a poststructural revelation of agency among Precontact indigenous people (see Restall 1998; Clendinnen 1987), the two agendas rarely come together.

Furthermore, historians readily acknowledge that their own perspectives prevent them from ever objectively reconstructing historical events but that the awareness of this limitation is what allows for valuable scholarship (Novick 1988). Positioned within the disciplines of Chicana/o and Indigenous Studies, my own work is not guided by a "salutary nonsense"[22] but instead recognizes that all scholarship is deeply embedded within a cultural and material context consumed and interpreted by myriad public communities. The choices regarding to which communities one seeks to be accountable constitute a choice of aesthetic. My work must meet the rigors of the academic community to be considered acceptable, but it also must take into account those communities that are implicitly affected by its publication. Within Ethnic Studies, then, *accountability* may be seen as an alternate constraining mechanism to the *objectivity* of cMd scholarship. Furthermore, I suggest that accountability may provide an even more rigorous check than objectivity alone. Examples may be readily found, but one of the most glaring comes from the scholarship on Aztec culture.

In 1977, Michael Harner proposed that residents of Tenochtitlan, the capital of the Aztec Triple Alliance, practiced cannibalism in order to compensate for a diet deficient in protein. This article was published by *American Ethnologist* and soon caused controversy (Hunn 1982; Ortiz de Montellano 1978; Price 1978). My point here is not about the arguments back and forth, especially since scholars (and, more importantly, indigenous people of the Western Hemisphere) have recognized for some time that the "three sisters" (corn, beans, and squash) are sufficient to maintain life without supplemental protein. Instead, I suggest that Harner's argument was perfectly acceptable under the framework of objectivity as a salutary nonsense, because he may easily claim to have been uninfluenced by the need to portray the Aztecs in a certain way and so only "assessed the data" (however it may have been collected). But clearly his article would not have been acceptable under the guidance of an accountability to communities other than those academic. That is, the argument only stands if one is predisposed to consider the "barbarity" or "savageness" of the Aztecs—an association that has existed in cMd cultural imaginaries since being constructed by sixteenth-century Spaniards.[23] In this and myriad other ways, appeals to objectivity have perpetuated inaccurate stereotypes and silenced dissenting voices inside and outside the academy. I suggest that an alternate choice of aesthetic would have had Harner concerned with the potential influence of this construction on his own "hypothesis" and so held him to a more rigorous standard.

Of course, accountability might be manipulated or otherwise subverted in many of the same ways as objectivity. For one, taking into account the consuming community might lead one to an overly sympathetic portrayal—perhaps even an outright attempt to create a "more positive" image than the data bear out. Within a postmodern context, however, such inability to define a single "correct" aesthetic is unavoidable. The most one can hope for is that any given scholar approaches his/her data with an intellectual honesty and a self-critical eye, regardless of methodological perspective, *and* openly recognizes the ramifications of his/her assumptions. Then, accountability is guided by the aesthetic a given scholar wishes to follow.

For the work presented here, my own sense of accountability— my guiding aesthetic—predominantly means three things: (1) I have avoided any gratuitous appeal to human sacrifice or shamanism as ready crutches that would play to the "mysterious" character of the ancient Maya within contemporary American cultural imaginaries; (2) I have emphasized historically contextualized human agency over Structuralist determinacy; and (3) I include ancient Maya scribes in my imagined audience.[24]

I have aimed thusly to develop an accountable historical context that will stage the treatment of Classic Maya intellectual inquiry. As a visual clue to recognizing this positioning, I have included two types of illustrations in this book. The first set is the standard-format archaeological drawings graciously provided by Merle Greene Robertson; the second was drawn in my own hand, pointing toward the filter impossible to remove in the realm of interpretation.

SCIENCE AT PALENQUE

As for the more specific task of considering an ancient science, we must take into account recent developments in the history of science that have demonstrated a need for viewing science as a social enterprise (e.g., Biagioli 1999; Latour 1987; Shapin and Schaffer 1985). The situation is now decidedly complex. We are attempting here to retrieve both the historical context for intellectual activity and the intellectual activity itself, which is part of the fabric of the original context. Although this observation complicates matters, it also provides us with a robust check on our work. We can no longer consider, for example, the practices of astronomy without considering the social processes supporting them or the historical events of which they were a part. As will be treated further in Chapter 2, astronomy, history, politics, and religion all must be taken together as responding to and influenced by common sociological pressures mediated by individual choice.

To contemporary historians of science, that the aforementioned disciplines both respond to and are influenced by sociological pressures and individual choice is a fundamental principle of investigation and might be considered obvious. Some of the reasons I make this point here—and a suggestion as to why the first attempt at a history of Classic Maya astronomy was not attempted until 2001 (Aldana 2001b)—can be found in the historiography in Chapter 2.[25] Here it is sufficient to note that when this approach is applied to the so-called 819-day count, two major themes emerge from Palenque's hieroglyphic inscriptions.

The first theme parallels the work already published on Palenque's history (Martin and Grube 2000; Robertson 1983; Schele and Freidel 1990; Schele and Mathews 1998). Namely, the Late Classic Palenque rulers found themselves in a position in which they were forced to legitimize their right to rule. We will see that both the motivation for this legitimation and the means behind its retrieval differ from previous interpretations, but the basic concern with local perspectives remains. The second major theme I recover from this geographically and temporally focused study is that the Palenque *ajawtahk* were also working to acquire a prominent position within *international* Maya society. Both of these themes became priorities during the reigns of two *ajawtahk* in particular, and both were realized through an astronomical development patronized under their tenures.

The larger motivation for this manuscript, therefore, is to explore the pressures on a given historical ruler and the means by which he negotiated them—a balance between cultural determination and individual human agency. In this case, we find that an important component of one ruler's exercise of agency found expression through the 819-day count. Because this count has proven enigmatic for so long and because it is powerful in revealing the agenda of this ruler, we will spend considerable effort treating this calendric construct. Its real value, however, is in providing us with a view into elite Maya society—in particular, the means by which the ruling elite limited power to a relatively small portion of the nobility. The material record makes it clear that the ruling elite maintained a coherent assemblage of symbols rhetorically supporting their societal positions. The continuity in usage of some of these symbols is transparent, as in the images patronized by Janaab' Pakal and his son Kan B'ahlam. For instance, the images stuccoed on the walls surrounding Janaab' Pakal's sarcophagus all carried the same two symbols of power: the manikin scepter (or K'awiil staff) and a shield bearing the image of the Jaguar God of the Underworld (see Figure 0.4). The son, Kan B'ahlam, dedicated two of his three major architectural constructs to the same two symbols—the Temple of the Foliated Cross to K'awiil and the Temple of the Sun to the Jaguar God of the Underworld (see Figures 4.1 and 6.4).

The question is, however, to what extent did this iconographic or material coherence reflect a crafted, historically motivated intellectual agenda. That is, do we see ancient Maya *ajawtahk* mechanically manipulating the same symbology—akin to Venus interpretations of the star

15

FIGURE 0.4: *A seated lord holding a K'awiil staff and a Jaguar God of the Underworld shield, from the walls of Janaab' Pakal's sarcophagus chamber*

war — or can we see an individual *ajaw* grappling with historical contingency through creative and unique means? Through the research compiled here, I argue for a specific creative spurt underlying some of the thematic coherence of the architecture and iconography of Late Classic Palenque. Here, I suggest that the 819-day count constituted an invention within a ritual language used by the ruling elite to hold power. We know from Postcontact sources (e.g., the *Books of Chilam Balam* and the *Popol Vuh*) that an esoteric language known as Zuyua formed one means of limiting access to rulership. In this book, I argue that the earlier Classic Maya also maintained such a language and that an extensive consideration of the 819-day count gives us a view

16

into one regionally and temporally restricted version of the language K'awiilil Zuyua. Thus, although an explanation of this calendric construct consumes a large portion of this text, its importance lies in its ability to reveal a more subtle version of Classic Maya intellectual history.

Chapter 1 sets up the treatment of the first (the local) theme by reviewing Janaab' Pakal's historical context. Set in the middle of the Classic period (ca. A.D. 650), the chapter introduces the ninth ruler of the Palenque dynasty, Janaab' Pakal, and the political situation within which he took the throne. In this chapter, I take apart Linda Schele and David Freidel's genealogically preoccupied interpretation of Janaab' Pakal's motives through use of recent reconsiderations of royal succession and a close reading of the hieroglyphic inscriptions. The result is a shift in attention away from dynastic sequence and toward the outcome of a lost military battle as understood within international political tensions. By the end of this chapter, we are introduced to the key protagonist in this history—Janaab' Pakal's eldest son, Kan B'ahlam—and the conditions under which he acceded to the throne. These conditions are important because they shed light on the motivation behind Kan B'ahlam's scientific patronage.

As a prelude to treating the nature of specific astronomical developments under Kan B'ahlam's reign, Chapter 2 considers the development of Mayanist scholarship on astronomy since the nineteenth-century work of Ernst Förstemann (1906). In this chapter, I argue that the absence of a history of Maya astronomy results from sociological issues among scholars investigating the ancient Maya, and not from lack of data. Emphasizing that local studies now will prove more enlightening than global modeling has been, I argue that the work of Classic Maya astronomers is still not well understood despite the longevity of its consideration. Furthermore, in Chapter 2, I detail the method utilized to recognize the first astronumerological puzzles as well as the ensuing methodology marshaled to recover the extent of the historical project patronized by Kan B'ahlam. I suggest that, in general, astronomical interpretation is inherently underconstrained— a condition producing the paradoxical situation in which the image of the astronomer remains consistent across studies but the specific astronomy recovered rarely does. I then suggest that the incorporation of further constraints will aid the endeavor of recovering Maya astronomy and discuss the specific development of the recovery contained herein.

Chapter 3 takes up the historical challenge of Chapter 1 and the methodological challenge recognized in Chapter 2 through an exegesis of three tablets housed within Janaab' Pakal's funerary monument, known as the Temple of Inscriptions. By contemplating these documents as a whole—rather than selectively mining them to corroborate externally derived hypotheses—we find that Janaab' Pakal's main concern was the reconstruction of the city's religious charter after the city was compromised by military defeat. Moreover, although modern approaches emphasize the sociological motivations for religious activity, the texts capture a profound concern with the *practice* of ritual activity. This aspect, too, must be taken into account.

Secondarily in Chapter 3, we find astronomical records supporting the rhetoric of precisely a religious legitimation within the texts. Chapter 3 begins the tandem exegesis of an astronumerology—an arithmetic language built around the periods of the planets. In this chapter, we encounter the first intellectual forays into the production of history using this mathematical language and the means by which the astronumerology was intended to be recovered. Key here is the recognition that the astronumerological language was deployed within hieroglyphic puzzles and that it served as one component in the *ajawtahk's* efforts to reestablish the city after defeat.

Chapter 4 applies the methodology from Chapter 2 to recover the utility of the long enigmatic 819-day count. Here we enter deep into the intellectual world of Late Classic Palenque. In particular, we find that what scholars had previously considered to be mathematical errors within the texts of Kan B'ahlam's architectural masterpiece were actually the bases of astronumerological puzzles. These puzzles grew out of the practice recognized in Chapter 3 but were here elaborated to a much greater extent. Also in this chapter, we confront the identification of Kan B'ahlam's intellectual collaborators, members of his royal court who were working toward this historical and astronomical construction.

Chapter 5 demonstrates that Kan B'ahlam's astronumerological intent played a role within a much larger project. Here we confront the metaphor of a mythological Creation behind his artistic and architectural patronage. This chapter further addresses the second major theme of the book, showing that Kan B'ahlam sought to ensure Palenque's status within international Classic Maya society. Specifically, the appeal to Classic Maya mythology argues that despite the city's peripheral geographic location and critical military defeat to another major city, Palenque was still a Classic Maya polity.

In Chapter 6, I look closely at the mythological appeal both as it was recorded in the hieroglyphic inscriptions and as it was reified within an esoteric astronumerological language as subtext. This chapter demonstrates that a central metaphor guided the intellectual work of Kan B'ahlam's royal court and that astronomy played an important role in its elucidation. Methodologically, this mythological consideration provides corroboration that the breadth of Kan B'ahlam's intellectual patronage grew out of a single vision.

Chapter 7 places astronumerology within the larger scope of Maya traditions. Here we find that although apparently quite esoteric, this mathematical language fits well among other recorded forms of Maya intellectual recreation. In particular, we find that the colonial Maya language of Zuyua provides an excellent framework for understanding the recovered astronumerology. Through Zuyua, we find that astronumerology's purpose was not only to help secure Palenque's place in Classic Maya society but also to ensure that it maintained that position for generations to come. Furthermore, we confront a set of clues suggesting that the basis of this astronumerology was no isolated endeavor by the *ajawtahk* of Palenque but part of an international alliance operating on political and religious levels.

Finally, the Epilogue broadly argues that this study reveals an "agency" within science/mathematics, and that such an agency would accord well with Kan B'ahlam's epistemological perspective.

With this roadmap, I lead the reader on a journey into modern interdisciplinary research. Because of its interdisciplinarity, I expect and welcome scholarly challenges and corroborations from different analytical lenses of the history I present here. It is my hope, however, that at some level the scope of this interdisciplinarity would look natural or "disciplinary" to the ancient Maya who originally composed the art, science, and literature treated herein.

NOTES

1. The Maya Long Count is the superstructure that anchors Classic period calendrics. See the prefatory material for an explanation.

2. The standard correlation is actually a family of solutions known collectively as the Goodman-Martínez-Thompson correlation (GMT). The correlation constant amounts to the number of days that must be added to the integer equivalent of the Long Count in order to produce a Julian date. The three members of the GMT family (each corresponding to a different prioritization of supporting data) are 584,283, 584,284, and 584,285. A good recent review of the correlation problem is given in Lounsbury (1992). For challenges to the GMT, see Aldana (2001a), David Kelley (1983), J.E.S. Thompson (1960:303–310), and Brian Wells and Andreas Fuls (2000).

3. See, for example, Aldana (2001b, 2005a) in which I demonstrate that the "star war" is, in fact, unfounded.

4. The numbering of Janaab' Pakal as ninth departs from convention but follows a hieroglyphic record naming Kan B'ahlam the tenth member of the dynasty. The rationale for following the inscription and going against convention is given in Chapters 2 and 4.

5. The term *Western* in reference to *European* is particularly inappropriate when considering civilizations of the Western Hemisphere. Moreover, to use simply *European* leaves out Europe's origins and various distinct contributors. Although not entirely satisfactory, I use *circum-Mediterranean-derivative* to include the contributions of Egyptian and Islamic cultures.

6. I realize that the term *K'awiilil Zuyua* is a mestizaje of languages since *Zuyua* is Yucatec Maya, and *K'awiil* is a Classic period deity in Classic Ch'olti'an; however, the term gets as close as possible to the concept I am trying to capture.

7. Most popular texts follow Linda Schele in referring to this king simply as Pacal (Schele and Freidel 1990; see also Coe 1993; M. Miller 1999). For a list of names and their variants in the literature, see the Note on Names in the frontmatter.

8. *Ajaw* is the Classic Maya term often translated as "king/queen" or "ruler." The plural form of *ajaw* takes the suffix -*tahk* (Houston, Robertson, and Stuart 2000, 2:25).

9. For a more detailed review of this organization, see Chase and Chase (1992); Coe (1993); Culbert (1991); Inomata and Houston (2001); Martin and Grube (2000); Schele and Freidel (1990); and Schele and Mathews (1998).

10. The other phonetically based writing system is denoted here as the Epi-Olmec or Isthmusian script. Although it has not been deciphered yet, it appears to have worked along phonetic lines. John Justeson and Terrence Kaufman (1992) have attempted the most recent decipherment.

11. For the most part, each city possessed its own Emblem Glyph. We will encounter two notable exceptions in Chapters 1 and 4.

12. See Coe (1992) for an entertaining account of the history of Maya hieroglyphic decipherment. For the shift in interpretations of Maya astronomy over time, see Rice (2004) and Chapter 3.

13. Despite my heavy reliance on hieroglyphic texts as primary source material, I generally will not reference the epigraphers behind the various decipherments being used because that information would shift the focus of the text to the epigraphers. Moreover, other sources already perform this function, most notably Martha Macri and Matthew Looper's recent catalog (2003). Interested readers should see Michael Coe's work on the history of the decipherment (1992) and the footnotes of any of Linda Schele's popular works, which are steeped in decipherment attributions (Freidel, Schele, and Parker 1993; Schele and Freidel 1990; Schele and Mathews 1998).

14. The adjective *k'ujul* derives from the noun *k'uj,* which is generally glossed as "god" or "deity." Matthew Looper (2003) uses "blood," following Linda Schele and Mary Miller (1986).

15. See Chapter 1 and later in this introduction.

16. David Stuart (2000a) has recently summarized the Maya hieroglyphic and archaeological evidence for connections between the two civilizations. Excavations are currently underway at Teotihuacan that appear to demonstrate connections to the Maya within funerary data (see http://archaeology.asu.edu/teo/moon/moon.en/moon.en.htm).

17. The end of the thirteenth *tun* shared the *chol qiij* with the end of the prior *k'atun,* for example, 9.8.0.0.0 **5 Ajaw** 3 Ch'en and 9.8.13.0.0 **5 Ajaw** 18 Tzek.

18. This description generally holds for most indigenous people of the Western Hemisphere.

19. I use *witz* here since the shrines mark religiously important mountains, or *witz.*

20. The *muwaan* ("hawk") sometimes substitutes for *chan.*

21. The Epilogue explains my rationale behind using quotation marks with the term *astronomy.*

22. "Salutary nonsense" is how Peter Novick (1988:7) describes the role of objectivity in cMd history.

23. See Aldana (2006b). The construction itself is quite intriguing. Sixteenth-century Spaniards had at least two reasons for creating the savagery of the Aztecs: (1) as a rationale for conquest; and (2) as a rejoinder to the Christian Reformation. The construction of the Other and Orientalism followed with the European Enlightenment period. Finally, modern notions of "prog-

ress" require that earlier civilizations be seen as inferior. One way to ensure the "backward" character of ancient Mesoamerica is to cast it as "barbaric," "savage," and, by corollary, "mysterious."

24. By using the term *imagined audience,* I am recognizing that the representation of the readers for whom I write can never accurately match the readers themselves. Any audience for whom I write must be imaginary either because I cannot accurately know its composition or because even those I do know may be disposed other than how I would expect them to be at the time of their reading. As a rhetorical guide, therefore, I include in this imagined audience an interest in what ancient Maya nobles might have considered interesting or entertaining in portrayals of themselves.

25. Floyd Lounsbury recorded a chronology of Maya astronomical developments in 1978, but it would be a stretch to consider it a history.

CHAPTER ONE

NEW LIFE AT B'AAKAL

Janaab' Pakal was born into the noble class amidst political turmoil. In the Classic Maya calendar, he "touched the earth" on 9.8.9.13.0 8 Ajaw 13 Pop, just over a year after the accession of the ninth[1] ruler of Palenque, Aj Ne' Ohl Mat (see Table 1.1). Aj Ne' Ohl Mat took the throne after Ix Yohl Ik'nal, the first attested ruling woman of a Classic Maya city, who ruled for over twenty years. Her rule must have been impressive, for it withstood attacks from two Usumacinta-region neighbors, Pia and Bonampak, allowing her to remain in power for longer than her contemporaries in the region (Grube 1996; Martin and Grube 2000:159; Schele and Freidel 1990:221–223). Her successor, however, was not so fortunate. Aj Ne' Ohl Mat held the throne in peace for only the next six years

TABLE 1.1: Palenque *ajaw* list

Ruler Number (according to Aldana)	Name	Ruler Number (according to Schele and Freidel)
0	U K'ix Kan	
1	K'uk' B'ahlam	1
2	[No reading]	2
3	Butz'aj Sak Chi'ik	3
4	Ahkal Mo' Naab' I	4
5	K'an Joy Chitam I	5
6	Ahkal Mo' Naab' II	6
7	Kan B'ahlam I	7
8	Ix Yohl Ik'nal	8
	Aj Ne' Ohl Mat	9
	Ix Sak K'uk'/Ix Muwaan Mat	10
9	K'inich Janaab' Pakal	11
10	K'inich Kan B'ahlam II	12
11	K'inich K'an Joy Chitam II	13
12	K'inich Ahkal Mo' Naab' III	14
13	K'inich Janaab' Pakal II	15
14	K'inich K'uk' B'ahlam II	16

(see Table 1.2). Then, on 9.8.17.15.14 4 Ix 7 Wo, while Janaab' Pakal was still a boy, the city came upon difficult times, suffering severe military defeat at the hand of the ruler of faraway Kalak'mul.

This last war in particular must have made an impression on eight-year-old Janaab' Pakal. Since Janaab' Pakal's parents were both of noble lineages, the event and aftermath undoubtedly impacted his everyday physical and social environments. In the hieroglyphic inscriptions of Palenque's royal temples, the war was recorded as *chak'aj Lakam Ja'* (the "chopping down of the city center"). Yet the Palenque under siege at this time was not the architecturally impressive city that modern visitors now see in ruin. The most recognizable constructs today—the Palace Tower and the Temple of Inscriptions—were not yet even in the planning stages during Janaab' Pakal's youth. We must be cautious, therefore, when interpreting the meaning of the phrase *chak'aj Lakam Ja'*. This chapter examines the physical, social, and political environments that framed this critical military loss and that set the historical context for Janaab' Pakal's reign.

HUMBLE ORIGINS

At the time of Janaab' Pakal's birth, Palenque was still a provincial town. Art historian Merle Greene Robertson and archaeologist Robert Rands suggest that at the time no more than a handful of permanent stone and mortar buildings occupied Lakam Ja', the city center (Rands 1974; Robertson 1985a:3). All other structures were organized in clusters around common areas and constructed of wooden walls and thatched roofs, which were open enough to allow for sufficient ventilation in the heat and humidity of the foothills bordering the Gulf Coast plains (Robertson 1985a:3). Preliminary surveys suggest that the bulk of such residences were located in the western part of the polity framed by the Picota and Michol rivers (Schele 1981:93) (see Figure 0.1).

East of this area, next to the Otolum River, we find the stone and mortar buildings, which most likely composed the residence of the ruling elite. Such an architectural inference is warranted since these structures possessed the same overall characteristics as the palace structures that would follow them, even though there were important differences. The engineering behind each phase, for instance, reveals two distinct traditions. In the earlier structures, the walls are significantly thicker, betraying a less elegant and less confident plan. Likewise, the vaulted roofs were constructed at a lower sloping angle than those of subsequent structures (Robertson 1985a:4).

The second tradition noted here consisted of a new elite residence constructed around the time of Janaab' Pakal's early reign.[2] In preparation for the new construction, the earlier structures and the area in between were filled to form a large platform. Upon the center of this platform, Palenque citizens built the structure today known as House E of the Palace Complex (Robertson 1985a:4) (see Figure 1.1). Interestingly, House E did not become a new standard for subsequent additions to the palace. Rather, this building was maintained as an anomaly within the greater complex that engulfed it. For one thing, the roof was set at a much steeper angle than any subsequent building at Palenque. As telling, House E is the only structure that did not possess a roof comb (Robertson 1985a:7).

The iconographic and symbolic differences between House E and all other constructions at Palenque are even more relevant to the discussion at hand. Namely, the exterior walls followed no convention, having been painted white and then covered with floating, abstract symbols (see Figure 1.1; Robertson 1985a:figures 29–52). Robertson (1985a:21) suggests that iconographically these symbols shared similarities with mural paintings at the great central Mexican city known as Teotihuacan, notably the co-occurrence of "goggle eyes." Although the direction of influence is still being debated within the scholarly community, the visual connection is little disputed.

The second difference consists of the unique symbolic link between House E and the cosmological region known as the Maya Underworld. Physically, the two are connected via a series of underground tunnels (Robertson 1985a:32–35). Within these tunnels, cosmic imagery, such as what David Stuart (2003) has called the Starry Deer Caiman, is both sculpted in stone and modeled out of stucco. We will consider this iconography and its referent in detail in Chapters 3 and 7. For now it is sufficient to note that House E functioned not only as part of a royal residence but, with its connections to the Underworld, as the ritual center of the polity as well.

Its ritual use becomes important when we take Mesoamerican war metaphors into consideration. Postclassic Central Mexican documents use images of temples on fire to represent conquered polities (Boone 2000:34); likewise, Classic Maya inscriptions refer to burning events as a part of war, which we will discuss later in this chapter. If the conquest of Palenque during Janaab' Pakal's youth involved the destruction or desecration of its ritual center, the focus of the destruction would have been directed toward the early — now filled in — structures of this complex. As a noble, Janaab' Pakal probably frequented this complex and therefore would have been reminded throughout his youth of the city's grave military defeat.

DYNASTIC REPERCUSSIONS

As for the social environment—and perhaps more significantly— no person took over the formal rule of Palenque after the war with Kalak'mul. The tablet that bears the hieroglyphic passage recording the event notes that after military defeat, the religious charter of the city was "lost," and the gifts that were regularly given to the gods at

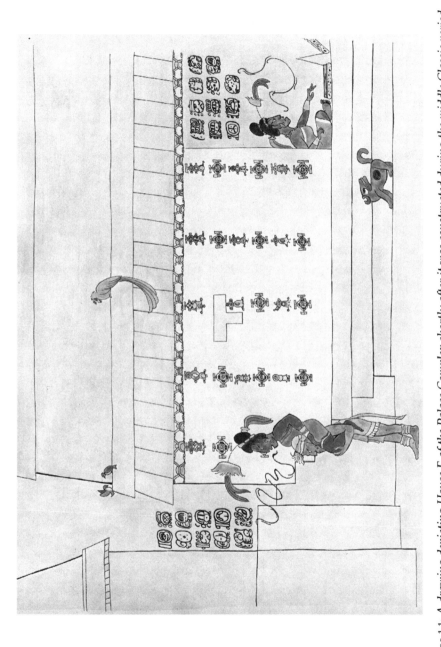

FIGURE 1.1: *A drawing depicting House E of the Palace Complex shortly after it was constructed during the middle Classic period*

the ends of calendric periods "could no longer be given." Instead, during the period after the war, the patron gods of Palenque were cared for by the primordial mother goddess, Ix Muwaan Mat.[3]

In order to understand the meaning of this gift-giving and to recover Janaab' Pakal's response to the tough times into which he was born, we must digress into a consideration of dynastic genealogy. The genealogical interpretation of the hieroglyphic text presented here differs from the generally accepted interpretation proposed by Linda Schele and David Freidel in 1990.[4] At the time of their proposal, the decipherment of the hieroglyphic script was in full bloom — a situation constituting a double-edged sword. On the one hand, the decipherment led to a new vision of the Maya world through the Maya's own words. On the other, a significant number of decipherments were insecure, and speculative interpretations were far more acceptable than they are now with a more subtle understanding of the script. Through an updated reading of the primary genealogical texts of Palenque, therefore, we can revise Schele and Freidel's interpretation to gain insight into Janaab' Pakal's tumultuous childhood.

In 1990, Linda Schele and David Freidel presented to the public the fruits of almost two decades of groundbreaking scholarship by a cadre of scholars gathered around the Mesa Redonda de Palenque (Coe 1992:193–217). Working from three primary sources — a set of tablets in the Temple of Inscriptions, texts carved into Janaab' Pakal's sarcophagus, and the tablets of the Triad Group[5] — Floyd Lounsbury, Peter Mathews, Linda Schele, and David Kelley reconstructed the entire dynastic sequence of Palenque into the Late Classic period. Of these sources, the Temple of Inscriptions provided a coarse overview of some of the important *ajawtahk* of Palenque. The Triad Group gave a more detailed listing for the earlier *ajawtahk*. And the sarcophagus lid recorded specific information about Janaab' Pakal's parentage. From these sources, Schele and Freidel (1990:219) presented the dynasty shown in Table 1.1.[6]

The trouble with this genealogy relative to the interpretation proposed in this book (and the main difference between the two numerical columns of Table 1.1) lies in the identification of Janaab' Pakal's mother as the tenth ruler of Palenque. In fact, nowhere is she explicitly recorded as having filled that role. Instead, her placement within the formal dynasty depends on an inferential link made by Schele and Freidel. The ambiguity necessitating some type of inference comes from their treatment of a hieroglyphic record in a carved tablet within the Temple of Inscriptions. Therein, right after a record of the above-mentioned battle lost to the Kalak'mul *ajaw*, and before the record of Janaab' Pakal's accession, the author of the tablet included the accession of a figure named Ix Muwaan Mat.

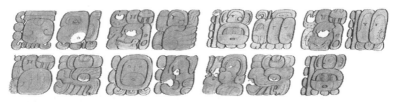

Less than a year (10.2) after Ix Muwaan Mat K'ujul B'aakal Ajaw became seated as ajaw, it was the k'altun of 3 Ajaw 3 Zotz' (9.9.0.0.0); it was the ninth k'atun. Muwaan Mat K'ujul B'aakal Ajaw gives the bundle of her gods for 9 bak'tun 9 k'atun.[7] (N11–P6)

The basis of Schele and Freidel's inference is stated explicitly in a footnote to their chapter on the dynasty of Palenque. They write:

[The] inference of the identity of the woman named in the Temple of Inscriptions as [Janaab' Pakal's] mother is based on the following pattern of data[8]:

1. The woman who appears in the equivalent chronological position in the death list on the sarcophagus lid is his mother, [Ix Sak K'uk'].

2. On the Oval Palace Tablet, the woman named as [Janaab' Pakal's] mother hands him the crown that makes him king, but his father is neither named nor pictured. The parent critical to his legitimate claim to the throne is his mother rather than his father.

3. His father, [K'an Mo' Hix], never appears in an accession phrase in any of the inscriptions of Palenque. Furthermore, [Janaab' Pakal] depicts [K'an Mo' Hix] only on the sarcophagus where he appears as the king's father and not as a king in his own right.

4. The goddess is born on a date deliberately contrived to have the same temporal character . . . as [Janaab' Pakal's] birth.[9]

They continue, "All of these factors emphasize that [Janaab' Pakal's] right of inheritance descended through his mother rather than his

FIGURE 1.2: *Name glyphs for Ix Muwaan Mat (left) and Ix Sak K'uk' (right)*

father." Additionally, they appeal to a purported pun built into the hieroglyphic word *k'uk'*, identified by Floyd Lounsbury (Schele and Freidel 1990:468).

The purported pun and the first and third points have been discredited by the ongoing decipherment, whereas the second and fourth will require more argument to refute. The pun recognized by Lounsbury was based on an identification of the acceding figure's name glyph as a heron with feathers in its mouth (Schele and Freidel 1990:468). Recently, the name glyph has been identified not as *bak'* ("heron") but as a *muwaan* ("hawk"), eliminating the viability of the pun (Macri and Looper 2003:96) (see Figure 1.2). Secondly, the first point — that Janaab' Pakal's mother and his ruling predecessor both precede him chronologically — does not necessarily imply anything provocative about their potential equivalence. It is a necessary condition but nothing more.

The third point actually contains an error of fact. Contrary to Schele and Freidel's assertion, Janaab' Pakal's father, K'an Mo' Hix, *is* named as an *ajaw* "in his own right" — three times in fact — and is named as such on Janaab' Pakal's sarcophagus and its lid. The inscription along the west edge of the lid explicitly names K'an Mo' Hix as K'ujul B'aakal Ajaw. Also, images on the sides of the sarcophagus depict K'an Mo' Hix twice as being reborn, and next to each of his portraits is his name followed by the *ajaw* title (see Figure 1.3). Moreover, on a public tablet on the façade of the Templo Olvidado, K'an Mo' Hix is listed as Janaab' Pakal's father (and Ix Sak K'uk' is identified as his mother).

FIGURE 1.3: *Record of K'an Mo' Hix as ajaw on the side of Janaab' Pakal's sarcophagus*

Now, it is true that K'an Mo' Hix does not appear in any accession phrase within the hieroglyphic inscriptions of Palenque that have been recovered thus far. But then neither does Ix Sak K'uk' unless we accept the inference that is under contention. The larger point that Schele and Freidel are attempting to make depends on the hypothesis that governs the interpretation they give. Namely, Schele and Freidel assume that the *ajawlel* must descend patrilineally and then apply this assumption to the early dynasty of Palenque, arguing that the reason for the extensive treatment of genealogy by Janaab' Pakal and his son (in the Temple of Inscriptions and in the Triad Group) is to legitimize their rule because it was not obtained patrilineally.

Although they admit in a footnote that there is no genealogical data supporting a specific relationship between Ix Sak K'uk' and Janaab' Pakal I (the namesake of her son), they fail to state that no data support a direct father-son relationship between any of Janaab' Pakal's predecessors (Schele and Freidel 1990:467; cf. Robertson 1985b:116). Their entire theory of Janaab' Pakal's and Kan B'ahlam's attempts at legitimation, therefore, rests on the assertions that for the Classic Maya as a whole, dynasties were ruled by fathers and sons and that any aberration required extensive justification. Schele and Freidel's (1990) readings, therefore, heavily reflected their own early concerns with the texts. With a nascent ability to read them, interpretations focused predominantly on dynastic successions and royal genealogies. This information was the most easily recovered and so became the focal point of scholarly attention — even if it may not have been the focus of the Maya who composed the inscriptions.

If instead we follow the work of Susan Gillespie, Patricia McAnany, and Ralph Roys, who note that father-son inheritance was preferred but not required and that the *ajawlel* could pass among a larger subset of the nobility (Gillespie 2001:470–473; Roys 1967), then the motivations behind the inscriptions considered here potentially change. Under this scenario, neither of Janaab' Pakal's parents would have to have been the reigning *k'ujul ajaw* for Janaab' Pakal to have acceded to the throne. All that would have been required was the fact that he was of an appropriate lineage. Whether his mother's or father's lineage was more important might then be debated without having to argue for either mother or father as the preceding ruler of Palenque.[10]

Without Schele and Freidel's assumptions, we may posit alternative motivations for the hieroglyphic inscriptions being considered here. We also now must seek a new means (other than strict patrilineality) for the Classic Maya to have maintained power within a small ruling elite class. Both of these issues will be addressed throughout the remaining chapters of this book with the latter constituting the focus of Chapter 7.

If Ix Muwaan Mat, the ruler directly preceding Janaab' Pakal, was not an alternate name of someone in his immediate family, we are left to ask who she may have been. Before attempting to answer this question, we should take into account the rest of the passage that noted her accession in the texts of the Temple of Inscriptions. Specifically, right after her accession and celebration of the *k'altun,* the text notes explicit restrictions on her reign.

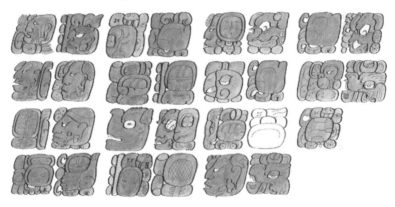

On the back of the ninth k'atun, god was lost; ajaw was lost. She could not adorn the ajawtahk of the first sky; she could not give offerings to the 9 Sky Yoch'ok'in, the 16 Ch'ok'in, or the 9 Tz'aak Ajaw. On the back of the 3 Ajaw k'atun, Ix Muwaan Mat could not give their offerings. Ix Muwaan Mat gives the bundle of her god. (O4–Q9)

Although she was able to perform some of the duties required of a K'ujul B'aakal Ajaw, others were left undone. To emphasize the point, the next hieroglyphic passage notes the accession of Janaab' Pakal and points out explicitly that he *was* able to interact with precisely those gods prohibited to Ix Muwaan Mat: the 9 Sky Yoch'ok'in, the 16 Ch'ok'in, and 9 Tz'aak Ajaw.

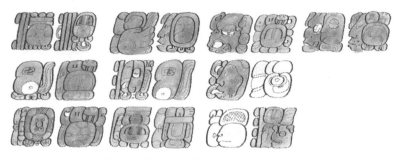

Seventeen years (17.13.12) after K'inich Janaab' Pakal K'ujul B'aakal Ajaw became seated as ajaw, it was the k'altun of 1 Ajaw 8 K'ayab (9.10.0.0.0). It was seated, the tenth k'atun. It was the half bak'tun of the ajawtahk Jun Ajaw, . . . 9 Sky Yoch'ok'in, the 16 Ch'ok'in, 9 Tz'aak Ajaw. (R9–S7)

Not only were there restrictions on her reign, but Ix Muwaan Mat served as *ajaw* for only a very short time, less than four years (see Table 1.2). She then passed the throne to the now twelve-year-old Janaab' Pakal. Although she was named with the formal title of *k'ujul ajaw* in the Temple of Inscriptions, it appears that her position was only a temporary fix.

Rather than appeal to a mortal regent for the identity of Ix Muwaan Mat, as did Schele and Freidel, we may actually turn to other hieroglyphic inscriptions at Palenque that mention a woman of this name. In the largest structure of the Triad Group, which we will treat in detail in Chapter 6, an inscription records that Ix Muwaan Mat was born, acceded to the *ajawlel* of Palenque, and bore a son in *primordial* times. Likewise, other deeds by her were cited elsewhere by later rulers (e.g., on the Palenque Temple XIX altar). A more literal reading of the Temple of Inscription texts, therefore, reveals that a deity might have some agency during the historical period after the defeat of Aj Ne' Ohl Mat. A more faithful reading would have the primordial deity taking charge of the city's ceremonial needs while no suitable mortal ruler was available (see also Martin and Grube 2000:161). Rulers were often in communication with ancestors and deities, and some deities (as we will see later) owned buildings during Classic times (Houston 1996; Houston and Stuart 1996).

In this sense, Ix Sak K'uk', Janaab' Pakal's mother, may have been an *ajaw* of Palenque, but she was not the mortal reigning K'ujul B'aakal

Table 1.2: Middle Classic dynastic transition

Date	Interval	Event	Source
9.7.10.3.8		Ix Yohl Ik'nal accedes	T.I. East
9.8.0.0.0	9.14.12	Ix Yohl Ik'nal celebrates *k'altun*	T.I. East
9.8.11.6.12	11.6.12	Ix Yohl Ik'nal dies	Sarc. lid
9.8.11.9.10	2.18	Aj Ne' Ohl Mat accedes	T.I. East
9.8.13.0.0	1.8.10	Aj Ne' Ohl Mat celebrates *k'altun*	T.I. East
9.8.17.15.14	4.15.14	Lakam Ja' is defeated	T.I. East
9.8.19.4.6	1.6.12	Aj Ne' Ohl Mat dies	Sarc. lid
9.8.19.7.18	3.12	Ix Muwaan Mat accedes	T.I. East
9.9.0.0.0	10.2	Ix Muwaan Mat celebrates restricted *k'altun*	T.I. East
9.9.2.4.8	2.4.8	Janaab' Pakal accedes	T.I. East

Note: T.I. East refers to the East Tablet in the Temple of Inscriptions.

Ajaw preceding Janaab' Pakal's position in the dynasty as inferred by Schele and Freidel (1990:223). Moreover, if we accept that Ix Muwaan Mat and Ix Sak K'uk' are distinct persons, during the period after Aj Ne' Ohl Mat's rule, the polity was without a formal *ajaw*—a situation alluded to by the restrictions placed on Ix Muwaan Mat's *ajawlel*. If we accept that these restrictions followed from her lack of mortality, the interpretation of the hieroglyphic text given previously much more closely fits the statement "god was lost; ajaw was lost."

From this perspective, it becomes even clearer that during his youth, Janaab' Pakal's world was in a state of limbo. Fortunately for the people of Palenque, Janaab' Pakal was no ordinary man. Unfortunately for us, the events that tested him were not explicitly recorded in stone.[11] As we have already noted, the next statement in the narrative at Palenque containing this early history leapfrogs over the early period of limbo, notes the accession of Janaab' Pakal to the *ajawlel* of Palenque, and records his celebration of the end of the tenth *k'atun* (East Tablet, Temple of Inscriptions). The continuation of the inscription also records a sketch of Janaab' Pakal's ritual activity between this period's end and his death. Thus, to gain insight into Janaab' Pakal's political rise to glory we must turn to the nearby kingdom now known as Tortuguero but then known by the same moniker of B'aakal.[12] After this geopolitical tour of Janaab' Pakal's political world we will return to the specific cases illuminating his international political activity.

ALLIANCES

Tortuguero was by no means a huge metropolis during the middle Classic period, which is very likely the reason that it shared the name B'aakal. Indeed, the small polity may have been established as an outpost of the larger B'aakal, using the same dynastic lineage and so keeping the same name.[13] Some time after his inauguration on 9.9.2.4.8 5 Lamat 1 Mol, Janaab' Pakal used his alliance with Tortuguero in order to benefit from the military prowess of that diminutive polity's ruler (Grube 1998). Although the alliance may have started much earlier, we know from Monument 6 that B'ahlam Ajaw, the Tortuguero *ajaw*, embarked on a series of military campaigns between 9.10.12.3.10 10 Ok 18 K'ayab and 9.11.2.17.4 10 K'an 17 Yax, while Janaab' Pakal was between the ages of forty-two and fifty-three. Part of the evidence that these polities were militarily allied comes from sources at other Maya cities, including Kalak'mul and Tikal (the archrival of Kalak'mul and Palenque's ally), and the larger political sphere that shaped Classic Maya culture.

Kalak'mul and Tikal were much larger polities and had been at each other's throats since the beginning of the Classic period (Aldana 2004b, 2006a; Martin and Grube 1995; Schele and Freidel 1990:165–197). Kalak'mul was one of the oldest of Classic Maya cities and its history appears to have extended back to ancient times. Some forty kilometers from Kalak'mul was the Preclassic giant city whose ruins are known as El Mirador. This city flourished from about 300 B.C. until around the end of the second century A.D. and now boasts the largest of all known pyramids within the Maya region. According to ceramic data, this city was depopulated around the beginning of the Classic period, precisely when Kalak'mul began to grow in earnest (Folan et al. 1995:329). The *sakbe* ("limestone road") connecting them suggests at least an important link between the two cities and may even suggest a population movement from one location to the other (Folan et al. 1995:313). If genealogical ties linked the cities, the *ajawlel* of Kalak'mul may be assumed to be among the oldest of ethnically Maya cities (see Frontispiece).

On the opposite side of the political spectrum lay the polity of Tikal. Unlike El Mirador, this polity's credentials did not rest solely in archaeological patterns but also were attested within hieroglyphic inscriptions. According to the texts recovered from the city, Chak Toh Ich'ak, Tikal *ajaw* during the fourth century, was the fourteenth member of the dynasty. Using a conservative estimate of fifteen to twenty years per reign puts the origins of the dynasty in the first century A.D.[14] We do not know if the relationship between Tikal and Kalak'mul was amicable during this early period. We do know, however, that Chak Toh Ich'ak's reign ended during the fourth century and that, in his wake, a new genealogical tributary entered the stream (Martin and Grube 2000:29–31; Stuart 2000). Here, at late fourth-century Tikal and Waxaktun, its nearest neighbor, we find the clearest evidence for intrusive contact into the Maya region by the highland Mexican metropolis known as Teotihuacan.

The Aztecs used "Teotihuacan" to name a city already in ruins by the time of the Aztec Triple Alliance (thirteenth through early sixteenth centuries A.D.). Translated variously as "City of the Gods" or "the Place Where the Gods Were Born," Teotihuacan was revered by the Aztecs, who considered the ancient city as the birthplace of their era — the Fifth Sun (Sahagún 1953; Taube 1993:41–44; Velásquez 1975). From archaeological excavation and interpretation, the city appears to have flourished between the first century B.C. and the sixth century A.D.[15] Situated in the Basin of Mexico, the city had over 150,000 inhabitants at its height. After A.D. 150, many of these people lived in apartment complexes whose construction was partially determined by the governing authority.

A hub of economic and ideological activity, Teotihuacan spread out to affect independent polities far from the Basin of Mexico in virtually all directions. To the north, remnants of a Teotihuacano astronomical interest dot the archaeological record at Alta Vista, situated just off the Tropic of Cancer (Aveni 2001:231; Aveni et al. 1982). To the south, stelae at Monte Alban show iconographic representations of Teotihuacanos visiting the local nobility (Coggins 1975, 1983, 1993; Marcus 1983). And to the east, ceramic, iconographic, lithic, astronomic, and hieroglyphic evidence reveals that the Teotihuacanos took an interest in the Maya region (Aldana 2001b:59–88; Braswell 2003; Coggins 1993; Harrison 1999:82–91; Stuart 2000).

The clearest evidence for the interaction between Teotihuacanos and the Maya can be found at Tikal. Contemporary hieroglyphic texts record "the arrival of strangers," who have been identified convincingly as Teotihuacanos (Harrison 1999:78–91; Martin and Grube 2000:29–31; Stuart 2000). With their arrival came the establishment of a new political order defined and controlled by the foreigners but integrated into Tikal Maya identity. Here we confront the first evidence of an *ajawlel* augmented by the title *kalomte* (Aldana 2003b, 2006a). Those *ajawtahk* carrying the *kalomte* title, and those allied with them, opposed the *ajawlel* of Kalak'mul, accounting for a vast amount of the recorded martial activity in the Maya world (Aldana 2003b, 2006a; Martin and Grube 1995; Schele and Freidel 1990:165–197; Stuart 2000).

The critical battle in this relationship came relatively early. As has been amply treated, during the reign of the sixth successor of the Teotihuacano interlopers, a smaller city switched allegiance from Tikal to Kalak'mul (Harrison 1999:101–104; Martin and Grube 2000:25–39; Schele and Freidel 1990:130–164; Stuart 2000). To solidify the change, Caracol (as the ruins of the smaller city are currently known) took up arms against Tikal and defeated its twenty-first *ajaw*, Wak Chan K'awiil. This defeat sent Tikal into a building hiatus lasting from 9.6.4.8.2 12 Ik' 0 Mol, through Janaab' Pakal's reign, and until the end of the thirteenth *k'atun* of the tenth *bak'tun*. During the intervening 140 years, the *ajawlel* of Kalak'mul solidified and expanded its domination over the Maya region. Recruiting smaller polities to fight most of their battles, Kalak'mul *ajawtahk* show up in the hieroglyphic texts of numerous Maya lowland cities under phrases such as *jubuy u tok' pakal . . . ukab'ijiiy Yuknom k'ujul Kan ajaw*, or "went down his flint and shield . . . under the auspices of Yuknom, ruler of Kalakmul" (Boot 2002; Martin and Grube 1995; Mathews and Willey 1991).

An attempt to reassert Tikal's position was taken up by the twenty-fifth ruler of Tikal, Nuun Ujol Chaak. His plans were challenged, however, by his own half brother, B'alaj Chan K'awiil, who had set up a splinter faction 100 kilometers from Tikal and then allied with the ruler of Kalak'mul (Houston 1993; Mathews and Willey 1991:55–57). The two kin engaged in a series of battles, instigated by B'alaj Chan K'awiil, that resulted in successive temporary ousters of each from their respective polities (Aldana 2005; Boot 2002; Houston 1993).

In records documenting this series of altercations, we find both explicit and implicit links to Janaab' Pakal, K'ujul B'aakal Ajaw. The explicit mentions come rather late in the establishment of Janaab' Pakal's renaissance. On 9.11.4.5.14 6 Ix 2 K'ayab, over 30 years after B'alaj Chan K'awiil took office at the smaller Tikal polity (41 years into Janaab' Pakal's reign and 100 years into the Tikal hiatus), B'alaj Chan K'awiil initiated an *ek'emey kab'* battle against his relative, Nuun Ujol Chaak, *ajaw* of Tikal.[16] (*Ek'emey* battles were specific types of battles that metaphorically invoked the meteors of the celestial realm as the arrows of the gods; Aldana 2001b, 2005.) The battle resulted in Nuun Ujol Chaak's banishment and an (undeciphered) action taken against the *ajawtahk* of Tikal (Dos Pilas Hieroglyphic Stairway 4). Afterward, Nuun Ujol Chaak teamed up with Janaab' Pakal, and the two aimed to return Nuun Ujol Chaak to the Tikal throne (see also Grube 1996:7–8; Harrison 1999:126; Martin and Grube 2000:42–43; Schele and Grube 1994:118–133).

In the inscriptions of Palenque, we read further that Nuun Ujol Chaak collaborated with Janaab' Pakal to capture a war palanquin from Itzamnaaj B'ahlam of Pa'chan (Yaxchilan), ally of Kalak'mul.[17] The texts of the Temple of Inscriptions at Palenque record that a little over two years after the battle between Nuun Ujol Chaak and B'alaj Chan K'awiil, on 9.11.6.16.17 13 Kaban 10 Ch'en, Nuun Ujol Chaak arrived at Palenque (West Tablet, Temple of Inscriptions; see also Grube 1996:7–8; Schele and Grube 1994:118–133). This statement effectively records a contract between the *ajawtahk* of Palenque and Tikal paid for in a time of political need.[18] It also tells us that during this time, while Tikal was in a position of disadvantage, Palenque was still able to maintain a relationship with the two *ajawtahk* in opposition to Kalak'mul.

There is implicit evidence that Tikal, Palenque, and Tortuguero were acting as military allies. Two of the final battles waged by B'alaj Chan K'awiil against his half brother were intentionally timed to commemorate anniversaries of events involving the three polities. This timing should not be taken lightly. As noted in the Introduction, completions of calendric cycles were of definitive import to Classic Maya rulers, and it is within them that we encounter the implicit links among Tikal, Palenque, and Tortuguero in opposition to Kalak'mul.

One of the battles conducted by B'ahlam Ajaw occurred on 9.10.17.2.14 13 Ix 17 Muwaan and was recorded as an *ek'emey* battle

(Aldana 2005a). After this battle, B'ahlam Ajaw "mountained" the bones of his captives in a ceremony that involved *u-sak ik'-il* (a part of their souls) and *chan* (the sky).[19] The important connection here is that B'alaj Chan K'awiil chose to conduct his own war against Nuun Ujol Chaak exactly 5,840 days—equivalent to ten canonical Venus cycles and sixteen *haab'*—after the aforementioned battle by B'ahlam Ajaw (Aldana 2001b:126; 2005a). The implication here is that B'ahlam Ajaw had something to do with Nuun Ujol Chaak's position as the K'ujul Mutul Ajaw (the ruler of Tikal). Since this battle brought by B'alaj Chan K'awiil occurred only six years after Nuun Ujol Chaak "arrived" at Palenque during his first ouster, we may argue parsimoniously that B'alaj Chan K'awiil chose the Chak Ek' anniversary for his battle because B'ahlam Ajaw was allied with Janaab' Pakal in his battle of 9.10.17.2.14. In some calendric conceptual space, then, B'alaj Chan K'awiil was attacking all three polities by invoking Ajaw Chak Ek' (Venus), the Sun, and part of the *chol qiij* (specifically, the day Ix).[20]

Lest one doubt this numerological intent by B'alaj Chan K'awiil, the scribes of the rebellious faction substantiated it further at their next opportunity. First Nuun Ujol Chaak regained his throne at Tikal, instigating another attack from B'alaj Chan K'awiil. This battle would be the final defeat of Nuun Ujol Chaak. B'alaj Chan K'awiil commemorated his victory with a *witzaj b'aak* ("mountaining of bones") parallel to B'ahlam Ajaw's ritual and timed to occur exactly one *k'atun* after the meeting between Janaab' Pakal and the exiled Nuun Ujol Chaak (Grube 1996:9; Martin and Grube 2000:43; Schele and Grube 1994:133). Thus it seems that B'alaj Chan K'awiil felt the need to numerologically tie his attacks against Nuun Ujol Chaak to the latter's affiliation with Palenque, yet when Venus and solar auspices did not produce the desired outcome, B'alaj Chan K'awiil settled for a *k'atun* commemoration.

Although not all political entities involved in this dispute were mentioned explicitly in the hieroglyphic records, we see here that some were invoked through a numerological subtext using commemorations of calendric cycles. This point is developed further in the astronomical treatments of Chapters 3 and 6. For now, it should be noted that although this example shows a Maya ruler timing his events according to a celestial meter, the type of timing differs drastically from that mentioned in the Introduction. As we will see in the next chapter, other scholars have argued for the timing of events by the dictates of celestial bodies; that is, the timing was mechanically triggered by a signal given by some celestial object. Contrastingly, here we recognize that celestial and calendric periods were utilized by B'alaj Chan K'awiil in a more complex discourse among humans and members of the celestial realm. This distinction, too, will become clearer as we move through the specific astronomy patronized by the Late Classic rulers of Palenque.

BACK AT HOME

Astronomical concerns aside, we find in the inscriptions of Palenque, Tortuguero, and Dos Pilas a series of records that demonstrates a web of alliances supporting Janaab' Pakal's (and his polity's) rise to prominence on the political stage set by Tikal and Kalak'mul. His alliance with Tortuguero quickly granted him enough prestige that he was sought out much later by the *ajaw* of Tikal while the latter was "on the run." Although not all of these military ventures were successful, these affiliations must have put Janaab' Pakal in a position to invest at home.

Architecturally, for instance, Janaab' Pakal first patronized the construction of what has become known as the Templo Olvidado. As we will see, this structure provided the inspiration for the first phase of his funerary monument, but he chose to build this temple in the "old" part of town, closer to the Early Classic residences (Schele 1981:94). Here is the tablet on the front pier that records Janaab' Pakal's parentage in public view. Next, Janaab' Pakal patronized House E of the Palace Complex. He added further to the Palace Complex with Houses B, K, L, and C before turning his attention to his funerary monument, the Temple of Inscriptions (Schele 1981:111). Janaab' Pakal thus maintained a concerted interest locally, building up the architecture of his city late in his rule and then governing the polity until he was over eighty years old.[21]

Also during his extended rule, Janaab' Pakal had two sons by his consort Ix Tz'aak Ajaw. The elder son was Kan B'ahlam II and was designated heir to the throne at six years of age, when Janaab' Pakal

was already forty. (K'an Joy Chitam, the younger son, eventually succeeded Kan B'ahlam II at the age of fifty-eight.) Despite his early designation, however, Kan B'ahlam did not accede to the throne of Palenque
until he was forty-eight, and he appears to have engaged very little
military activity (Grube 1996). So we may well ask what he did for the
first thirty years of his adult life and how he occupied himself once he
took the throne.

In the following chapters, part of my aim is to answer these questions. I argue that with so much time on his hands, Kan B'ahlam was
able to dedicate himself to intellectual and esoteric pursuits (Robertson
1991:8–12). One such pursuit, or at least his patronage of it, resulted in
a calendrical invention of the 819-day count. This count served to elaborate a religious analogy that would architecturally, artistically, and
scientifically place Palenque firmly within the Classic Maya world.
Such an invention, though, was intimately tied to the state astronomy
of its time, and so to properly understand it, we must first review a bit
of what modern scholarship tells us about Classic Maya astronomy,
along with how we came to know it.

NOTES

1. Here, I am using *ninth,* although it appears that the Palenque *ajawtahk*
following this ninth ruler would not have assigned him this number. For further discussion, see additional information found in this chapter and also in
Simon Martin and Nikolai Grube (2000:168).

2. Robertson (1985a) argues for dating the construction to the late sixth or
early seventh century, certainly by "the end of the seventh century," by implicitly invoking the GMT correlation. Linda Schele and Robert Rands (Schele
1981:111), however, have suggested a significantly later Long Count date of
"9.11.0.0.0 +5 tuns."

3. This reading differs from that published by Schele et al. (1992) and
comes from a close reading of the text by the author in collaboration with
Shannon Plank in 1999.

4. Martin and Grube (2000:154–175) present a shorter sketch of Palenque's
dynastic history that is much more in line with the version presented here. As
Schele and Freidel treat the reigns of Janaab' Pakal and Kan B'ahlam more
extensively, their interpretation takes center stage here.

5. Most of the literature refers to this complex as the Cross Group after
early attempts to find vestiges of Christianity in Maya religion. The largest of

the three temples houses an iconographic construct that bears resemblance to a cross but is now referred to as a world tree. This tree is at the center of the cosmos and helps to hold up the sky. Since the more important characteristic of this architectural complex for the Maya was its triadic form, I refer to it as the Triad Group (see Chapter 5).

6. Martin and Grube (2000:168) note that if only the "non-problematic" rulers are taken into account, Kan B'ahlam is the tenth member of the dynasty.

7. Note that there is no mention in the text of celestial bodies as proposed by Schele and Mathews (1998). Their inference was based on a calendric pattern proffered by Michael Closs (1994). See Aldana (2001b, 2005a) for the explicit argument against an astronomical reading.

8. I have changed the names to reflect the orthography adopted in this manuscript or recent decipherments in order to avoid confusion.

9. Elided was a reference to another footnote on calendrical contrivance.

10. Given the evidence we have so far, though, the issue is still unresolved. As noted, in the sarcophagus lid text, K'an Mo' Hix is named K'ujul B'aakal Ajaw and Ix Sak K'uk' is recorded without any title whatsoever. When Ix Sak K'uk' is named on the Oval Tablet, again she goes without recognition as an *ajaw, k'ujul,* or otherwise. Also, this tablet was commissioned by Janaab' Pakal's second son, K'an Joy Chitam. The names accompanying the images carved around Janaab' Pakal's sarcophagus, however, carry *ajaw* titles. Here, though, Ix Sak K'uk' is labeled K'ujul B'aakal Ajaw whereas K'an Mo' Hix is named *ajaw* of an as yet unidentified site.

11. An alternate possibility, of course, is that this history was recorded but has not yet been recovered by archaeological excavation.

12. These two cities shared the same Emblem Glyph.

13. The same phenomenon occurred at Tikal, the results of which we will see later, but see also Harrison (1999:123) and Boot (2002).

14. One inscription from Tikal records a period-end celebration taking place at the turn of the fifth *bak'tun,* ostensibly pushing the history of Tikal back to circa 1000 B.C. This record, however, was commissioned by the twenty-seventh ruler of Tikal, Jasaw Chan K'awiil and may not have been meant to be taken literally. This concept will be explained in more detail later. See also Martin and Grube (2000:22–23).

15. For an excellent survey of Teotihuacan, see Pasztory (1993).

16. Stuart and Houston argue that Nuun Ujol Chaak was the half brother of B'alaj Chan K'awiil (Schele and Grube 1994:118–119).

17. Apparently the *ajawtahk* of Tikal were able to keep this war trophy since a reference to this palanquin is made later by one of Nuun Ujol Chaak's descendents (Grube 1996:7; Schele and Grube 1994:118–133).

18. Schele and Grube (1994:124) make a similar inference: "Apparently the [Tikal *ajaw*] went to battle with [Janaab' Pakal]. We are not told what he wanted or what happened between the two rulers, but we think it likely that [Nuun Ujol Chaak] was looking for help in his wars against [Kalak'mul]." (Bracketed names have been changed to maintain consistency with the rest of this book.)

19. "13 Ix 17 Muwaan . . . witzaj b'aak, bolon-?-na-ja u sak ik' il ?-ik'-yax?-chan, B'ahlam Ajaw, K'ujul B'aakal Ajaw." Schele and Grube (1994:120) understand this ceremony as "perhaps the taking of relic bones from the captive's dead body."

20. Much later a successor's panegyrist rearranged the inscriptional record of B'alaj Chan K'awiil's campaigns (Aldana 2005a). In doing so, he attempted to follow the practice—common by the middle Classic—to first record the attack by one's enemy before recording the martial victory of interest (Grube 1996:3; Houston 1993:108).

21. Janaab' Pakal's age at death had been a point of contention, and an entire session at the 2003 annual meeting for the Society of American Archaeology was devoted to revisiting the question with new data. Early tests suggested that the skeleton in the sarcophagus was only forty to fifty years old at the time of death—far short of the eighty-three years stated in the inscriptions. New osteological tests verified that the inscriptions were accurate.

CHAPTER TWO

RECOVERING MAYA ASTRONOMY

The study of Maya astronomy and calendrics by cMd scholars has a much longer history than is usually treated in the Mayanist literature. Most references begin with the groundbreaking work of Ernst Förstemann in the nineteenth century, over 100 years before the modern decipherment of the hieroglyphic script. Although his work is of uncontestable import, careful attention paid to colonial history reveals a more complex relationship between European and Maya scholars (Aldana 2001b: 273–312; Clendinnen 1987:154–160; Farriss 1984:286–319; cf. Boone 2000:2). This complexity affected the retrieval of Maya astronomy and thus the interpretations of Maya culture during the nineteenth and twentieth centuries. In this chapter, I review the early colonial engagement

45

between European and Maya intellectuals and the palimpsest that it created within modern approaches to recovering Maya astronomy. In order to address—and in some ways overwrite—this palimpsest, we then review the methodological inspiration for my research in the following chapters.

ANDRES DE AVENDAÑO AND LOST KNOWLEDGE

One of the most extensive studies of Maya ritual calendric knowledge must be attributed to the seventeenth-century Franciscan, Fray Andres de Avendaño. Although other servants of the Spanish crown before and after him wrote chronicles of Maya history or set out to record indigenous "customs" by royal order, Avendaño's literacy was sufficient for him to suggest a Maya conversion to Christianity through a reading of Maya hieroglyphic prophecies (G. Jones 1998:202).

One of the most interesting aspects of Avendaño's work, though, was not that he was reading Maya hieroglyphic manuscripts (codices) but that he was reading them so late. Twentieth-century scholars of the Maya—most vociferously J. Eric Thompson—commonly held the belief that Europeans had never been able to read the hieroglyphic script, much less understand its ritual content (Thompson 1972:3–5). Yet the words of more than a few sixteenth-century Europeans directly contradict Thompson's position. Fray Antonio de Ciudad Real, for example, claimed that some of his colleagues during the mid-sixteenth century achieved literacy in the Maya script. In his *Relación breve y verdadera*, Ciudad Real wrote: "Only the priests of the idols, called *ah kins* in that language, and an occasional noble understood these figures and letters [hieroglyphs]. Afterwards some of our friars understood them, knew how to read them, and even wrote them."[1]

Thompson was quite well versed in the Colonial period literature and in 1972 responded to Ciudad Real's claim in his *Commentary on the Dresden Codex*:

> The remark that some friars learned to write in these characters must surely refer to their use in a Testerian system for instructing converts in the Pater Noster, creed, etc., such as had developed on the Mexican plateau by 1589, when Ciudad Real wrote. The friars had no reason for learning to write the old pagan texts for which

Maya hieroglyphics were mainly employed and which were not
adaptable to Christian instruction. (Thompson 1972:4)

Here, Thompson is referring to a genre of pictorial catechisms that
have been called Testerian "after the Franciscan Jacobo Testera who
used paintings to help instruct the indigenous people in the Christian
religion" (Boone 1998:161). Thus, Thompson is claiming that Ciudad
Real was confused—that Ciudad Real witnessed friars painting pictorial catechisms and mistook the product for hieroglyphic texts.[2] An
additional complication that Thompson ignores is that Ciudad Real
was referring specifically to friars in the Maya region (using the term
ah kin, or *aj k'in* in the new orthography), and the Testerian script was
only used in Nahuatl regions.

Even if we follow Thompson and deny the ability to read the hieroglyphs to those who made the claim during the middle sixteenth century—within a generation of initial contact between Maya and European—how are we to deal with the knowledge that Avendaño was
reading and manipulating Maya prophecies over 100 years later? One
might suggest that the answer lies in Avendaño's uniqueness and his
negotiation with the Itza Maya of the central Petén—according to Spanish categorization, those Maya across "the frontier" (Farriss 1984). It is
much easier to visualize a Maya *itz'aat* ("learned one") producing and
consulting hieroglyphic manuscripts late in the seventeenth century if
we place him in the "backwaters" of Guatemala. Yet, even this allow-
ance creates a logistical problem since Avendaño only visited Tah Itza,
the "last Maya kingdom," twice—hardly enough time to acquire a fluency in the hieroglyphic script (G. Jones 1998:189; Villagutierre Soto-
Mayor 1983).

This apparent contradiction finds resolution in the differentiation
between two types of European knowledge regarding the Maya generated during the Colonial period. One form was passed down to Thompson. This perspective we recognize even in the early seventeenth-
century writings of the French Jesuit, Claude Duret. Of indigenous
books from Honduras, Duret noted that "the learned Indians understood and deduced the change of the seasons, a knowledge of the Planets, of the animals, and of other natural things, since antiquity: a thing
full of great curiosity and diligence. [Diego de Landa] thought that this

was all enchantment, an art of Magic, and obstinately held that [the books] should be burned, and he forced them to be placed in a fire" (Duret 1613:939–940).[3] In *Universal Languages* . . ., Duret then gives an account of a fellow Jesuit who consulted "les anciens de Tescuco, de Tulla, & Mexique" in order to learn of native histories, books, and calendars. In this account, Duret describes the type of writing used by these "sages Indiens": "Since their letters and characters were not sufficient, like our own letters and writings, they could not express with them all words, but only the substance of ideas" (Duret 1613:940).[4] Indeed, Duret provides a fitting description of Central Mexican (e.g., Mexica or Mixtec) writing, but it does not hold for Maya writing (Boone 2000; Brotherston 1995:10–20). Since, across the Atlantic, Duret did not distinguish between the two cultures or forms of writing, the distinction became lost for scholars in Europe.[5] Therefore, the recognition of the phonetic nature of Maya writing—and so the possibility of decipherment—never occurred to them.

For those scholars living among the Maya, however, an entirely different situation appears to have transpired. In a sixteenth-century plea to the Crown for more support across the "frontier," Fray Francisco de la Parra (1547:2) suggested that the men going to Yucatán, Guatemala, and Honduras had to be of "supple mind, young, and strong" in order to write dictionaries of the indigenous languages and to learn Maya customs by living among the Maya. These were the men who had the opportunity to learn the hieroglyphs and who acquired the cultural exposure to comprehend the role of these native writings in native cultures. These men may well have been the same ones who Ciudad Real described as recognizing the phonetic character of the script and recording it as such. Unfortunately, the writings of these men have been lost either to deterioration or to burial within the archives of Europe.[6]

We have evidence, however, for specific intellectual exchanges between Spanish priests and indigenous intellectuals. The *Books of Chilam Balam* provide clear evidence of appropriations of European knowledge into indigenous learning.[7] These books preserved the transmission of knowledge westward and were appended into the eighteenth century. We will examine one part of the *Book of Chilam Balam of Chumayel* in Chapter 7. As for the eastward transmission, it appears that the social discontinuity between the scholars studying "languages of the universe," such as Claude Duret, and those working in the trenches, such as Francisco de la Parra, produced the chasm of unfamiliarity with the hieroglyphic script that confronted the Mayanists of the nineteenth and twentieth centuries. Had there been more (or better) communication across the Atlantic (granted, not an easy proposition at the time), the ability to read and write the hieroglyphic text may not have needed a twentieth-century decipherment.[8] Thus, this gap—the one of the *lost* ability to read the hieroglyphic script—has contributed to the understanding (or misunderstanding) of the ancient Maya by scholars since the end of the seventeenth century. This loss also allowed for the central place of astronomy in the interpretations of Maya studies during the nineteenth and twentieth centuries.

THE NEW MAYA SCHOLARSHIP

A century and a half after Avendaño left the Petén, a new type of European arrived to take his place. These men experienced cultures and environments drastically altered through the colonial enterprise. Just prior to the beginning of the eighteenth century Avendaño visited an active Maya ceremonial center operating in the tradition of the Precontact Maya. The men of the nineteenth century, however, wandered about overgrown, dilapidated groups of architectural ruins long abandoned. Although both groups euphemized their activities through the rhetoric of "discovery," the latter group illustrated and photographed their "findings" and nested them within entertaining accounts of their adventures (Coe 1992:99-123).[9] The more careful of these men produced records of architecture and hieroglyphic writing that are still useful today (Maler 1908; Maudslay 1974 [1889]; Stephens 1996).

Just as Duret had worked independently of de la Parra, a group of scholars remained comfortably at home to stumble upon the literary products of the people who had abandoned the ancient structures visited by their more intrepid contemporaries. One man in particular, Ernst Förstemann, found himself in a position analogous to that encountered by modern scholars who come upon looted Maya artifacts. Förstemann attempted to find meaning in a document without

49

known provenance buried in the Dresden Library. His training in grammar, linguistics, and mathematics put Förstemann in a fortuitous position to uncover some of the mystery held within the several-hundred-year-old manuscript now known as the Dresden Codex.

By 1887, Förstemann had recovered from this document the fundamental components of the Maya calendar (Coe 1992:107). From the patterns of bars and dots in tabular form on nearly every page, the German linguist built on previous recognitions of the vigesimal mathematical system used in ancient times. In the vast majority of cases, these bars and dots served as coefficients for a set of twenty "day signs." The combination revealed a 260-day round structurally identical to the count used by the Aztecs (and all other members of Mesoamerican cultures reaching back to the Olmec). This 260-day count, Förstemann recognized, fit into a larger calendric system with the Long Count and the *haab'*.[10]

With the calendar securely deciphered, Förstemann was free to explore the patterns in the Dresden Codex that were constructed with calendric dates. One of the most influential of the patterns he found on pages 46–50 of the manuscript. Herein, Förstemann recognized recurring periods of 584 days, first broken down into sub-periods of 236, 90, 250, and 8 and then tabulated for larger periods of 2,920 days. The key for Förstemann was the proximity of 584 to the average synodic period of the planet Venus.[11] This information allowed for the four sub-periods to be recognized as reasonable approximations to the observable phases of Venus (i.e., morning visibility, superior conjunction, evening visibility, and inferior conjunction; see Aveni 1980, 2001; Lounsbury 1978:776–788). Furthermore, Förstemann noticed that a period of 2,920 days was extremely close to the period of commensuration between 8 solar years (2,921.9 days) and 5 Venus Rounds (2,919.6 days). With these correspondences, Förstemann postulated that this table served as an ephemeris for Venus.[12]

A second table, immediately following the Venus table, suggested lunar cycles to Förstemann, so he eventually ascribed a heavy astronomical content to the document (Coe 1992; Förstemann 1906). With ostensibly little else to work with on an intellectual level, Förstemann's colleagues fashioned cultures of the now "lost" Maya civilization based substantially on these celestial revelations. Hence, ironically enough, most twentieth-century archaeological interpretations of Maya intellectual culture were based on an "unprovenanced artifact" (Coe 1992).

By the early twentieth century, Mayanists had access both to Förstemann's interpretations of the Dresden Codex and to a growing corpus of photographic records of Classic period hieroglyphic inscriptions — texts preceding the Dresden Codex by some 300 to 600 years. Looking for meaning in these hieroglyphic texts without having the ability to read them, scholars soon found astronomical cycles embedded throughout the Classic period inscriptions as well, from the Venus and eclipse cycles of the Dresden Codex to tropical year calculations and sidereal lunar periods in the stelae of Copán and Yaxchilan.

Some of these careful studies achieved a degree of lasting success. In the 1930s, John Teeple (1931:53–61) recovered a lunar count from within Classic period inscriptions and suggested a pattern among them that, with slight revision (Aldana 2001b, 2004b), still holds today. Most, if not all, of his and his contemporaries' studies, however, based their work primarily on mathematical consistency without much regard for social context or utility. When interpretations were made, weight was given to astronomical importance. For example, Teeple (1931) used dates recorded in stone at several different cities to argue for an adjustment to the Maya approximation to the solar year. An altar from Copán, he went on to argue, depicted the sixteen astronomers in some grand congress accomplishing this feat.[13]

The ensuing proposal of a Maya astronomical obsession held for most of the twentieth century.[14] Without a reading of the hieroglyphic script in which dates were embedded, scholars focused on an astronomer-priest/farmer model of Maya society. The great cities were thought to have been built by *milperos* (rural maize farmers) who lived in thatch-roofed houses in the outskirts of town under the supervision of astronomer-priests who alone occupied the impressive monuments (Coe 1992:132–135; W. Fash 1991:10). Although phonetic hypotheses regarding the script were formed and debated during this period, no one produced a reading that countered this interpretation or, more importantly, that was entertained for long without severe attack (Coe 1992:123–144). Therefore, astronomy became the soul of Maya culture; to know the ancient Maya was to know their calendrics and their astronomy.

TABLE 2.1: Summary of date intervals at Piedras Negras

Series	Initial Date to Inaugural Date, Same Series	Initial Date to Initial Date Next Series	Initial Date to Inaugural Date, Next Series	Inaugural Date to Inaugural Date, Next Series
1	?	?	?	1.15.16.13 (35+ years)
2	13.1.8 (12+ years)	1.19.3.1 (38+ years)	3.1.9.0 (60+ years)	2.8.7.12 (47+ years)
3	1.2.5.19 (22+ years)	1.17.7.13 (36+ years)	3.5.14.11 (64+ years)	2.3.8.12 (42+ years)
4	1.8.6.18 (28– years)	?	2.17.2.6 (56+ years)	1.8.13.8 (28+ years)
5	?	?	?	5.11.17 (5+ years)
6	?	?	?	17.16.16 (17+ years)
7	1.11.10.17 (31+ years)	?	?	?

Source: Proskouriakoff (1960:461, table 1).

A DIFFERENT PUZZLE

Playing with dates remained popular methodologically well through the 1950s, but one scholar in particular changed the course of Maya studies by toying with them under a different initial assumption. In 1960, Tatiana Proskouriakoff found among the inscriptions of Yokib (Piedras Negras) a sequence of dates that implied the recording of *historical* — not astronomical — cycles.

Her choice of city on which to perform the analysis was ideal. At Piedras Negras, archaeologists had recovered a series of monuments that marked very frequent and regular intervals. A subgroup of these monuments shared the same artistic motif: a human figure sitting within a niche, framed by a band of symbols that rested on some sort of animal (see Figure 2.1). In the analysis of seven series of stelae, each containing one of these motifs, Proskouriakoff recognized an intriguing historical pattern (see Table 2.1). She concluded from this pattern that the intervals among the recorded dates corresponded to periods between births, accessions, and deaths of the members of a ruling dynasty (Proskouriakoff 1960). The scenes, then, consistently depicted

FIGURE 2.1: *Piedras Negras Ruler 4, moments after posing for depiction on Stela 11, showing his accession to a Celestial Dragon throne*

the inauguration of a ruler as his seating on a throne, and the accompanying inscription provided the vitals of his personal history.

With this decisive (and divisive) work, the historical thesis was born. This thesis held that the content of the inscriptions did not primarily concern the movements of celestial bodies (at least not explicitly) but instead recorded critical events in the political lives of mortal people. Combined with the slow but insistent reception of Yuri Knorosov's phonetic hypothesis and Heinrich Berlin's recognition of Emblem Glyphs, the emphasis of the inscription dates was transformed (Coe 1992). Scholars began to utilize dates to anchor the names of specific *ajawtahk* within the reconstruction of Classic Maya ruling dynasties, changing the rubric behind Maya studies. Now, to know the Maya was to know their dynastic histories (as noted in the last chapter), not the astronomy in which they were supposedly engaged.

This interpretive move thrust astronomy behind the scenes, for if the inscriptions really did record mainly dynastic and ritual records, astronomy had to be relegated to subtext. Of course this shift did not end investigations into Maya astronomy. Scholars suggested that rulers still could have used astronomy to time historical accessions and public rituals, arguing that the *application* of the science still could be recovered by modern scholarship even if the "science" itself was not the main concern of the texts.[15]

Just as astronomy was being pushed into the background, however, a trend developed east of the Atlantic with the potential to challenge this displacement. These seeds of change had nothing to do with the ancient Maya. During the 1960s and 1970s, interest rose in the astronomical endeavors of prehistoric cultures around the world (Aveni 2001; Ruggles 1999). The result was the birth of a new field of study.

ENTER ARCHAEOASTRONOMY

The seminal works of archaeoastronomy attempted to reveal east of the Atlantic a "megalithic science" within the construction of sites such as Stonehenge and Newgrange. During the 1960s and 1970s Alexander Thom and Gerald Hawkins claimed to find a sophisticated astronomy encoded in the placement of megaliths relative to the movements of celestial bodies (Hawkins 1965; Ruggles 1988; Thom 1967). The hypothesis that the alignments of stones marked astronomical orientations was not an unreasonable one; where these scholars found difficulty was in the method with which they proposed to test it. The authors of these studies suggested that the intent of the builders could be accessed through statistical analyses alone. Mathematical consistency was proposed to determine whether or not a particular alignment of a monument was intentionally constructed to mark some celestial phenomenon (Thom 1967).

Critiques of this method soon formed within and outside the community of archaeoastronomers (see, e.g., the repartee between Aveni [1992] and Kintigh [1992]). What is important here, though, is that something of this approach made its way into Mesoamerican studies. Researchers, principally Anthony Aveni and Horst Hartung, began to parallel the inscription-based work of pre-decipherment Mayanists with studies of astronomically oriented architecture.[16] To a degree, archaeoastronomy was an external project that was imported into Maya studies. Originally developed in Europe to explain the features of pre- or non-historic cultures, archaeoastronomy was used in Maya studies with little adaption to fit the needs or directions of this new application. Ironically, early efforts to recover Maya astronomy had been based on an artifact far removed from its original, albeit unknown, location (the Dresden Codex), and now methods created outside Mesoamerica were brought in to reveal yet another version of Maya astronomy.

Accordingly, one of the largest problems facing early archaeoastronomical studies was that of academic legitimation. The very formulations of their arguments put archaeoastronomers outside of any preexisting disciplines. Their appeals to statistical analyses, however, resonated with the methods of the New Archaeology. Also aiding their cause was that the case for Maya archaeoastronomy was easier to make than it was for other civilizations. With the long tradition of astronomical study—however questionable it had become—it was no great stretch to begin to integrate archaeoastronomical finds into the cultural reconstructions of the day (Carlson 1976; Schele and Fash 1991; Schele and Larios 1991). This backdrop set up a complicated scenario as captured by Anthony Aveni (2001:4):

> Because [archaeoastronomers] tend to frame their arguments in the scientific jargon of their specialty, the anthropologists either blindly accept their propositions out of awe and reverence for the complexity of language and scientific method or they refuse to consider an argument because they cannot comprehend the intricacies of positional astronomy delineated in tracts that were never intended for a nonscientific audience. Conversely, many outrageous astronomical assertions have been uttered by untrained anthropologists, who, with a little understanding of elementary astronomy, could have carried their theories a long way.

This lack of critical engagement was quite unfortunate as it allowed Mesoamerican archaeoastronomy to develop outside of the theoretical debates of the time.[17] Much of the archaeoastronomical literature culled from Maya hieroglyphic texts was but a "thin" form of interdisciplinarity. These scholars aimed to legitimize themselves through quantitative astronomical arguments and then borrowed anthropological and/or historical material to bolster their claims. Often, unconnected elements of cultural data that seemed to address the statistically recovered astronomy were utilized without consideration of whether there was some historical connection there. Thus, ethnohistory, archaeology, ethnography, and iconography were all loosely brought together to contextualize an astronomical find.[18] Although methodologically questionable, this aspect of the research probably served the community to a degree in that it allowed the work to address a wide audience, thereby increasing its chances for academic acceptance. That is, since the technical astronomical argument was often outside the familiarity of most anthropologists, archaeoastronomers needed a different hook to catch the interest of traditional anthropological subdisciplines. Instead of a hook, though, they set about casting a large net, pulling together enough variety to appeal to a number of different specialties.[19]

None of these theoretical or methodological difficulties, however, prevented archaeoastronomers from rapidly producing provocative results. The architectural construct known as the Group E complex (after its map location at Waxaktun) is one such example. Recognized by Frans Blom in 1924, the complex comprised three temples on a platform built on the eastern edge of a plaza near the center of Waxaktun (Aveni 2001:289; Aveni and Hartung 1986). In the center of the plaza, a square, cardinally oriented structure faced this platform. From a landing on the east-facing staircase of this central structure, one could witness the positions of the solar year. Off the corner of the southernmost temple, the sun could be seen rising on the winter solstice (see Figure 2.2). Similarly, the northernmost temple marked the summer solstice, and the central structure marked the equinoxes (Aveni and Hartung 1986).

The Templo Mayor at Tenochtitlan, as well as solar and Venusian alignments in Yucatán, presented similar observationally compelling arguments for intentional alignment to astronomical events (Aveni 2001:235–244, 273–279). So, difficulties aside, the work of archaeoastronomers corroborated holdover sensibilities that indeed the Dresden Codex contained material of interest more broadly in Classic Maya culture, even if astronomy was not the explicit content of the hieroglyphic inscriptions. The confidence produced by these results apparently spurred researchers to return to pre-Proskouriakoffian tactics and to look again at intervals among the dates of various texts for evidence of astronomical activity (Dütting 1985; Schele and Freidel 1990; Tate 1985).

During the 1980s and 1990s, less complex studies followed mid-twentieth-century practices, showing, for example, that several dates in the inscriptions of Yaxchilan were separated by multiples of lunar periods or that specific recorded dates appear to have coincided with equinoxes or solstices.[20] In other cases, scholars claimed to find correspondences between the dates anchoring a specific glyph and the "events" of a given planet.[21] These authors then inferred that the anchored glyphs must have been appellations for planets, implying the renewed significance of astronomy in hieroglyphic inscriptions. Here scholars suggested that—despite the predominant concern with human historical events—certain celestial historical events were of sufficient import to have been recorded as well.[22] Taken together, these studies promoted the image of Maya astronomers as completely analogous to their ancient Chaldean and Greek counterparts.[23]

Some of these studies followed standard archaeoastronomical methodology in relying principally on statistical correlations to justify their conclusions (Aveni and Hotaling 1994). Others relied more on the coincidence of specific recorded dates and planetary positions as generated by computer programs (Closs 1994; Dutting 1985; Freidel, Schele

FIGURE 2.2: *The moon anticipates the winter solstice sunrise, rising off the corner of the southernmost temporary structure on the Group E platform at Tikal during the Early Classic period*

and Parker 1993; Milbrath 2002; Tate 1985). In some of these cases, however, the specific content of the inscriptions was not taken into consideration. For example, one study sought to correlate all celestial references in the corpus of hieroglyphic inscriptions to their purported observed referents. A significant number of the supposed celestial references, however, were actually records of historical figures' names, which happened to include celestial components (Aveni and Hotaling 1994; for identification of names, see Aldana 2001b, 2005a).

Actually, this problem was recognized decades ago. J.E.S. Thompson wrote in 1972 that "over thirty years ago I was able to show that Ludendorff obtained a higher percentage of astronomical phenomena on dates that had been incorrectly deciphered than on those correctly deciphered" (23). Thompson also addressed a claim for finding a pattern of purported Jupiter cycles "with results so decisive that, were it a matter of pure chance, there would be less than one chance in ten million of hitting these nails on their heads. . . . [T]he situation is repeated with Smiley's one chance in ten million scoop for dates which in many cases were never recorded in the codex" (1972:23). In other words, many archaeoastronomical arguments have leaned on statistical computations demonstrating that patterns recovered from glyphic texts could not have resulted from pure chance—even when the patterns themselves depended on faulty interpretations. Despite these complications, the results of the more recent studies have generally been accepted (Coe 2005:228; Freidel et al. 1993; Harrison 1999:122; Martin and Grube 2000:16).

Other scholars have suggested that the astrologer's role may have been even greater in contributing to intellectual culture. David Kelley (1980), for example, implied that early Mesoamerican astronomers systematically encoded the planetary identities of the gods in the calendrical dates with which they were generally associated.[24] According to his hypothesis, a base date had been used that when combined with the synodic periods of the planets, would reveal the association astrologers made between the calendric names of the gods and their planetary identities.[25] Thus, when one Jupiter round after 12 Lamat 1 Pop resulted in the day 7 Kimi 14 Wo, Kelley (1980:S22–S24) identified Jupiter with the Maya God M and Mixcoatl—the Mexica god characterized by the day 7 Death. Here, Kelley was explicitly arguing for a Maya (actually, pan-Mesoamerican) astronomical method.

Dennis Tedlock (1992) presented a theory somewhat similar to Kelley's, but he restricted his study to speakers of Mayan languages. Tedlock attempted to demonstrate that the same astronomical events were being referenced in the story of Creation told within Kan B'ahlam's Triad Group (which we will treat in Chapter 4) as those in the several-hundred-year-younger and several-hundred-mile-distant Dresden Codex. These references, he claimed, revealed the Maya identities of the planets such that he was able to name Venus as Jun Junajpu, the sun as Junajpu, and the moon as Xbalamke (D. Tedlock 1992). Although these results differed from Kelley's, both of these studies suggested a more complicated job description for the Classic Maya astronomer and specifically targeted the retrieval of indigenous astronomical method.

Kelley's and Tedlock's studies appealed to a standard Mesoamerican pantheon, portable across culture and time. Their hypothesis has been challenged by others (Gillespie and Joyce 1998). Furthermore, they do not corroborate each other in their deity assignments, and neither do many of the other studies of their time. As noted previously, the resulting views of astrologers' duties remain relatively consistent, but the results those astrologers supposedly obtained rarely were.

A large part of the problem lies in methodology. Specifically, several of the aforementioned studies rely heavily on two factors that possess great potential for producing false positives. The first is that a correlation between the Maya and European calendars must be chosen in order to reconstruct the positions of the planets on the dates associated with certain events. This reconstruction is problematic because no calendar correlation has yet been proven and also enough "events" occur in any night sky to produce patterns that can be imbued with meaning by modern researchers.[26]

The second (and more daunting) factor is that even if the dates recorded in the inscriptions were strictly regulated by politics and had nothing to do with astronomical cycles, there should still be detectable astronomical cycles among them. That is, if a set of dates is not planned by astronomical events, then these dates may be considered random relative to such events. Given enough random dates, it is the mathematical rule that some patterns will still emerge among the dates coincidentally.[27] Hence, not only should one expect to find astronomical cycles in long strings of dates, but if they are not intentional, one may also expect that interpretations of such cycles will generally contradict each other across a number of independent studies. This result is precisely what we find in many of the aforementioned studies and again echoes Thompson's (1972:23) thirty-year-old (albeit overstated) observation: "If astronomers contradict each other so flatly on this matter, it is pretty clear that all are wrong."

Another aspect of this methodology that has created some of these contradictions comes from ignoring historical context. Both Kelley and Tedlock in particular gathered together data from sources separated substantially in both space and time.[28] Analytically, they may have found significant patterns tying all of this data together, but they have not sufficiently established how transmission may have occurred to justify the connection between the different sources in the first place. The possibility again arises here that they have aggregated enough dates to generate interesting patterns in randomness—an observation also made in the abstract by Matthew Looper (2003:32), who critiques the bricoleur's approach to interpreting Classic Maya art. Although this methodology by no means characterizes archaeoastronomical research as a whole—or even that treating Maya culture— it does appear to characterize the core approach in the field to hieroglyphically recorded astronomy.

HISTORICAL MOVES

When I began my research, I intended to focus on the history of astronomy during the Colonial period in Yucatán and Guatemala with only a brief treatment of Precontact astronomy to set the background. But a coherent background became quite elusive. In order to choose among the various versions of Maya astronomy found in the literature, I decided to base my decision on scholarly method. Because of my appreciation for the rigor in his approach, I focused my early attention on re-deriving Floyd Lounsbury's arguments in particular.

Floyd Lounsbury began his academic training as a mathematician but switched to the study of languages upon entering graduate school (Coe 1992:197–198). When his attention turned to the intellectual artifacts of the ancient Maya, Lounsbury thus was able to weigh textual and astronomical evidence equally. Moreover, in all of his mathematically based work, Lounsbury sought the Maya method leading to the recovered results. In the *Dictionary of Scientific Biography*, Lounsbury

(1978:768) demonstrated a clear Maya appeal to arithmetic algorithms in the performance of tedious calculations. Such an approach proved tremendously insightful when Lounsbury went back to treat some of the same inscriptions from which Teeple had culled his lunar results. It was through these studies that I began to appreciate the logic of what Lounsbury called "contrived numbers" (1976:218).

I eventually worked through Lounsbury's writings during my off-time from digging through the archives of the Arzobispado in Mérida. Without access to an extensive library, I was content to play with the texts from the Palenque Temple of Inscriptions, using Lounsbury's articles, my notes and handouts from David Stuart's class on Maya hieroglyphic writing, and a pocket calculator. By the end of the summer I came across an anomalous passage in the third tablet of the Temple of Inscriptions, which will take center stage in the next chapter. Once the academic year started, however, I suspended further treatment of the anomaly.

I picked up the thread again in time to present the Venusian periods in the third tablet of the Temple of Inscriptions the following summer as part of a work in progress in Berlin at the Max Plank Institute for the History of Science for the International Laboratory's conference on the Material Culture of Calculation. By the end of summer 1998 — again working in my off-time from archival research (this time in Seville) — I became convinced that I would make no headway into Colonial period astronomy without first coming to terms with Precontact astronomy. Thus, I needed a strategy to avoid the methodological difficulties pointed out previously.

Having in the meantime gained a substantial familiarity with Lounsbury's corpus of writings, I was convinced that he had developed — and most faithfully adhered to — the most rigorous methodology for recovering Mesoamerican astronomy. In particular, with regard to astronomical periods and what he called "contrived numbers," Lounsbury's work rested on three premises: (1) the dates in question spanned a substantial number of days such that contrivance would have been warranted; (2) the events or people indicated by the dates were connected in some relevant way other than simply by the numbers linking them;[29] and (3) a larger theme or issue underlay the connections, leading to the intent for such connections in the first place. Lounsbury's work resulting from this methodology did not challenge orthodoxy and implied that the court astrologer functioned as a mystical secretary for the Classic period *ajawtahk*. By combining their numerological skills with astronomical phenomena, the skywatchers were apparently able to set future dates, manipulate historical ones, or select from a set of alternative dates to imply relationships across vast intervals of time.

From this reading of the scholarship, I began my own investigation into hieroglyphically recorded Maya astronomy with a new set of constraints in order to adequately avoid the trap of detecting only "pattern in randomness." In addition to the points made by Lounsbury, I also maintained that the numerological reconstruction itself could not be the source of a glyphic decipherment; rather, it could only augment what had already been deciphered. Second, historical context could not be ignored; that is, mechanisms and means of transmitting concepts had to be taken into account in order to make use of two sources separated significantly by space and/or time.

I did not intend to ignore mathematical consistency. Rather, I was now taking mathematical tractability as necessary but not sufficient to demonstrate that a given interpretation of an apparent astronomical pattern was secure. Thus, it followed that any acceptable interpretation would have to be mathematically coherent. With these guidelines in mind, I began the first step of the study that would advance my comprehension of the astronomy within the hieroglyphic texts of the Temple of Inscriptions.

Ideally, I would have liked to reconstruct the method behind the purported astronomy in the Temple of Inscriptions solely through means that I knew would have been accessible to a Classic Maya *itz'aat*. Therefore, I focused my initial efforts on looking for textual clues and computing intervals, using both computing seeds and a calculator. I soon realized, however, that my fluency in the hieroglyphic script may have been adequate to detect the most blatant clue left by the author of the text in the Temple of Inscriptions, but it was not sufficiently reliable to ensure detection of all of them.

In order to proceed systematically, I set up a hypothesis. Namely, if the utilization of Venusian periods was of major significance to the astronomy in the Dresden Codex (still the best understood artifact of

Table 2.2: Table of intervals from the Temple of Inscriptions' tablets that contain factors suggesting contrivance

First date	Source	Second Date	Source	Interval	Factor(s)
9.6.0.0.0	TIE	9.12.11.4.10	TIW	47,250	378
9.6.1.10.3	TIE	9.11.0.9.7	TIW	35,624	584
9.6.18.5.12	TIE	1.0.0.0.0.8	TIW	1,534,216	116
9.7.5.0.0	TIE	9.12.10.0.0	TIW	37,800	378
9.8.11.9.10	TIE	9.12.11.5.18	TIW	28,728	378, 399
9.8.11.9.10	TIE	9.12.11.12.10	TIW	28,860	260, 780
9.8.13.0.0.	TIE	9.12.3.6.6	TIW	25,326	378
9.8.17.9.0	TIE	9.12.10.0.0	TIW	26,100	116
9.8.17.15.14	TIE	13.4.12.3.6	TIW	1,326,848	584
9.8.17.15.14	TIE	9.12.0.6.18	TIW	22,504	116
9.9.2.4.8	TIE	1.0.0.0.0.8	TIW	1,518,400	260, 365, 584
9.9.2.4.8	TIW	1.0.0.0.0.8	TIW	1,518,400	260, 365, 584
9.8.7.14.7	TIW	9.11.0.9.7	TIW	18,980	260, 365
9.12.3.6.6	TIW	9.12.10.0.0	TIW	2,394	399

Notes: TIE refers to the East Tablet of the Temple of Inscriptions and TIW refers to the West Tablet. This table does not include all pairs of dates that contain astronomical periods as factors. I have left out of this list, for example, intervals that argue against necessitating contrivance for their inclusion in the narrative. Predominantly, these intervals were composed of period ends (e.g., 9.6.0.0.0–9.6.13.0.0) and carry along 260 and 780, which is probably why ends of thirteenth *tuns* could be commemorated by recently inaugurated *ajawtahk*.

Maya astronomical activity), other puzzles built on astronomical periods also might be present among the intervals of the text. Indeed, Lounsbury purported to find such records in later texts from Palenque, so the hypothesis was not entirely original (Schele and Mathews 1991). To determine whether astronomical cycles were built into the intervals separating recorded events, I engaged a mathematically brute-force method. I developed an algorithm that generated the intervals between all pairs of dates in the three tablets of the Temple of Inscriptions and then checked to see if these intervals comprised significant astronomical numbers. I assumed the following set of numbers may have been used for contrivance: 116, 260, 364, 365, 378, 399, 584, 780, 819, 2,392, 3,276.[30] The output of the program is summarized in Table 2.2.

For comparing only a few dates, this procedure can be carried out relatively easily by hand. The number of distance numbers generated for n dates, however, may be computed as

$$\sum_{i=2}^{n} (i-1) ,$$

which quickly becomes computationally overwhelming. Since we are checking the divisibility of these distance numbers by the astronomical periods listed previously, the total number of computations for this project comes to ten times this sum, which reaches a magnitude of 100 for only five dates. The tablets of Janaab' Pakal's funerary temple contain over forty distinct dates, yielding over 7,000 intervals to check. Hence I resorted to the services of a computer. The reader should note, though, that the individual computations also could have been performed by an ancient Maya *itz'aat* and an *itz'aat* would not have had to perform so many calculations since the subtle clues unavailable to me would have been readily accessible to him.[31] Therefore, in theory, I am using a method for understanding the inscription that might have been used to compose it and that could have been used to solve the numerological puzzles by the ancients.

After generating the results summarized in Table 2.2, my first observation was that all the planetary periods showed up as factors of the resulting distance numbers. Thompson's caveat warns, however, that this apparent connection might be attributed to statistical probability, as might be the number of times each shows up. Before moving on to any interpretation of Table 2.2, therefore, I had to evaluate whether the presence of these factors represented the result of pure chance or whether they were intentionally included in the formation of the text. To do so, I began by considering the distribution of astronomically relevant date pairs within the texts. If the factors were produced randomly, we would expect them to be relatively evenly distributed across all three tablets. As shown in Figure 2.3, distribution is clearly concentrated in the West Tablet, the one that is the most jumbled chronologically.

This visual clustering, along with its specific placement, spurred me to look at the specific textual connections made by the numbers. But I was concerned that a textual exegesis would still not be enough. Although there seemed to be enough mathematical consistency to suggest that a mathematical method was behind the set of patterns (confirming part of my hypothesis), to determine whether these patterns held any significance I would have to venture out of the abstract mathematical world and into the cultural space that purportedly generated this set of patterns. To demonstrate that the patterns reflected historical

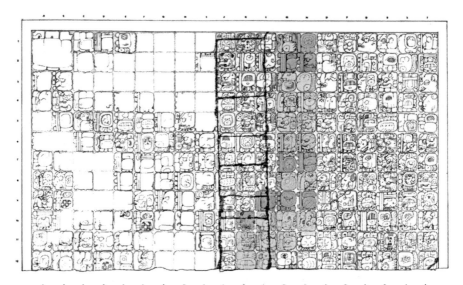

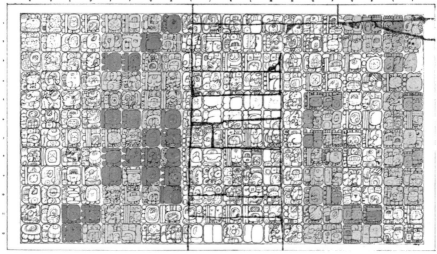

FIGURE 2.3: *Distribution of the numerological associations in the tablets from Janaab' Pakal's funerary monument. The shaded passage in the East Tablet covers the accession of Aj Ne' Ohl Mat through the defeat of Palenque by the Kalak'mu ajaw; the darker shaded glyphs are those dates with astronumerological connections. The first shaded passage in the West Tablet corresponds to the text bounded by the two 5 Lamat 1 Mol dates; the other shaded passages are astronumerologically related to the East Tablet.*

intent, I had to be able to engage the means by which intent might be corroborated.

At this point I faced three separate issues. First, I needed to figure out how these patterns were generated. Second, I had to determine whether the specific astronomical numbers that fell out of the study were actually significant. Third, I needed to be able to answer why they were generated in this venue.

The first question basically set up a puzzle-solving endeavor. Chapters 4 and 5 spell out the puzzle as I recognized it and identify the 819-day count as the key to its solution. The second question was a bit trickier to answer in that we have to take into account aspects of Maya culture that are not explicitly noted in these texts. Nevertheless, the necessary connections come from reliable sources and are spelled out in Chapter 7. The most difficult part was generating a reasonable response to the third question, because we must explicitly confront the attempt to establish historical intent. When considering this question, what first came to mind were Anthony Aveni's caveats regarding the recovery of Mesoamerican astronomy.

In particular, Aveni (1980, 2001:4) consistently warned (and continues to warn) that we must not allow our own perspectives of what astronomy is to govern our recovery of what astronomy has been. In other words, the ultimate challenge is to not allow the biases of our own cultural history to direct the interpretations we make of astronomies independently maintained in "other" cultures. Although important, this caveat is not sufficiently prescriptive to engage a specific astronomical problem.

Stepping back, though, I recognized a set of opposing viewpoints that seemed to frame perceptions of ancient astronomy. On one hand, modern scholars not familiar with astronomy are confronted with a cultural lack of interest in observing celestial bodies and relatively few such objects that can penetrate the current light pollution. To them, astronomical events, such as heliacal rises, maximum elongations, or planetary conjunctions, are esoteric and it is difficult to see their possible relevance. On the other, modern astronomers, archaeoastronomers, and even astrologers can identify several "significant" celestial events in just a week's time—plenty of evidence to argue for ancient interest and to provide ready interpretation. On a level of practicality, therefore, an argument for Maya astronomical method must overcome non-astronomically minded modern scholars' cultural blinders and, at the other extreme, find a means to manage a seeming overabundance of potential data.

According to my reading of historian of science Bruno Latour's work, the key would be to focus on the historical practice of Maya astronomy, in effect reintroducing the ancient astronomer. Namely, an ancient Maya *ajaw* would not have had to wait long for something to turn up in the night sky that could be "read" as an omen appropriate to her/his stately needs.[32] The astronomer responsible for reporting potentially useful omens to the *ajaw* would have needed two things: a model of the universe sufficiently accurate to predict regular astronomical events and, more importantly, a cosmology that identified certain events as important.[33] Most of the nuts and bolts of ancient Mesoamerican models had been worked out early in the history of Mayanist activity.[34] In my own work, though, I seemed to be confronting a relatively novel — and extensive — application of a new tool. How could I best demonstrate from its application that this or any given tool had been recovered properly and that its intent was as described?

Here I turned to the study of the social maintenance of language, although the language in question was not verbal but mathematical. My hypothesis became that the best possible corroboration of a tool's existence would be if I could demonstrate the mathematical soundness of a tool *and* its sensible place in its historical context. The difficulty now was in establishing what constituted a sensible place.

The social study of science (e.g., history and philosophy of science; studies of scientific knowledge) over the last several decades has demonstrated that science is never an autonomous project. Rather, the individuals engaged in science, as well as the social, political, and religious influences acting upon those individuals, impact the practice of science in myriad ways.[35] Perhaps especially in ancient societies, science does not occur in a cultural vacuum, a critical consideration for any methodology. The motivation for a given science should also be reflected in other cultural expressions; likewise, political and social pressures on certain intellectual activities may very well be exerted on scientific activities. In short, such an approach requires that a given recovery of science fits well in a recovery of that science's historical and intellectual context.[36] Chapter 6 accepts this challenge and demonstrates the synchronic answer to the why question and Chapter 7 places that response in its diachronic framework.[37]

Like so many other Maya epigraphers, I had cut my teeth on the famed texts of Palenque. By using a new analytical lens to view these texts, however, I have been able to tease out a substantially revised history of this Classic Maya city. Once I had explored the overall intellectual historical context of this set of patterns, I felt I had enough to write up my interpretation for the dissertation and for presentation at two international conferences: the History of Science Society Annual Meeting in Vancouver in 2000 and the IV Mesa Redonda de Palenque in Chiapas, Mexico, during the summer of 2002.

For now, we must recognize that it was the *lost* ability to read the hieroglyphic script that resulted in the early emphasis on finding astronomy in Maya intellectual culture. Although patterns within calendric dates revolutionized the scholarly understanding of Maya culture, that revolution came through a historical—not an astronomical—hypothesis. Hence, astronomy continues to hold an enigmatic position within the field of Maya studies. The following chapters do not completely dissolve this ambiguity. Rather, by returning to Teeple's and Lounsbury's interests, we begin to recover the place of astronomy in one historical place and time and so gain a perch from which to view a broad landscape of Classic Maya elite history. With this backdrop in mind, we now turn to an esoteric knowledge embedded within three inscriptions at Palenque and the light they shed on the intellectual work of Palenque's royal court.

NOTES

1. The Spanish can be found in Ciudad Real (1873). This translation is taken from Thompson (1972:4). Coe (1992:139-140) quotes the same passage, although with a different translation coming from Brinton (1890:234-235) yet attributed to Fray Alonso Ponce (probably through confusion generated by the title).

2. Here Thompson follows Cyrus Thomas, who considered the recorded language to have been "in a transition stage from the purely ideographic to the phonetic." Quoted in Coe (1992:117).

3. "[L]es sages Indiens tenoient comprinses, et deduictes la distribution de leurs temps, la cognoissance des Planettes, des animaux, et des autres choses naturelles, avec leurs antiquitez: chose pleine de grande curiosité et diligence. Il sembla à quell que pendant, que tout cela estoit un enchantement, et art de Magic, et soubstint obstinement que l'on les devoit brusler, de forte qu'ils furent mis en feu."

4. "[P]ourceque leurs escritures & caracteres n'estoient pas si suffisants, comme nos lettres & escritures, Ils ne pouvoient exprimer de si pres les paroles, ains seulement la substance des conceptions."

5. Valentini espoused the same opinion in 1880 (Coe 1992:119).

6. Notable missing documents are those produced by sixteenth-century cosmographer Francisco Dominguez — with the aid of Gaspar Antonio Xiu — and by Avendaño, who was mentioned previously.

7. I have also argued that the Paris Codex is a Postcontact document based on its astronomical content (Aldana 2001b). Likewise, Michael Coe has argued that the Madrid Codex was written in part on Spanish paper (Coe and Kerr 1998:181). These texts might be seen as further examples of knowledge transmission from east to west.

8. A similar discontinuity in knowledge maintenance provided another type of error and resulted in the debate of 1550, in which Bartolomé de las Casas, who traveled throughout the Western Hemisphere and advocated a more sympathetic approach to indigenous people, was matched against Juan Gines de Sepulveda, *the* humanist of his time, who relied on books for his information and authority and never traveled outside of Europe.

9. I use the term *findings* although now it is commonly acknowledged that these structures were not lost; they were simply unknown to cMd populations for a given period of time.

10. See prefatory section "Note on Maya Calendrics," pp. xxv–xxviii.

11. The synodic period is the time it takes for a celestial body to return to a specified position relative to the sun when viewed from the earth.

12. See Aldana (2001b, 2003a) for a new interpretation suggesting that the table works more effectively as an oracular tool than as an ephemeris.

13. This hypothesis was not seriously challenged until 1977, when John Carlson revealed the assumptions behind the calculations that supported this interpretation to be extremely tenuous. Indeed, part of his argument anticipated the focus of this work that, in this case, enough dates were pulled together such that patterns could be expected out of randomness. The decipherment of the script eventually brought along the readings that named the figures as the sixteen members of Copán's ruling dynasty.

14. The story is entertainingly described by Michael Coe in *Breaking the Maya Code* (1992). For more on this interpretation, see any of the recent popu-

lar treatments of Maya culture, such as William Fash (1991:91) and Prudence Rice (2004) or refer to the original texts of Sylvanus Morley, John Teeple, or J.E.S. Thompson.

15. The literature on the timing of ceremonies by astronomical events is substantial. In the popular literature, see Coe (1993) or Schele and Freidel (1990). For the scholarly literature, see specific cases cited later in this chapter.

16. See principally Aveni (1980, 2001), which contain a summary of his early work in the field.

17. In some ways, this issue continues to pose difficulties to the community of archaeoastronomers. The last major archaeoastronomy conference (the 7th Oxford Conference on Archaeoastronomy [2004]) was dedicated to exploring the "relationship between anthropology and archaeoastronomy."

18. See, for example, the Rain-Maize-Venus complex by Closs, Aveni, and Crowley (1984) and by Sprajc (1996). Also see Carlson (1993) on the Venus Wars. Against this complex, see Aldana (2001b:89–134; 2005a). Even Aveni's revision (2001:169) includes interpretations that are not based on updated hieroglyphic records.

19. A later example of this same phenomenon occurs in Freidel, Schele, and Parker's *Maya Cosmos* (1993). In a piquant review published in the *Cambridge Archaeological Journal* (1995), virtually every reviewer negatively criticized the material from their realm of expertise yet praised or accepted the material outside of their training.

20. See Dütting (1985); and Tate (1985).

21. By *events* I mean phenomena such as planetary conjunctions and heliacal rises. See Aveni and Hotaling (1994); Closs (1994); Justeson and Fox (1978); and Lounsbury (1978). Also see Bricker, Aveni, and Bricker (2001).

22. See especially Closs (1994) and Schele (1992); but cf. Aldana (2005a).

23. The standard references for the work of these early Mediterranean scientists include Neugebauer (1952) and Van der Waerden (1974).

24. Kelley (1980) attributes no explicit authorship to any one cultural group, but for the identities to have been pan-Mesoamerican as he claimed, the association had to have been made relatively early.

25. Many of the Mexica and Mixtec gods were known by Calendar Round names in addition to their personal names; for example, Quetzalcoatl was also known as 9 Wind.

26. For European Renaissance astrological ephemeri, see Aldana (2001b); Kelley (1983); as well as Thompson (1960).

27. For the theoretical justification of this phenomenon, see a general text on combinatorial mathematics, especially the section on the Ramsey Theory in Erickson (1996). For a discussion intended for a nontechnical audience, see Paulos (1988).

28. Kelley attempts to use data from all of Mesoamerica; Tedlock combines Postclassic Yucatec with Colonial K'iche and Classic Usumacinta sources.

29. The connections referred to here are understood broadly to encompass social, political, or religious intentions.

30. These numbers represent integer approximations that respectively correspond to the synodic period of Mercury, *chol qiij*, Lounsbury's computing year, *haab'*, the synodic period of Saturn, the synodic period of Jupiter, the synodic period of Venus, the synodic period of Mars, the duration of one station in the 819-day count, the lunar formula used at Palenque, and a complete 819-day count cycle.

31. Extremely large numbers of computations performed by hand are not unheard of from ancient times. Johannes Kepler, for example, claimed to have performed thousands of calculations in his work on Mars for the *Astronomiae Nova*.

32. This interpretation does not have to be considered as pure political manipulation without belief in the omens themselves. Instead, the ruler might have viewed the sky as a rich resource of information with frequent potential answers to his questions.

33. In my opinion, defining this cosmology is one of the greatest stumbling blocks. Several authors argue that Maya astronomers would have been qualitatively interested in such phenomena as maximum elongation or retrograde motion. Such hypotheses, however, seem to rely heavily on cMd visions of the sky.

34. Aveni's *Skywatchers* (2001:4) summarized the field, aiming to provide "a bridge to connect the established disciplines of astronomy, archaeology, culture history, and the histories of astronomy and religion. It is intended to serve as a platform for the exchange of ideas among students of these seemingly disparate fields."

35. For a variety of results drawn from various contexts, see Biagioli (1999); Daston and Park (1998); Fleck (1981); Galison (1997); Latour (1987); Shapin and Schaffer (1985).

36. Beyond the problem of contextualization, I confronted the issue of translation across languages and between cultures. For more information on this issue, see Aldana (2001b); Clifford (1988); Tambiah (1990); Taussig (1987).

37. While at Palenque, I had the good fortune of meeting Moises Morales, local Maya ambassador to the archaeological site. After my presentation, Don Moises approached me to bring to my attention that a colleague and good friend of his had been working on a bit of the same problem. Specifically, Christopher Powell of the University of Texas, Austin, had written a Master's

thesis on the subject of the 819-day count concurrent with my own research. Powell's methodology, however, concentrated strictly on mathematical tractability (Powell 1998). Whereas this can now be taken as independent corroboration for the work I presented at the Mesa Redonda and is of decided importance, mathematical tractability served only as the beginning of my work. Namely, it is one thing to demonstrate a consistent set of mathematical patterns; it is quite another to reveal the religious, historical, and political motivations behind them.

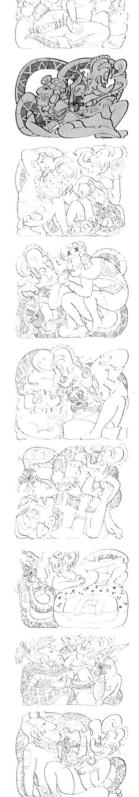

CHAPTER THREE

CONSTRUCTING PORTALS

Approximately 150 years after the death of Janaab' Pakal, at the end of the Classic period, the city of Palenque was abandoned. Its structures lay dormant for several centuries thereafter, slowly reclaimed by the forest. Interest in the ruins remained local until the end of the eighteenth century when representatives of the Spanish Crown visited the site in search of collectibles (Griffin 1974; Schele and Freidel 1990:460). Soon named after the nearby town of Palenque, the ruins attracted further visitors who made drawings of a number of carved tablets found in three small temples. Over the next 100 years, these drawings made their way into the nascent Mayanist literature, eventually piquing John Teeple's mathematical interest, as noted in the last chapter.

Teeple recognized that a portion of the calendric dates in many Classic Maya inscriptions contained lunar information. Maya scribes had included the moon age after the Long Count date, usually sandwiched between the *chol qiij* and the *haab'*.

It is fifteen days after the arrival of the second goddess moon. X3 is the name of the twenty-nine days.

By convention, moon ages were recorded as days elapsed since first appearance, and each lunation was assigned to a supernatural patron (for complications, see Satterthwaite 1951). For the Classic Maya, three patrons (a goddess, the Jaguar God of the Underworld, and Death) governed up to six months each in accord with local numerology (Aldana 2001b, 2006a; for earlier work, see Linden 1991; Satterthwaite 1959; Schele et al. 1992; Teeple 1931).

Before the advent of archaeoastronomy, Teeple recognized that lunar data in several Palenque inscriptions produced an intriguing question that introduces the central problem addressed in this chapter. Notably, three dates possessing lunar records corresponded to times approximately 3,000 years before the Classic period. Teeple recognized that either the scribes at Palenque were privy to extremely old records of the moon or the moon age was calculated based on an approximation to its synodic period (see Table 3.1). Taking the latter scenario as the more likely, Teeple was able to determine the Maya approximations used in these texts as 81 moons counted as 2,392 days—or 29.5308642 days per month (Teeple 1931:65).

Some forty years later, Floyd Lounsbury argued that Teeple had recovered examples of a specific type of interval—one intended to do more than simply record an ancient event. Lounsbury (1976:218) proposed that the dates from mythological times were constructed to parallel historical events such that both might be considered "like-in-kind." To illustrate, Lounsbury made use of the date 12.19.13.4.0 8 Ajaw 18 Tzek, the birth date of the primordial mother figure Ix Muwaan Mat and the first date listed in Table 3.1. This date and the birth of Janaab' Pakal, 9.8.9.13.0 8 Ajaw 13 Pop, both occurred on the same day

TABLE 3.1: Teeple's data from Palenque for determining the Maya synodic period of the moon

Monument	Long Count	Calendar Round	Moon Age (days)
GI's Temple	12.19.13.4.0	8 Ajaw 18 Tzek	5
GIII's Temple	1.18.5.3.6	13 Kimi 19 Kej	26
GII's Temple	1.18.5.4.0	1 Ajaw 13 Mak	10
Stela 1	9.12.6.5.8	3 Lamat 6 Sak	19

Source: Adapted from Teeple (1931:65).

in the *chol qiij*: 8 Ajaw. The large number of days that separated the two births was therefore a multiple of 260 days. This correspondence is not so surprising or infrequent, but Lounsbury dug deeper to find that the large interval also contained other "significant" factors connecting the two events: 364, the "Maya computing year"; 780, the synodic period of Mars; and 819, the period of a cycle recognized for some time but as yet not explicated.

Lounsbury dubbed this phenomenon—of which he found a number of other instances—a "contrived number" (Lounsbury 1976:215; 1978). These date pairs were not serendipitously linked by fate, he claimed, but intentionally manipulated by Palenque astronomers to effect certain "like-in-kind" relationships, using both astronomical and calendric cycles.

Lounsbury's "like-in-kind" proposal stemmed from his understanding of the Palenque inscriptions as heavily concerned with dynastic legitimation (Schele and Freidel 1990:223). We will see in the pages that follow that a concern with legitimation was important but also that a fuller historical treatment reveals more subtlety and intricacy than Lounsbury or his colleagues expected. We will find that there were both practical dynastic purposes for calendric contrivances as well as religious motivations and also that such a practice does not mandate an interpretation of deterministic history. The practical purposes fit into a tradition for maintaining—or recovering—the rights and responsibilities of the ruling elite. These responsibilities included the specific rituals that were required of a *k'ujul ajaw*. The story of Janaab' Pakal's relationship to certain rituals then becomes the main concern of this chapter, and it begins with the treatment of the historical context and textual function of mathematical contrivance itself. Along the way, we will confront compelling evidence for the astronomical identities of mythological figures embedded within an astronumerology.

COSMIC CENTER

We do not have to accept Lounsbury's "like-in-kind" theory to believe that some sort of mathematical contrivance was intentional. The Postclassic Dresden Codex, for example, explicitly records other instances of precisely this type of number (Thompson 1972; see also Box C.1). Unlike the codex records, however, in the Palenque inscriptions the numbers are not recorded explicitly; they arise only in the intervals between pairs of dates.

If the contrived numbers noted by Lounsbury are merely patterns recoverable among dates, we must inquire as to their purpose since the Maya scribe writing the text was the only person assured to have known of their existence. Lounsbury never demonstrates that a Classic Maya ruler would have known about, or even looked for, these contrived numbers. He does, though, offer the suggestion that the contrived numbers were puzzles meant only for the gods—a hypothesis we will take up again in Chapter 7. For now, we leave their purpose ambiguously defined in order to explore the issue further without prejudice. To address the security of *any* possible interpretation of intent, we turn to an examination of the texts that contain these contrived numbers.

When we consider the earliest inscriptions at Palenque in which contrived numbers can be found, we come across a textual anomaly that appears to have been intended as a signal by the author of the inscription. These earliest texts come from the funerary monument of the ninth member of the Palenque dynasty, K'inich Janaab' Pakal. As noted earlier, the maturation of Janaab' Pakal's reign brought with it the blossoming of the city's architecture. No longer the simple one-mound city center, Palenque now displayed Classic Maya architectural forms. Specific to our interest here, Janaab' Pakal initiated the structure that would house his body in the Underworld upon his passing. This structure has become known as the Temple of Inscriptions (see Figure 3.1). Hung within the temple at the top of this monument were three stone tablets, dubbed the East, Middle, and West tablets of the Temple of Inscriptions by modern scholars. As we saw in Chapter 1, Linda Schele, David Freidel, and Peter Mathews reconstructed much of the Early Classic dynastic history of Palenque from these tablets (Coe 1992). But there is more to be learned from these texts than the city's dynastic sequence. A larger message is revealed through a treatment of the texts as a whole—a treatment we now undertake.

The first tablet, the East Tablet, begins in formulaic fashion with a list of the early Palenque *ajawtahk.*

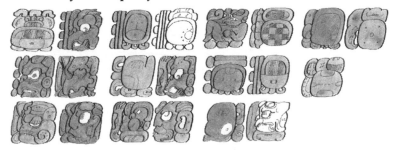

9.4.0.0.0 13 Ajaw 18 Yax, he gave it, the bundle of the gods GI, GII, and GIII. Over thirteen years earlier (3 k'in 10 winal 13 tun), he was seated with the white headband, Ahkal Mo' Naab', K'ujul B'aakal Ajaw. (A1–B12)

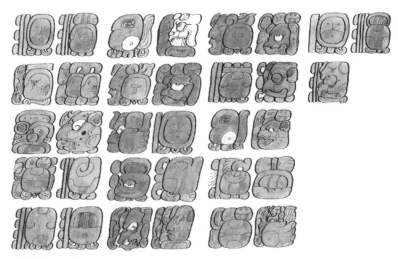

13 Ajaw 18 Kej is the fifth tun; it is the k'atun of the gods of Kan B'ahlam K'ujul B'aakal Ajaw. Almost ten years (9.14.12) after she became seated with the headband, Ix Yohl Ik'nal K'ujul B'aakal

Ajaw, it was the k'altun of 5 Ajaw 3 Ch'en [9.8.0.0.0]. Ix Yohl Ik'nal K'ujul B'aakal Ajaw gave the bundle of her gods. A year and a half (1.8.10) after Aj Ne' Ohl Mat K'ujul B'aakal Ajaw became seated as ajaw. It was the k'altun of 5 Ajaw 18 Tzek [9.8.13.0.0], the thirteenth tun. (I10–N2)

Here we recognize royal accessions and religious ceremonies as the basic content of most of the stelae texts at other Maya cities (as noted in the Introduction). Moreover, the monotonous progression of the narrative implies that during this early time, the city was going through a period of relative normalcy. This normalcy was characterized by the regular accession of *ajawtahk* and their subsequent commemoration of period ends, which involved the giving of gifts to the gods. This time of apparent peace and prosperity long preceded Janaab' Pakal's birth.

A little over halfway through this tablet, however, a break occurs in the formulism. After the accession of Aj Ne' Ohl Mat and his celebration of the 9.8.13.0.0 period end,[1] the *ajaw* of Kalak'mul brought war to Palenque (as we saw in Chapter 1).

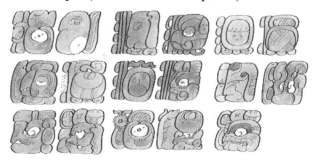

It was forgotten, the tun seating witnessed by Aj Ne' Ohl Mat K'ujul B'aakal Ajaw.
    Shortly after (6.14) 13 Ajaw 18 Mak [9.8.17.9.0], Lakam Ja' was chopped down on 4 Ix 7 Wo [9.8.17.15.14] by the authority of the K'ujul Kan Ajaw. (M3–M11)

The inscription suggests that the defeat was severe. The ceremony critical to Aj Ne' Ohl Mat's reign as *k'ujul ajaw*—the celebration of the *k'altun*—was forgotten as a result of the lost battle. Moreover, immediately following the defeat, the inscription continues with the record of Ix Muwaan Mat's accession (see Chapter 1). Through the restrictions

FIGURE 3.1: *Current view of the Temple of Inscriptions, Janaab' Pakal's funerary monument*

placed on Ix Muwaan Mat's ritual activities discussed above, the text makes clear that normalcy had ended and the kingdom was now facing crisis.

In an elegant rhetorical move, the East Tablet ends with a record of Janaab' Pakal's accession to the throne two years after the *k'altun* on 9.9.2.4.8 5 Lamat 1 Mol and his celebration of the end of the tenth *k'atun*, seventeen years later.

Contrasted with the second half of the East Tablet, the Middle Tablet appears to be purely celebratory and (as noted previously) to omit what we would want to know about how Janaab' Pakal transformed the polity from a humbled city into a powerful player in Classic Maya society. But there are subtleties within the details of the tablet that suggest great import behind the content that is explicitly presented.

The Middle Tablet narrative begins thirty-seven years after Janaab' Pakal took power, a full *k'atun* after the last record in the East Tablet and right in the middle of B'ahlam Ajaw's military rampage through the region.

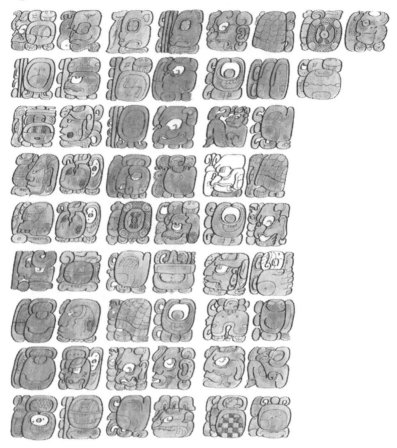

It is the chumtun of 12 Ajaw 8 Kej. It is the eleventh k'atun. Twelve becomes ajaw.

The Jeweled tree was born of the earth; the 5-ZIP-tree was born of the earth. The celestial burden; the earthly burden.

There is a necklace; there are earspools.

The 9 Sky Yoch'ok'in, 16 Ch'ok'in, 9 Tz'aak Ajaw.

It happened on the 12 Ajaw k'atun. It was overseen by the k'atun ch'ajom K'inich Janaab' Pakal K'ujul B'aakal Ajaw.

He gives the sacrificial bowl hat; it is the bundle of GI.

He gives the K'ak' Chanal Huh Chaak hat; it is the bundle of GII.

He gives the white paper hat; it is the bundle of GIII.

The juntan of the gods, K'inich Janaab' Pakal K'ujul B'aakal

Ajaw takes the paper headband on the throne of the three gods, GI, GII, and GIII. (A1–E9)

This section is composed in two parts. The first part is framed by the notation that all of this is occurring at the end of the eleventh *k'atun*, on 12 Ajaw 8 Kej. This first portion comprises three actions. First, a patron of the *k'atun* is named as presiding *ajaw*. Next, two tree births are recorded, referred to as the *ikatz* ("burden" or "charge") of the earth and the sky. Third, there is an implicit presentation of the adornments of precisely those gods who were denied offerings while Ix Muwaan Mat was *ajaw*. These three actions were overseen by Janaab' Pakal as he celebrated the *chumtun*.[2]

Also required on this period end was the giving of gifts to the patron gods of Palenque, and this gift giving constitutes the second part. Here, different hats were given to the three patron gods as their "bundles." Apparently in reciprocity, Janaab' Pakal ties on the paper headband as a symbol of rulership on the altar of these three gods.

The second half of this tablet follows the same formula. It begins with a record of the next major period end, 9.12.0.0.0, followed by a new figure presiding over the *k'atun*.

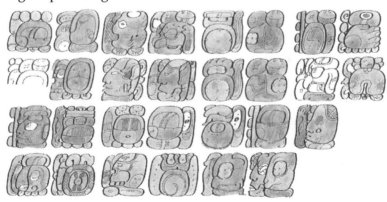

It is his third chumtun on 10 Ajaw 8 Yaxk'in, the twelfth k'atun. K'inich Janaab' Pakal K'ujul B'aakal Ajaw oversaw it. Ten becomes ajaw. The Jeweled tree matured.[3]

The West ajawtahk and the East ajawtahk descend.[4]

They seated themselves, the 9 Sky Yoch'ok'in, the 16 Ch'ok'in, and the 9 Tz'aak-bu Ajaw. It is Janaab' Pakal's second taking of the white paper headband on the altar of the gods. (F9–J3)

Here again, a *chumtun* brings with it a new numeric *ajaw*. Next, the text references one of the previously mentioned births, but this time only the tree associated with the sky is noted and here it is said to have matured. The "descent" that follows is presumably of celestial *ajawtahk*, perhaps as a result of the maturing of the celestial tree. But more importantly, those gods who were left out after Lakam Ja' was sacked now were able to seat themselves. Following this section, three long passages document not only the hats that were part of the bundles of the patron gods as on the last *chumtun* but also their earspools and necklaces.

Over these two parts of the tablet, therefore, we witness a ritual progression. After the defeat of Palenque by the Kalak'mul *ajaw*, Ix Muwaan Mat was unable to tend to the 9 Sky Yoch'ok'in, the 16 Ch'ok'in, and 9 Tz'aak-bu Ajaw. On Janaab' Pakal's first period end, 9.10.0.0.0, these gods possessed the *k'atun*. On Janaab' Pakal's second period end, 9.11.0.0.0, these three gods' adornments were named. And on his third period end, 9.12.0.0.0, the three gods, the 9 Sky Yoch'ok'in, the 16 Ch'ok'in, and 9 Tz'aak-bu Ajaw, were able to (re)seat themselves. This progression, however, appears to have been dependent on a second process.

To understand this second process, we must refer to Maya cosmology as considered in Chapter 1. Namely, the terminology used to describe the military defeat of Palenque in the East Tablet referred to an action on animate objects: *chak'aj* refers to a "chopping down" and most often it has been taken as a metaphor for sacrifice (as exemplified in the historical case of Waxaklajuun Ub'aah K'awiil; W. Fash 1991:129; Looper 2003:76; Martin and Grube 2000:205). After this chopping/killing as the major event disrupting normalcy at Palenque, on his second *chumtun* Janaab' Pakal oversees the birth from the earth of two entities: one is described as the *ikatz* of the sky; the other is the *ikatz* of the earth. Then, on his third *chumtun*, Janaab' Pakal oversees the maturing of the entity that is the *ikatz* of the sky. This maturing is implicitly responsible for the celestial descent of the East and West *ajawtahk*. And bringing this all together, it is this descent that apparently allows for the seating of the 9 Sky Yoch'ok'in, the 16 Ch'ok'in, and the 9 Tz'aak-bu Ajaw.

In other words, the main concern of the Middle Tablet is with the process that reopens a portal of communication between the inhabitants of the sky and the earth. This reopening constitutes a repairing of the religious charter at Palenque, which actually took some doing. It was not until 9.12.0.0.0 (almost sixty years after Janaab' Pakal took office) that the polity had returned to the ritual normalcy that it enjoyed before the defeat by the Kalak'mul *ajaw*. This progression is also evident in the types of rulership recorded over time. The text tells us that Janaab' Pakal's third *chumtun* corresponded to his second tying on of the white headband on the altar of the gods. Indeed, when he was inaugurated, as recorded on the East Tablet, he was said to have been seated into the *ajawlel* but, unlike all *ajawtahk* preceding Aj Ne' Ohl Mat, this seating was not with the white headband (see Figure 3.2). This privilege, it seems, was lost with Aj Ne' Ohl Mat. So it was only at the 9.11.0.0.0 period end that this privilege had been recovered. We will see later a role for the construction of House E in this implied reconstruction. For now, though, the important point is to recognize that the Middle Tablet was entirely dedicated to the religious work necessary to re-legitimize the polity.

Finally, the third tablet of the Temple of Inscriptions, the West Tablet, prophesizes the continued stability that would follow Janaab' Pakal's ritual accomplishments. Namely, it begins by repeating Janaab' Pakal's *chumtun* of 9.12.0.0.0 10 Ajaw 8 Yaxk'in, but then it provides us with a bit more information.

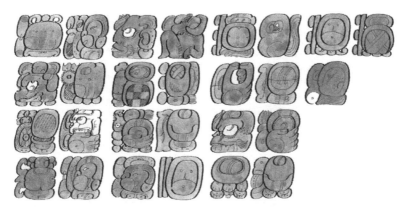

The k'atun ch'ajom K'inich Janaab' Pakal is the juntan of the gods. He ties on the paper headband on the throne of the three gods GI, GII, and GIII. He appeases the heart of the god of the 10 Ajaw 8 Yaxk'in chumtun. And then he appeases the heart of the successor person of the heart of the 8 Ajaw 8 Wo chumtun. (A1–D2)

85

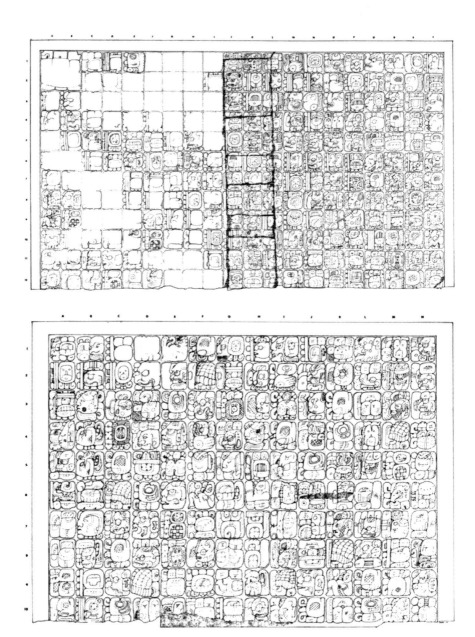

FIGURE 3.2: *The three tablets from the Temple of Inscriptions (illustrations by Merle Greene Robertson)*

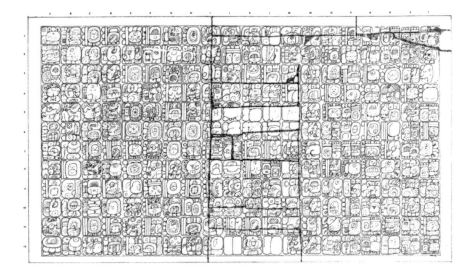

The text is telling us that what was elaborated in the Middle Tablet, transpiring on 9.12.0.0.0 10 Ajaw 8 Yaxk'in, amounted to satisfying the patron of the time period. This interpretation would seem to confirm our reading that the maturing of the celestial *ikatz* noted in the Middle Tablet allowed for a renewed communication between cosmological realms — whatever form this communication actually may have taken.

After this clause, the text begins to make predictions about future events. The first is not too bold, but before long the predictions move into the thousands-of-years range. The first prediction claims that on 9.13.0.0.0 8 Ajaw 8 Wo, the deity charged with the time period will be appeased (A11–D2, West Tablet, Temple of Inscriptions). This reading implies that whether or not Janaab' Pakal was alive for the next period end, the duties of the *ajawtahk* would still be performed.

The next prediction jumps 140 years into the future, claiming that it would take this long to complete the adornment of the *ch'ajom* for the Matawiil *ajaw* and the Palenque *ajaw*. The text here seems to preserve a sense of the scale that the Classic Maya rulers were working in. We saw in the Middle Tablet that it took some 60 years for the religious charter to be reconstructed; here we see that it takes over 140 years to properly adorn the *ch'ajom* for both Matawiil and B'aakal.

The point of these first passages of the West Tablet, then, is to demonstrate that Janaab' Pakal was not looking to change things in the short term. He was not managing the success of his polity to ensure that citizens looked back fondly on his reign. Rather, Janaab' Pakal was attempting to fundamentally reconstruct the rights and responsibilities of his rule so that his successors could carry on the duties he had retrieved. That this third prediction is for a period of seven generations after Janaab' Pakal's reign probably was not mere coincidence. The time interval goes from 9.13.0.0.0 to 10.0.0.0.0 to cover seven *k'atuns*. If each *k'atun* (approximately twenty years) was conceptualized as a generation, then we have here seven generations—a framework common to indigenous conceptions of time.

The set of predictions following this prophesied appeasement, though, changes the character of the narrative significantly and opens a window illuminating the rest of the material in this book.

A TEXTUAL CLUE

The first passages of the West Tablet mimicked the East Tablet in orderly progression. The East Tablet moved through the ancient past, exhibiting the ritual normalcy presided over by the early *ajawtahk* of Palenque. Likewise, the beginning of the West Tablet predicted an extension of a new normalcy (established by Janaab' Pakal) into the foreseeable future. Nearly a quarter of the way through this third tablet, though, the prose becomes erratic. At this point, the narrative jumps from times in the distant future to times in the historic past and then into the virtually inconceivable past. These chronological gymnastics are then followed by a jumble of references that have no real theme other than that they relate to Janaab' Pakal's (or his wife's) life history. First we will review these textual passages; then we will see that the reason behind their order comes not from rhetorical interests but from astronomical ones.

After the chronology has jumped 140 years forward to mark the end of the tenth *bak'tun*, the text moves 4,000 years into the future with the end of the first *pik'tun*.[5] In loose translation, the text reads:

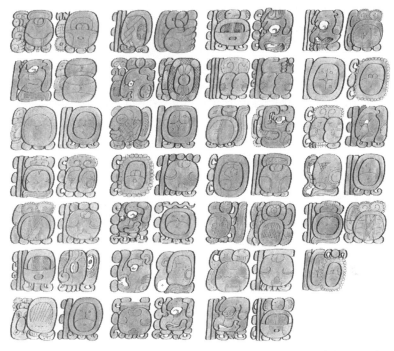

He appeases the heart of . . . person of the mat, person of the wind, on 10 Ajaw 13 Yaxk'in, 1 pik'tun [1.0.0.0.0.0]; it will happen.

Twelve years (12.3.8) after K'inich Janaab' Pakal was born on [9.8.9.13.0] 8 Ajaw 13 Pop, then he tied the headband on himself, K'inich Janaab' Pakal, on [9.9.2.4.8] 5 Lamat 1 Mol. This was two years (2.4.8) after the 3 Ajaw 3 Zotz' chumtun.

One million two hundred forty-six thousand eight hundred and twenty-six years (7.18.2.9.2.12.1) after Mi-[square-nose] became ajaw on 1 Manik 10 Tzek, K'inich Janaab' Pakal K'ujul B'aakal Ajaw became ajaw.

Four thousand years (10.11.10.5.8) later, it will happen, 5 Lamat 1 Mol on 1 pik'tun and 8 days. After the chumtun of 10 Ajaw 13 Yaxk'in [1.0.0.0.0.0], then it will happen, 5 Lamat 1 Mol. (D8–H10)

The text appears to be continuing the predictions into the deep future by suggesting that there will still be a "person of the mat," a "person of the wind," tending to the religious needs of the dynasty 4,000 years later. But this date of 1.0.0.0.0.0 10 Ajaw 13 Yaxk'in actually serves as a frame for an odd passage. Between the statement that this period end "will happen" and a second one four columns over, an inserted clause makes a couple of cryptic references. First, the clause gives redundant information, providing the dates of Janaab' Pakal's birth and accession on 8 Ajaw 13 Wo and 5 Lamat 1 Mol, respectively.[6] The clause then reminds the reader that this accession occurred very shortly after the 3 Ajaw 3 Zotz' period end — the restricted *chumtun* presided over by Ix Muwaan Mat on the heels of the defeat to the Kalak'mul *ajaw*. The next clause refers back over a million years into the past, noting that a primordial figure became *ajaw* long before Janaab' Pakal did. And then the passage states that the 10 Ajaw 13 Yaxk'in *pik'tun* end is only eight days before the same Calendar Round as Janaab' Pakal's accession: 5 Lamat 1 Mol.

In its English translation, I present this passage as suggestive that something other than the "usual" information is being presented here (Aldana 2001b, 2004a). To the Classic Maya reader, the passage must have induced suspicion that something was going on beneath the surface of the text. Although the overall message of the tablets — glorifying the deeds of Janaab' Pakal after the city was militarily devastated — may have remained relatively clear, the organization of the text was unjustifiably odd. For one, the reader would have asked why a future anniversary was taking up space in a dynastic history when it was associated with no explicit event. Anniversary dates of this type would occur every fifty-two years after Janaab' Pakal's accession date and, indeed, this one was close to a major period end, but why was this one singled out?

The answer lies in the type of anniversary this would be. Janaab' Pakal's accession had occurred on 5 Lamat 1 Mol, 9.9.2.4.8. Because the date eight days after the end of the *pik'tun* would be a Calendar Round anniversary of Janaab' Pakal's accession, the time interval separating the two dates had to be a multiple of both 260 and 365. Now, 365 possesses 73 as a factor as does 584, the canonic synodic period for Venus. Since there are eight 73s in 584, a reader of the text had only to determine if the interval between 9.9.2.4.8 and 1.0.0.0.0.8 was divisible by 8 to show that the interval was also a multiple of Venus cycles (Aldana 2004a). This calculation easily could have been performed on the spot with a bag of computing seeds or a codex table of multiples (see Figure 3.3).

At this point, we need to ask whether this correspondence was mere coincidence or was there some other reason for Venus's involve-

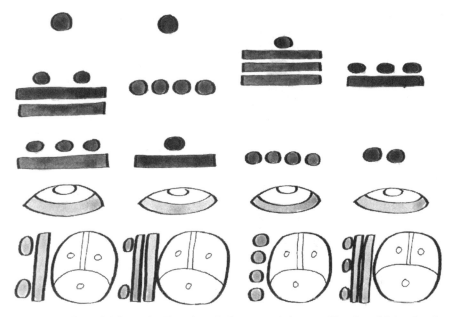

FIGURE 3.3: *Page 24 from the Dresden Codex, containing a table of multiples for the period of Venus*

ment in this passage. An answer comes from an observation already noted: the anniversary occurred *eight* days after the end of the *pik'tun* (Aldana 2004a). To the astronomically savvy, the number eight numerologically implicated the planet Venus since eight was the canonic number of days of disappearance between its visibility as evening star and morning star (as noted hundreds of years later in the Dresden Codex). Eight is also the number of solar years necessary to realign the solar and Venus calendars (8 x 365 = 2,920 = 5 x 584). Therefore, the long interval anchoring no explicit event, the emphasis on the number eight, the blatant marking of other anniversaries, and the ease of determining the presence of Venus cycles all come together to suggest a numerological subtext (Aldana 2001b, 2004a).

To a Classic Maya reader, these clues would not have been overly taxing intellectually to find and solve. In fact, they appear to have been intentionally "loud" to get the reader thinking and looking for other such clues and/or contrivances, of which there were several more to be found. Although the implicit association between Venus and Janaab'

Pakal may have been obvious to the Classic Maya reader, it will take some work for us to recover the meaning here.

ASTRONUMEROLOGY

The author of these tablets did not rhetorically flag the other puzzles in the same way, but they follow a similar pattern of clues for solution and carry the bulk of the numerological message. Working through this set of clues, we will be in a position to recognize a system of astronumerology invented at Palenque along with the reasoning behind the (apparent dis)organization of the latter portion of the West Tablet.

After the record of the end of the first *pik'tun* (containing the implied Venus reference), the text on the West Tablet of the Temple of Inscriptions goes on to record a number of events in the life of Janaab' Pakal along with some events undertaken by supernaturals. Near the last third of this tablet, the reader confronts another passage that reaches back into the distant past:

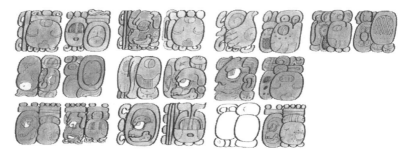

Three years (3.6.6) after the 10 Ajaw chumtun, then he arrived with the ?-Sun on 7 Kimi 19 Kej.[7] It was almost 3,967 years [9.7.11.3.0] after the appeasing of the bright Death Ajaw on 1 Kimi 19 Pax [13.4.12.3.6].[8] He said it for the work of GI on the ocean. 7 Kimi 19 Kej, it was the conjuring of the k'atun ch'ajom K'inich Janaab' Pakal.[9] (O5–R2)

Like the last section containing an astronumerological subtext, in this passage the ancient event is framed by references to a conjuring performed by Janaab' Pakal. First, the text states that he arrives with some form of the sun on the date 7 Kimi 19 Kej. Then, the last statement notes that this arrival constituted a conjuring by Janaab' Pakal. The impli-

TABLE 3.1: Names of mythological figures

Hieroglyphic Name	Popol Vuh Name	Classic Correlate
[GI$_{father}$]	Jun Junajpu	Jun Ajaw
[GI$_{son}$]	Junajpu	Ajaw
Unen K'awiil	—	—
[GIII]	Xbalamke	Yax B'ahlam Ajaw
Ix Muwaan Mat	Xkik	—
	Kame	Kimi

cation, therefore, is that three years after the 9.12.0.0.0 *chumtun*—the period end corresponding to the "maturation" of the Jeweled tree—Janaab' Pakal was making use of the portal for communication that had just been completed. Furthermore, the conjuring itself appears to have included some sort of utterance in which Janaab' Pakal was remembering the activity of GI on the primordial seas during Creation times. Between references to the 7 Kimi event, the text notes an appeasing of the heart of a Death Ajaw on the *chol qiij* date 1 Kimi. The following reference to GI's "work" on the ocean is far from clear to interpret, but the elements that we have recovered already are sufficient to begin the decipherment of the underlying message. Such a decipherment, however, requires a familiarity with Classic Maya Creation mythology, to which we now turn in the version presented by Dennis Tedlock.

Again, fitting within most traditions of the indigenous Western Hemisphere, Maya Creation was the product of many supernatural beings. Two of these, Jun Junajpu[10] and Vukub Junajpu (both of the older generation of gods), were twins who roamed the primordial earth and were great seers but found greatest delight in playing ball. Eventually, the games of the twins disturbed the *ajawtahk* of the Underworld who then summoned Jun Junajpu and Vukub Junajpu into their domain to play against them. The Underworld, however, was a dangerous place and the twins were tricked and killed by the lords Jun Kame (1 Death) and Vukub Kame (7 Death) (see Table 3.2). After his defeat, Jun Junajpu's head was severed and placed in a calabash tree to remain animate there in a forest of the Underworld.

Some time thereafter, Xkik, the daughter of one of the lesser lords of the Underworld, wandered into the forest and came across the calabash tree. Still in the tree, the head of Jun Junajpu spoke to the young maiden and spit a seed into her hand, causing her to become pregnant. When her father learned that she was with child and could not tell him the father's name, he demanded her death. Because of the compassion of her would-be executioners, however, she escaped and found her way to the house of Jun Junajpu's mother, Xmukane, affectionately referred to as Grandmother. And indeed Xmukane soon became the grandmother of the Hero Twins, Junajpu and Xbalamke, Xkik's sons. These two went on a series of exploits, taming the unruly inhabitants of the unformed universe, tending to their family's milpa, and hunting game.

Eventually, as fate would have it, they came across the gaming equipment of their father and likewise proceeded to annoy the *ajawtahk* of the Underworld. Unlike their father and uncle, though, the twins passed all the tests launched at them by the inhabitants of the Underworld. They eventually cheated mortality and defeated Jun Kame, Vukub Kame, and their entire cohort. The twins then resurrected their father before entering the sky to become the sun and moon.

Turning from the account preserved in the *Popol Vuh* to Classic Maya sources, we find specific painted images that expand on the account of Jun Junajpu's resurrection. In particular, several ceramic vessels reveal the process of Jun Junajpu's rebirth (Kerr photo 3033). As one ceramic cup from Guatemala shows, there were three parts to his resurrection. First, Jun Junajpu actually was birthed out of the Underworld as the god of maize (see Figure 3.4). Next, reborn full-grown, he was transported to a second location by the so-called Paddler Gods by canoe. He was then left to be ritually dressed by young women to assume his honored role.

Not only preserved in ceramic art, these stories would have been preserved in codices and recounted at public rituals during Classic times. The story, then, would have been familiar to all of the nobility and very likely most of the commoners of the day. Thus, the reasoning behind the quotation from the West Tablet may be found within the story captured by this mythological sketch. The two *chol qiij* dates in the hieroglyphic passage, 1 Kimi and 7 Kimi, corresponded to the names of the highest-ranking lords of the Underworld (Jun Kame and Vukub Kame). These were the deities responsible for the death of Jun

FIGURE 3.4: *Rebirth of the father of the Hero Twins as the Maize God (after Kerr photo 3033)*

Junajpu and his brother, Vukub Junajpu. The use of one and seven as paired coefficients of the same day name, however, was also a mathematician's shorthand for invoking that day name with all possible coefficients.[11] Thus, 1 Death and 7 Death imply all lords of the Underworld; likewise, Jun Junajpu and Vukub Junajpu represent all lords of the Middleworld.

Taking into account numerological and mythological associations, then, the reader of the third tablet confronts a ritual event conducted by Janaab' Pakal correlated to an event by GI, such that the day names, 1 Death and 7 Death implied the presence of all lords of the Underworld. Here we have found a gateway into an extensive numerological puzzle.

The defeat of the older generation of twins, Jun Junajpu and Vukub Junajpu, hermeneutically relates to a defeat of all lords, which calls to mind the passage in the East Tablet "god and lord are lost." The reader will recall that this passage immediately followed the record of the Palenque battle lost to the army of Kalak'mul. Accordingly, we may return to Lounsbury's hypothesis noted at the beginning of this chapter and check for a contrived number between the dates in these two passages. Doing so, we find that the interval between 13.4.12.3.6 1 Kimi 19 Pax (Death Ajaw's appeasing) and 9.8.17.15.14 4 Ix 7 Wo (battle with Kalak'mul) is a multiple of 584 days—once again, the canonic period of Venus. The explicit numerological connection through Venus, therefore, is between the military defeat of Palenque and a set of events by Janaab' Pakal that themselves bring along GI and the Lords of Death. The meaning of these associations is found through the rest of the numerology and the ensuing implicated mythology.

Turning to the 7 Kimi date corresponding to the ceremony performed by Janaab' Pakal, we encounter a connection invoking Jupiter and Saturn. Specifically, the interval from 9.12.3.6.6 to 9.12.10.0.0 was 2,394 days, or six Jupiter cycles, and that from 9.12.3.6.6 in the third tablet to 9.8.13.0.0 of the first tablet was 25,326 days, or sixty-seven Saturn periods. This last date, 9.8.13.0.0, was the first *tun* seating celebrated by Aj Ne' Ohl Mat and was recorded immediately before his accession date. It may appear that these connections are relatively random, but if we step back, we note that all of these numerological chains connect the same two textual passages: 9.12.3.6.6 corresponds to Janaab' Pakal's ceremony on 7 Kimi and 9.8.13.0.0 directly precedes the battle on 4 Ix 7 Wo. The implied puzzle, therefore, has expanded to include Janaab' Pakal, GI, Aj Ne' Ohl Mat, One Death and Seven Death, Venus, Jupiter, and Saturn, but the puzzle is captured by only two isolated textual passages.

The last two planets, Saturn and Jupiter, have been associated with the supernatural beings known as the Paddler Gods (Aldana 2001b:56, 163). This observation makes sense since they travel together (in close proximity) across the night sky for long periods of time. I suggest that it is not too great a stretch to see them as companions in a journey, or Paddlers. Perhaps more suggestive, the inscriptions betray a strong association between the Paddler Gods and *k'atun* ends. For the mathematically aware, Saturn and Jupiter are strongly associated with *k'atuns* since they carry a periodicity of observability (7,182 days) very close to the length of a single *k'atun* (7,200 days) (cf. Hall 1998). These two oarsmen also show up frequently in mythological scenes painted on ceramic vessels (see Figures 3.4 and 3.5). Generally, they are shown together transporting one or more passengers in a canoe—hence their name. Most notably, however, they often are depicted transporting the Maize God. Recalling that in Classic Maya mythology GI gets resurrected as the Maize God, we find resolution to this complex pattern. Namely, the numerology is bringing together the death and resurrection of Jun Junajpu, Janaab' Pakal, the Paddler Gods, and Aj Ne' Ohl Mat through the periods of Venus, Saturn, and Jupiter. As complex as it may seem, a nearly identical set of associations between an historical *ajaw* and this set of deities has been found elsewhere in the archaeological record.

A series of incised bones recovered from the burial of Jasaw Chan K'awiil, twenty-sixth ruler of Tikal, bear other images of the Paddler Gods (see Figure 3.5). As elsewhere, they are carrying the Maize God (identifiable by his headdress) along with a host of animals. Relative to the imagery of the vessel in Figure 3.4, here the artist has isolated the canoeing scene. The text on the incised bone, though, identifies the Maize God as Jasaw Chan K'awiil himself. By substituting the dead *ajaw* for the Maize God in the mythological scene, the artist was demonstrating a kinship between a deceased ruler and GI as the Maize God (Schele and Miller 1986:270).

FIGURE 3.5: *Image from an incised bone extracted from the tomb of Jasaw Chan K'awiil*

We find that the numerology of Janaab' Pakal's tablets tells the same story. If we take the earlier numerological puzzle (that between Venus and Janaab' Pakal's accession anniversary on 1.0.0.0.0.8) as a clue that Janaab' Pakal is being associated with Venus, then so far we have the Paddler Gods as Jupiter and Saturn and Janaab' Pakal as Venus. If we also bring in the long attested association between Venus and the father of the Hero Twins, then here Janaab' Pakal is being given a numerological headdress identifying him as the Maize God. Thus, the numerological connection between the battle and the ceremony brings along the celestial Paddler Gods, Jupiter, and Saturn. We now have a specific mythological event that captures all of the associations made by the numerology in the texts (see Figure 3.6).

There is one difference between numerology and mythology, however, and that is that through the numerology a fourth being is also involved: Aj Ne' Ohl Mat. If we push the analogy, we might now see Aj Ne' Ohl Mat in the Paddler Gods' canoe with Janaab' Pakal as the Maize God. Such an interpretation makes sense historically and ritually. That is, Palenque fell on hard times with the military defeat under the reign of Aj Ne' Ohl Mat—the history in the first textual passage in the numerological puzzle. This fall was the historical and ritual event that required mending.[12] The second textual passage in the puzzle describes Janaab' Pakal's use of the portal he worked so hard to reconstruct over the first fifty-seven years of his reign (9.9.2.4.8–9.12.0.0.0). That he was able to use the portal for conjuring makes it clear that his repairs were successful. Moreover, the numerology tells us that the mending work took the form of Janaab' Pakal's becoming the Maize God for his polity.

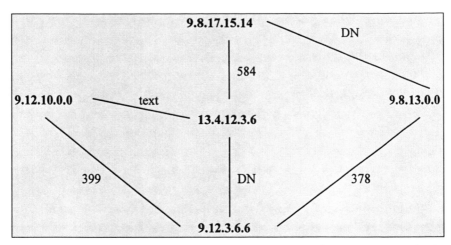

FIGURE 3.6: *Resurrection numerology based on information from two passages in the East and West tablets of the Temple of Inscriptions*

This numerological message was important enough to be encoded three times. Picking up where the above puzzle left off, the accession of Aj Ne' Ohl Mat on 9.8.11.9.10 8 Ok 18 Muwaan was linked directly to the day on which Janaab' Pakal "entered the road," 9.12.11.15.18 6 Etz'nab 11 Yax — a Maya metaphor for death (or something that happens to one shortly thereafter). Specifically, 2^2 x 19 Saturn rounds and 2^3 x 3^2 Jupiter rounds was the link between Aj Ne' Ohl Mat's accession and the beginning of Janaab' Pakal's journey through the Underworld. Whereas in the examples mentioned previously and in other instances, intermediary dates connected the Paddler Gods to Janaab' Pakal and Aj Ne' Ohl Mat — demonstrating the role of the battle with Kalak'mul — here the correspondence was direct. Although the repetition in numerology may seem excessive, the numerological subtext clearly told the same story: that both Janaab' Pakal and Aj Ne' Ohl Mat would be transported together to the abode of the *ajawtahk* by the Jaguar and Stingray Paddlers.

Although powerful, the story told in the numerology is not completely unexpected given the story of the inscriptions already presented. In fact, these numerological puzzles serve mainly to augment the narrative, creating larger analogies without writing them out explicitly in the textual account. Yet we would be wise to inquire whether there is any corroborative evidence that the rather elaborate message we have extracted from the astronumerology and this reading of the texts was indeed intended. In fact, two independent forms provide corroboration.

One means for this corroboration comes from the observation that for the retrieval of the duties of the Palenque *ajawtahk*, Janaab' Pakal would have needed some place to conduct the rituals noted previously. By looking to the architectural patronage of Janaab' Pakal's early reign, we find evidence for just such a place.

House E — the anomalously decorated member of the Palace Complex described in Chapter 1 — was the first to be constructed on top of the platform at the ritual center of the city. Modern researchers have combined ceramic, architectural, and glyphic data to place the construction of House E within fifty years of Janaab' Pakal's birth (Schele 1981:95, 111).[13] Along with its temporal relevance, the imagery adorning House E's façade takes on specific import. As mentioned previously, abstract floating images decorated the façade of House E (see Figure 1.1). We may infer that the relationship between the imagery and the architectural function of the structure remained constant throughout its life since, unlike other buildings that were painted in different colors over the centuries, House E only had one decorative design maintained since it was first built (Robertson 1985a).

The specific images adorning House E's façade can be found in places suggesting that they denote a ritual substance — precious material accessible by the *ajaw* (Houston and Stuart 1996; Schele and Miller 1986:284). Moreover, Merle Greene Robertson and Linda Schele have suggested that this iconography is related to hallucinogenic plant usage (Robertson 1985a). According to Peter Furst (1974), to whom they refer, and aside from all the extra baggage carried by appellations of "shamanism" (see Klein et al. 2002), such plants at least enabled communication across the borders between cosmological worlds — precisely the concern of the Middle Tablet inscription.

Certain other architectural features corroborate a cosmological aspect to House E, which in turn associates the structure with the content of the texts of the Temple of Inscriptions. For one, the designer of the new construction included a tunnel through the mound fill to connect the early palace structures with a stairway that opened into the southwest corner of House E. This tunnel physically connected the Middleworld to the Underworld. And the cosmological theme was not left unmarked. As mentioned in Chapter 1, archways within this tunnel bear stucco sculptures of the two halves of the Celestial Dragon, the primordial being who was used to form the earth and sky (Aldana 2001b:239–246). We will see the explicit hieroglyphic record describing the mythological event in Chapter 7. Here, we will review the story in order to explore the ramifications of the Celestial Dragon's placement in House E.[14]

As attested throughout Mesoamerican Creation mythologies, the world was formed through a rather violent act (Aldana 2001b:25–30, 239–246; Arellano Hernández 1995). One of the more complete versions of the story comes from a sixteenth-century French translation of an Aztec myth within the *Histoyre du Mechique* (De Jonghe 1905). Therein, Tlaltecuhtli, a great crocodilian creature with mouths on each of its joints, threatened the stability of the primordial waters. Two important Creation deities, Tezcatlipoca and Quetzalcoatl, set out to quell Tlaltecuhtli in order to make the world safe for its eventual inhabitants. The Central Mexican Hero Twins transformed themselves into their *naguales* (*wayob*) and wrapped themselves around her until finally they tore her apart.[15] The other deities then felt that Tlaltecuhtli had been wronged, so they decided to fashion her two halves into the world: one half becoming the earth laid upon the primordial seas, and the other half held up by four deities to form the sky.[16] For the Classic Maya, the Celestial Dragon represented the upper half, with her image visible as the Milky Way (Aldana 2001b:25–30; Stuart 1995b, 2003).

The Celestial Dragon, then, took on particular importance for Classic Maya culture. Namely, it appears that *k'ujul ajawtahk* entered into her body upon death (Aldana 2001b; Plank 2003; Stuart 1995a). When new *ajawtahk* acceded to the throne, they were depicted sitting on a Celestial Dragon throne—an act symbolizing their access to the rest of the dynasty (see Figure 2.1). The Celestial Dragon thus represented the connection between living and deceased *ajawtahk*.

Yet another representation of the Celestial Dragon makes this case explicitly for Palenque. Early excavations revealed a throne in the subterranean structures connected to House E. The Celestial Dragon's body frames the hieroglyphic inscription with its two heads at either end of the frontal text. Recently deciphered by David Stuart, the text refers to the all-important 9.11.0.0.0 period end, corresponding to the births of the sky and earth trees noted in the Middle Tablet of the Temple of Inscriptions.

? ?-white breath, opening through the sky, opening through the earth at the Celestial Dragon place. It is the house of K'inich Janaab' Pakal K'ujul B'aakal Ajaw, [occurring] just after the 12 Ajaw 8 Kej (9.11.0.0.0) chumtun. (A–N)

As Stuart (2003) noted, the first part of the phrase is eroded and the second glyph is undeciphered, so we cannot know precisely the meaning of the whole text. What follows, however, is extremely suggestive given the throne's architectural, iconographic, hieroglyphic, and now numerological context. The next phrase Stuart reads as "?-sak-ik' numil ta chan numil ta kab [Celestial Dragon]-nal." The *?-sak-ik'* glyph is one that refers to the "breath or life spirit of rulers and nobles" (Stuart 2003:2). The next couplet rests on the translation of *numil*, which Stuart (2003:2) correlates to the Ch'orti' word for "opening, passage, conduit, lane, . . . flow." Where "opening" is perhaps the least suggestive of possible translations, "passage" and "conduit" provide a reading perfectly in line with the above interpretation of the tablets in the Temple of Inscriptions. Here, then, we have a conduit through the sky and earth at the Celestial Dragon place, which, the next passage tells us, is the house of Janaab' Pakal. Accepting the caveat that we have not translated the beginning of the inscription, it appears that here we have textual and iconographic evidence that the 9.11.0.0.0 period end was critical to the royal ritual life of the city. Specifically, this altar implies that House E was a Palenque locus for communication between the inhabitants of the sky and earthly realms.

Finally, within House E itself, still more iconography reinforces the association with the Underworld. At the end of the southeast corridor, a low bench abutted the wall. Framing the corridor and bench, an artist painted the maw of a great bearded serpent.[17] From similar imagery at Copán, Linda Schele and Mary Miller (1986:284) have shown that this jaw signifies an entrance to the Underworld. Furthermore, scenes painted on Classic period ceramic vessels give us an idea of how the framed bench was likely used. Urns or mummy bundles[18] may have been set on the low bench in House E so that the reigning Palenque *ajaw* could have conjured the remaining *k'uj* of the previous *ajawtahk* out from the Underworld using this space as a conduit.

Bringing these observations together, I suggest that if the previous locus for such communication was destroyed when "chopped down," leading to the loss of "lord and god" (as mentioned in the East Tablet), then House E was the architectural response by Janaab' Pakal that reopened the portal of communication. Thus, if we recognize that with its hallucinogenic and Underworld iconography and with its passageway leading physically and ritually into the Underworld, House E must have been the primary ritual passageway at Palenque. Further, if it was constructed during Janaab' Pakal's early tenure — that is, for the 9.11.0.0.0 period end as implied by the Celestial Dragon throne text — it seems reasonable to conclude that this architectural structure reified the portal that Janaab' Pakal reopened for the 9.11.0.0.0 *chum-tun*, allowing the gifts to be given once again to the gods as recorded explicitly in the Middle Tablet of the Temple of Inscriptions (cf. Robertson 1985a:17–18, 40).

Even if the architectural sequence cannot be dated with sufficient resolution to solidify this interpretation, yet another architectural feature adds to the plausibility that this structure was being referenced in the texts.[19] The feature in question is known as an Ik' window, taking the form of a T and symbolizing "wind" or "breath." Robertson (1985a:10) reports that with its ten Ik' windows House E has the largest number of Ik' windows of any structure at Palenque. Two of these are prominently located on the front of the building (see Figure 1.1). Further, some of these "windows" did not actually penetrate through the walls, such that Robertson (1985a:11) notes that she has been led "to believe that the *shape* was more important than the penetration of the wall." So, if we recall the connection between Ik' and the soul of the *ajaw*, a plethora of Ik' symbols would seem a suitable means of symbolizing the purpose of this structure.

If House E, therefore, reifies the portal of communication alluded to within the inscriptions, we might ask whether the other messages we have extracted from the texts are corroborated elsewhere at Palenque. In fact, the analogy of Janaab' Pakal as the Maize God can also be found on the well-known sarcophagus lid within his funerary monument, the Temple of Inscriptions itself.

As noted previously, Janaab' Pakal borrowed the architectural layout from the Templo Olvidado for the structure that would house his remains in the Underworld (Schele and Freidel 1990:225). The sarcophagus chamber was then entombed within a large pyramidal mound that maintained a small passageway from the chamber to the temple on top of the mound. The temple itself was broken up into several spaces. The East and West Tablets were hung on two large walls separating the front section from the interior. On the back wall of the inner chamber, just above the tunnel leading to the sarcophagus chamber, hung the Middle Tablet—the one dedicated to the recovery of the portal of communication. The same message, we will see, was recorded at the other end of this tunnel.

Janaab' Pakal's own image centers the iconography of his sarcophagus lid (see Figure 3.7). David Stuart (personal communication, 1996) has argued that the recumbent position taken by the *ajaw* follows the standard depiction of a newborn—or in this case reborn—being.[20] Moreover, in this reborn position, Janaab' Pakal wears the garb of the Maize God, just as Jasaw Chan K'awiil did on the incised bones found in his tomb.[21] More telling, Janaab' Pakal is framed by the jaws of the Underworld. Referring back to Maya mythology, we recall that Jun Junajpu was brought out of the Underworld to be reborn as the Maize God. Here, the artist has depicted Janaab' Pakal playing precisely this role.

Appearing to rise from Janaab' Pakal's midsection as he comes forth from the jaws of the Underworld is an image of the world tree—a portal between levels of the cosmos.[22] We will see in Chapter 6 that this tree is depicted elsewhere at Palenque, and that in its other setting, it appears to be labeled with the hieroglyphic name of the tree that is reborn of the earth, noted in the Middle Tablet in the temple above

MERLE GREENE '75

FIGURE 3.7: *Janaab' Pakal's sarcophagus lid (illustration by Merle Greene Robertson)*

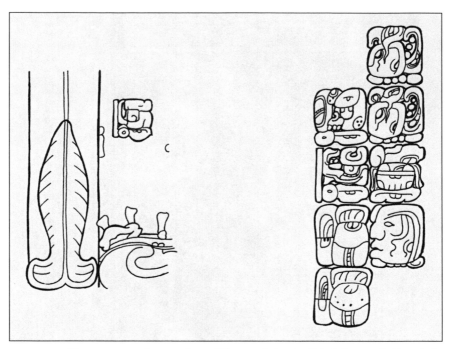

FIGURE 3.8: *Name next to the tree from GI's temple in the Triad Group (left) and the passage from Janaab' Pakal's funerary monument noting the rebirth of the sky burden (chanal ikatz) and the earth burden (kab'al ikatz) (right)*

the sarcophagus chamber (see Figure 3.8). We, therefore, have here a complete reiteration of the message extracted from the inscriptions and the numerology it contained. Namely, Janaab' Pakal was reborn as the Maize God and reestablished the cosmological portal of his city. As if to add an exclamation point, Janaab' Pakal's own lineage was carved around the perimeter of the sarcophagus; these were the *ajaw-tahk* ("lords") who were "lost" but now were rebirthed to reconstitute the portal between worlds (see Figure 1.3). Image, text, architecture, and numerology, therefore, all tell the same story.

Lest we doubt the Creation theme on this lid, we may appeal across time and locale to the Mixtec Codex Borgia. Pages 49 through 53 of the manuscript show a set of world-tree births from supernatural entities during Creation times. The interesting part here is that we are given a sequence of tree births. Here, the four trees of the four directions are set up first. Then, the codex shows a person falling into the jaws of

FIGURE 3.9: *World Tree in the Codex Borgia*

the Underworld immediately preceding a separate scene depicting the birth of the fifth tree — the tree at the center (see Figure 3.9). Paralleling the birth of the Maya Maize God, this fifth tree is depicted as a fruit-bearing stalk of corn. The sequence, then, may be understood as demonstrating the role of the Maize God (and by extension of the role of the *ajaw*). Once the world is constructed (either the sky is raised by the four trees or the physical Mesoamerican city is built), the Maize God/resurrected *ajaw* sits at the center and manages the conduit between cosmological realms. The imagery of Janaab' Pakal's resting place, therefore, was not appealing solely to a local story but to a pan-Meso-american conceptualization of Creation.

We began this chapter by following Lounsbury's clues that signaled the possibility of a mathematical contrivance at work below the surface of the hieroglyphic texts of Palenque. We have since found that such contrivance was far more extensive than Lounsbury had perceived. What is particularly interesting is that the production of historical narrative followed a recoverable method based on numerological contrivance. In the next chapter we will address the heretofore ill-understood 819-day count and its specific role in Classic period Palenque's historical method. This new understanding will constitute a key step in demonstrating the method's much more extensive application by Janaab' Pakal's son, Kan B'ahlam. Therein, we will see that this astronumerology is no figment of a numerical imagination but part of Kan B'ahlam's programme for building on Janaab' Pakal's newly recovered religious charter and extending it as one part in a scheme to make a name for Palenque in the greater Maya world.

NOTES

1. For an explication of the period end, see prefatory material on the Maya calendar.

2. Note that in the B'aakal inscriptions, *k'altun* substitutes freely for *chumtun*.

3. Here I take *ta-ki-ja* as the Ch'orti' *takij*, which means to dry or harden. With regard to maize, however, it refers to the drying that ripens.

4. Several scholars have followed Michael Closs in seeing this record as having to do with Venus (e.g., Schele and Mathews 1998:105). The association derives from a misreading of the verb as having to do with the planet Venus as well as a misreading of the glyph blocks at G8 and G9 (Aldana 2001b, 2005a).

5. *Pik'tun* is the reconstructed name for the period of 20 *bak'tuns*, or 2,880,000 days.

6. Note that here it is recorded that he tied on the headband, but it does not state that the headband was white or that it occurred on the altar of the gods.

7. The glyph block at P6 is significantly eroded, but two parts can be made out distinctly. The first element is the *ti* prefix denoting a preposition. The last element is K'IN-ni, or *k'in*. The part in the middle modifies the noun (*k'in*)

but suffers the most erosion. Therefore, I translate the passage as "with the ?-Sun."

8. Mythological time pivoted around the date 13.0.0.0.0 4 Ajaw 8 Kumk'u. For time thereafter, the 13 acted like a 0, such that 13.0.0.0.0 + 1.0.0.0.0 would be 1.0.0.0.0. See later discussion and Lounsbury (1978).

9. The glyph at Q2 is significantly eroded, but a thumb is identifiable on the left-hand side. This position accords well only with the "hand-grasping-fish" — *tzak* — conjuring glyph. Schele and Mathews (1998:108) also read it this way.

10. In Classic times Jun Junajpu's name was GI, and it is not clear that he had a twin brother. The short review given here, however, follows the sixteenth-century account given in the *Popol Vuh* (e.g., D. Tedlock 1985). The names of many Mesoamerican gods corresponded to days in the 260-day count. Thus, 9 Wind was a name for Quetzalcoatl in Aztec culture. And many of GI's events occur on the date 9 Ik'. Similarly, in the *Popol Vuh*, Jun Junajpu corresponds to the day 1 Ajaw in the Classic calendar.

11. Starting with 1 Ajaw, a jump to the next day name Ajaw (+20 days) yields a coefficient of 8; next is 2 Ajaw, 9 Ajaw, and so forth, until the last Ajaw before we return to 1 Ajaw is 7 Ajaw. See D. Tedlock (1985:234). This practice still occurs among the K'iche.

12. As noted previously, this scenario also makes sense of Kan B'ahlam's record of himself as the tenth *ajaw* of B'aakal (Martin and Grube 2000:168).

13. Schele (1981) has it at five years from 9.11.0.0.0 and so constructed under Janaab' Pakal's reign, but Robertson (1985a:7) has it "built during the reign of [Janaab' Pakal's] grandmother [Ix Yohl Ik'nal], first woman ruler of Palenque, who reigned from A.D. 583–604."

14. The Celestial Dragon is elsewhere referred to as the Star Caiman (Stuart, personal communication 1998), the Starry Deer Caiman (Stuart 2003), and the Cosmic Monster (Freidel et al. 1993; Stone 1985).

15. The name Tlaltecuhtli ends with the masculine suffix *-tecuhtli*, but the creature is referred to in the text as feminine.

16. As translated by scholars over the last few centuries, this story does not show up in Postcontact Maya texts. My colleagues and I have recently shown, however, that this absence comes from the translation process and not from the original documents (Aldana et al. n.d.). We have shown that both the *Popol Vuh* and the *Books of Chilam Balam* contain references to this version of Creation.

17. See Robertson (1985a:figure 67) for a reconstruction of the imagery.

18. See, for example, those mummy bundles shown in Kerr Vessels 1081, 1645, and 1813.

19. Recently, epigraphers have proposed that the name of House E is given in the Tablet of 96 Glyphs as Sak Nuk Naah, "white skinned house" (Stuart, personal communication, 2006). If this reading bears out, the overall interpretation here is further strengthened.

20. Janaab' Pakal's sarcophagus lid has been interpreted many times (Robertson 1985a; Schele and Freidel 1990; Schele and Mathews 1998; Schele and Miller 1986). The main difference in interpretation between my account and those listed here is that I follow Stuart in seeing Janaab' Pakal as being reborn from the Underworld, whereas others have argued that Janaab' Pakal is falling into the Underworld (see especially Schele and Mathews 1998:116).

21. Waxaklajuun Ub'aah K'awiil *kujul ajaw* of Copán wears the same attire on Stela H in the Great Plaza (see Figure 0.2).

22. As described in the *Book of Chilam Balam of Chumayel*, the trees hold up the sky: "Then, after the destruction of the world was completed, they placed a tree to set up in its order the yellow cock oriole. Then the white tree of abundance was set up. A pillar of the sky was set up, a sign of the destruction of the world; that was the white tree of abundance in the north. Then the black tree of abundance was set up in the west for the black-breasted *pixoy* to sit upon. Then the yellow tree of abundance was set up in the south, as a symbol of destruction of the world, for the yellow-breasted *pixoy* to sit upon, for the yellow cock oriole to sit upon, the yellow timid *mut*. Then the green tree of abundance was set up in the center of the world as a record of the destruction of the world" (Roys 1967:100).

CHAPTER FOUR

ERRORS AND IDENTITIES

As mentioned previously, twentieth-century Mayanists Floyd Lounsbury, Linda Schele, and Peter Mathews focused much of their early attention on working out the dates associated with the first rulers of the Palenque dynasty. I suggest that Janaab' Pakal's historians faced a similarly difficult task with the commissioning of the tablets in the Temple of Inscriptions. These court historians were charged with the assignment of reaching back in time in order to link the events of Creation explicitly to those of the beginning of Palenque's dynastic history. The reason for the challenge here comes from the fact that for times as early as those of the first rulers, the people living in the area of Palenque most likely had not yet subscribed to Classic Maya culture per se.

At this very early period, before the first stone buildings of what would become the ritual center of Palenque were built, it is quite possible that the Long Count had not been used in cities along the Usumacinta River. The earliest Long Counts in the Maya area have been found at Tikal around 8.14.0.0.0 (Stela 29; Harrison 1999:66); Palenque was much smaller than Waxaktun or Tikal at this time, so if its leaders were recording dates at all, they probably followed the practice common throughout Mesoamerica, that is, recording events only by Calendar Rounds. Janaab' Pakal's historians, then, would have found only the Calendar Round dates for these early events in their records or oral traditions. Since each Calendar Round recurs every fifty-two years, these historians would have confronted more than one possible placement in the Long Count for each date. It was left to them to determine which of the Long Count possibilities best reflected the needs of the history being composed. Without another framework, this process meant computing all possible Long Count matches for a given Calendar Round date within some prescribed interval. For more than a couple ambiguous events—as we saw in Chapter 2—this process would have led to a huge number of calculations.

Undoubtedly, the scribes performing these computations would have developed some algorithms to aid them in their enterprise (Lounsbury 1978:768). For the earliest royal events at Palenque, we will discover that the enigmatic 819-day count functioned as the perfect tool for facilitating these types of calculations (Aldana 2001b:145–150; 2004a). In this chapter, we consider the 819-day count relative to the results obtained in Table 2.1 but also with respect to the content of the Triad Group texts. First, we unpack the meaning of the 819-day count, then we consider some specific uses to which it was put.

RECONSTRUCTING TOOLS

Upon Janaab' Pakal's passing, his son Kan B'ahlam II took the throne. Kan B'ahlam focused his architectural program on a Triad Group built behind Janaab' Pakal's funerary temple. From the inscriptions in these three temples, we find the first occurrence of the so-called 819-day count.[1] This count has proven enigmatic to the community of Mayanists since its recovery by J. Eric Thompson in 1943. Not universally used by Maya kingdoms, 819-day count records have been found by archaeologists so far only in the texts of cities located along the Usumacinta River and to the south at Copán and Quirigua (Lounsbury 1978:811; Thompson 1960). In mathematical and epigraphic terms, the count is readily tractable; only its meaning has remained elusive. Here we will see that the meaning becomes clear when considered relative to the exegesis of the astronumerology in the Triad Group inscriptions.

The 819-day count is characterized by four calendric stations, each associated with a cardinal direction.[2] Explicitly, these "stations" correspond to the consecutive *walaj K'awiil-nal* or "raising of the K'awiil-nal" in the order east, north, west, and south. Each station remained active for 819 days until K'awiil-nal was raised in the next direction (hence this is really a 3,276-day count). A complete record of the count gives the number of days from the beginning of the active station to the current date, is followed by the phrase *walaj K'awiil-nal*, and ends with the cardinal direction in which it is raised.

It is 19 k'in 14 winal after 1 Kawak 7 Yax when the Nal-K'awiil was set up in the west.

Much (though definitely not all) of the ambiguity of the count lies in the referent *K'awiil-nal*. To understand this term, we may break it up into two parts. *K'awiil* is the personification of royal blood and, as an idol, is received by an *ajaw* at his/her inauguration (Stuart 1995a; see Figure 0.3). *Nal* most often is used as a suffix to refer to place. Thus we might read the combination as "the place of K'awiil." The accompanying verb noted above is that of "raising" or "erecting," so we might interpret the count as guiding the ritual circuit for the placement of a representation of K'awiil.[3] Although possible, a more intriguing alternative comes from a consideration that *nal* also functions as a word carrying the meaning "ear of corn."[4] Here, though, we confront the difficulty of finding meaning in "raising the ear of corn made of royal blood" unless we appeal to the iconography of the temple dedicated to K'awiil himself.

According to the texts within the three temples, the smallest structure of the Triad Group is dedicated to one of the three patrons of Palenque: Unen K'awiil, or "infant K'awiil." The imagery centering this text bears an animated stalk of maize with human heads in place of corn ears (see Figure 4.1). That Mesoamericans saw humanity as made of corn is well attested (Taube 1993). It, therefore, may simply be that this image represents this concept alone. Yet the stalk's face and the fact that Kan B'ahlam stands on its right in order to give offerings to it suggest otherwise. One implication, then, is that this image is actually a representation of a deified maize plant bearing human offspring. Mythologically considered (as we have just seen), the Hero Twins are the sons of the Maize God, so this cornstalk may symbolically become a representation of the lifeblood of the first *ajawtahk*. In other words, this image may be seen as an iconographic conflation of Nal (as corn) and K'awiil (as royal blood and the owner of the temple), that is, Nal-K'awiil. Under this guise, the "raising of the Nal-k'awiil" is more specifically the organic generation of a representation of the dynastic lifeblood around a cosmic ritual circuit.

So if this Nal-k'awiil Count included a cosmic ritual circuit, the next natural question is why use 819 (or 3,276) days? Scholars have long noticed that the number has cosmic importance since it can be factored into three numbers important to Maya culture: $7 \times 9 \times 13 = 819$ (also $4 \times 819 = 3,276$). Numerologically, seven was the number of the Earth; nine was the number of levels to the Underworld and the number of lords of the night;[5] and thirteen was the number of the sky as well as half of the numerology of the *chol qiij* (and four was the number of the sun). If nothing else, 819 possessed a natural aesthetic.

But the construction of the 819-day count also may have grown out of the basic program of Maya astronomy. Without appeal to the use of fractions in their mathematical calculations, Maya astronomers developed a method to determine the synodic periods of the planets that involved choosing a specific point in the planet's cycle, for instance, first morning visibility to begin the count.[6] Complete cycles were then tallied in numbers of days. At each completion, the astronomer looked for the tally as a factor of the total number of days—a circumstance that would give him his "canonic" value for the period of the planet.

114

FIGURE 4.1: *Tablet in Unen K'awiil's temple of Kan B'ahlam's Triad Group (illustration by Merle Greene Robertson)*

Say, for example, that an astronomer chose to verify the period of Venus. For a good record, she might have gathered 583, 587, 583, 585, and 582, giving her a total of 2,920 days for five cycles. In Maya numerals she would have divided 8.2.0 by 5. Since she would have been an experienced computer, she would have known immediately that "a shell in the basement"[7] meant divisibility by five, so here she would have her "canonic" value for the period of the planet: 584. Of course there would be variation from this value on a cycle-to-cycle basis due to inherent astronomical phenomena as well as meteorological contingencies, but given that for the Maya the planets were willful beings, such variation would have been expected. On the other hand, the longer the totals were tallied, the closer one would have approached the canonic periods when restricted to integer values. As a limiting case, then, the canonic values may very well have been expected to be exact.[8]

If such a method was instituted any time during or before the Early Classic, all of the planetary periods in Table 4.1 would have been determined by the time of Kan B'ahlam's court. Thus, a visionary astronomer might have taken up the numerology that potentially lay within; that is, each characteristic number could be broken down into its prime factors as also shown in the table. What someone in Kan B'ahlam's service recognized in doing so was the significant overlap between the factors of the *chol qiij*, the computing year, and the periods of Saturn, Jupiter, and Mars. This astronomer then extracted the numbers common to all and discovered that a "new" cycle would tie them together: $3^2 \times 7 \times 13 = 819$ days, of which there would be 2^2 in a complete period (Aldana 2001b, 2004a).

Because 819 (and 3,276) was constituted of sacred factors (7, 9, 13 [and, in the case of 3,276, 4]) and captured the factors of the periods of the planets, Kan B'ahlam may have seen this number as the discovery of a great truth. He alternately may have found this congruity simply to be expected as ratification of Maya cosmology. Either way, Kan B'ahlam and his court scholars were able to put this number to good use.

Using the numerology of 3,276, an astronomer would have been able to track the cycles of Saturn, Jupiter, Mars, and Mercury over huge periods of time with relative facility (Aldana 2001b:148).[9] Pre-

TABLE 4.1: The basis for Palenque's astronumerology[1]

Cycle	Characteristic Number	Factors
Mercury	116	$2^2 \times 29$
Chol qiij	260	$2^2 \times 5 \times 13$
Computing year	364	$2^2 \times 7 \times 13$
Haab'	365	5×73
Saturn	378	$2 \times 3^3 \times 7$
Jupiter	399	$3 \times 7 \times 19$
Venus	584	$2^3 \times 73$
Mars	780	$2^2 \times 3 \times 5 \times 13$
Nal-k'awiil	819	$3^2 \times 7 \times 13$

Note: 1. Compare this list to that found in Carlson (1981:206).

viously, if someone knew the positions of the planets within their respective cycles on a given day and wanted to determine the position of that planet on some day in the past or future, she would have had to divide the interval separating the two dates by each of the periods of the planets individually. Such division would have been quite time-consuming given the clumsy periods of the planets: 116, 378, 399, and 780. Unquestionably, astronomers would have developed arithmetic algorithms for simplifying calculations. The 819-day count, as we will see in a later example, may be considered one such elegant algorithm.

COMPUTING HISTORY

Recalling that Middle Classic Palenque historians only had Calendar Round records for the events of the early rulers of the city, the 819-day count would have facilitated their charge tremendously. In composing the early history, they would have had a few constraints already in place—very likely enough to reveal the specific dates unequivocally. But the authors of the Triad Group inscriptions did not go with a straightforward choice based on these constraints. Instead, in the tablets within the largest of the three temples, they recorded a distance number implying that U K'ix Kan, the first ruler of Palenque, acceded on the 11 Kaban 0 Pop of 5.8.17.15.17—a date almost 1,600 years before Janaab' Pakal's accession. The text following these Calendar Rounds continued with the births and accessions of six more early rulers of

Palenque. The sixth, however, is the same *ajaw* identified in Janaab' Pakal's mausoleum inscriptions as Ahkal Mo' Naab' II — *ajaw* during the seventh *k'atun* of the tenth *bak'tun*. Doing the math, we appear to have a time span of almost four *bak'tuns* (5.9.0.0.0 to 9.6.0.0.0, or over 1,500 years) during which only seven men ruled.

In their treatment of the Palenque dynasty, Linda Schele and Peter Mathews suggested not that these were the Maya analogues of the Christian Biblical men of extreme longevity but instead that U K'ix Kan was the first ruler of the city and K'uk' B'ahlam (the ruler recorded immediately after U K'ix Kan) was the first in the lineage that produced Kan B'ahlam II (Schele and Mathews 1991). Hence, according to Schele and Mathews, the three and a half *bak'tuns* between U K'ix Kan and K'uk' B'ahlam and the rulers governing them were irrelevant to the theme of the inscriptions and so went unrecorded.

As we saw in Chapter 1, this interpretation requires the assumption that each ruler is the son of the previous one listed, starting with K'uk' B'ahlam. We have already noted, though, that although direct inheritance was the convention, it was by no means the rule. Further, this interpretation left Schele and Mathews with another anomaly in this first portion of historic text: the distance number mediating between K'uk' B'ahlam's birth and his accession is not commensurate with the Calendar Round dates recorded. That is, 8.18.0.13.6 5 Kimi 14 K'ayab to which was added an interval of 1.2.5.14, does not result in the 1 K'an 2 K'ayab (8.19.15.3.4) date recorded. This anomaly Schele and Mathews (1991:89) left as unexplained scribal error.

If we consider the construction of the history, rather than just its interpretation, we encounter an alternate explanation. As noted previously, the authors of the text may have looked to the Calendar Round date as an element of freedom. For the date of U K'ix Kan's accession, for example, without an explicit anchoring to a Long Count date, the Calendar Round gave historians a scope of about 2,800 years within which to find significant numerological associations. On the late end, assuming normal life spans for K'uk' B'ahlam and his successors, U K'ix Kan's own accession date of 11 Kaban 0 Pop could have been as late as 8.17.8.11.17. As for the early end, the first three *bak'tuns* mark the period of much of the mythistory recorded in the Triad Group, culminating in Ix Muwaan Mat's accession on 2.1.0.14.2 9 Ik' 0 Yax. Hence,

TABLE 4.2: Determining the Long Count position of U K'ix Kan's liminality

Free-floating Calendar Round	Long Count	Difference from Midpoint (days)	Astronumerologically Related Dates	Interval Factors
1 K'an 2 Kumk'u	5.7.11.8.4	14,160	1.18.5.4.0	364
11 Kaban 0 Pop	5.8.17.15.17	4,647	9.6.18.5.12	116
Midpoint	5.9.10.14.4	0	—	—
1 K'an 2 Kumk'u	5.10.4.3.4	4,820	—	—
11 Kaban 0 Pop	5.11.10.10.17	14,333	—	—

the earliest possibility for U K'ix Kan's accession would have been 2.10.17.17.17 11 Kaban 0 Pop.

If we hypothesize that Kan B'ahlam's historians were interested in anchoring the Calendar Round to an astronumerologically related Long Count—such as those we saw in the Temple of Inscriptions—then these historians first had to compute the fifty possible Long Counts for the placement of the two Calendar Rounds. Next, they would identify the figures or events with whom they were interested in making associations. Finally, they would have to compute the resulting intervals to check if there were any useful periods within them. The authors then were left to determine which dates would have been most auspicious or which best served the purposes of the text.

What we find is that the date that was chosen, 5.7.11.8.4, had both practical and numerological characteristics to recommend it (Aldana 2001b:170–174; 2004a). If the Palenque historians considered every possible date as equally acceptable, they would have been required to perform the above calculations for fifty-two pairs of dates, because the interval between K'uk' B'ahlam's earliest recorded date, 8.18.0.13.6, and the last recorded date from mythical times, 2.1.0.15.2, is 986,364 days, or just shy of 52 × 18,980. As we have seen, processing fifty-two dates would be unreasonably unwieldy, but it appears that Kan B'ahlam's historians had a way out. U K'ix Kan held a liminal position between the figures enacting Creation and the counted members of the Palenque dynasty. Apparently, the Palenque historians took this genealogical position seriously and attempted to place his dates of birth and accession mathematically between the two periods (see Table 4.2). By adding half of the above interval to the earlier date, they would have confronted a Long Count position of 5.9.10.14.4 4 K'an 7 K'ank'in.

Although situated in the middle of the interval, this Long Count did not correspond to the desired Calendar Round of either birth or accession (1 K'an 2 Kumk'u or 11 Kaban 0 Pop). The key, then, would be to find which of the possible Calendar Rounds closest to 5.9.10.14.4 would produce the numerologically best result.

Two sets of dates would have suited the purposes of the Palenque historians. Either 5.7.11.8.4 1 K'an 2 Kumk'u and 5.8.17.15.17 11 Kaban 0 Pop or 5.10.4.3.4 1 K'an 2 Kumk'u and 5.11.10.10.17 11 Kaban 0 Pop would match the two free-floating Calendar Rounds and be as close as possible to the midpoint, 5.9.10.14.4. In order to choose between them, the next step would be to determine if either pair could be astronumerologically tied to the rest of the text, which would require a significant number of calculations. This is where the 819-day count would prove useful.

All that is needed here is a set of tables containing multiples of the relevant astronumerological periods (much like those found in the Dresden Codex). A Palenque astronomer would start with multiples of 819.[10] This astronomer would have considered Saturn and Jupiter first since their periods were the best captured by the method. For Saturn, commensuration between 378 and 819 comes at $18 \times 819 = 14{,}742$. If the historians were interested in connecting U K'ix Kan to Unen K'awiil's birth, for example, they would start by calculating the interval between 1.18.5.4.0 and 5.7.11.8.4 (= 499,044). Here the astronomer would look for multiples of 819 that are near 499,044. Most likely, the tables would have provided multiples up to 10 and then multiples of 10 such that the astronomer would come up with $3 \times 147{,}420 + 3 \times 14{,}742 = 486{,}486$. Then he would calculate the difference: $499{,}044 - 486{,}486 = 12{,}588$. This last number would be compared to the table of multiples of 378 where the closest number is 12,474. The discrepancy here ($12{,}588 - 12{,}474 = 114$ days) prevents the inclusion of whole Saturn periods.

Moving on, the astronomer would then look to Jupiter periods: $3 \times 155{,}610 + 2 \times 15{,}561 = 497{,}952$ and $499{,}044 - 497{,}952 = 1{,}092$. The closest multiple of 399 to 1,092 is 1,197, so here again he would not have found commensuration. However, 1,092 is an easily recognizable multiple of 364 ($3 \times 364 = 3 \times 365 - 3$). Thus, the astronomer would simply have to check to see if 497,952 is a multiple of 3,276 (since $9 \times 364 = 3{,}276$). First

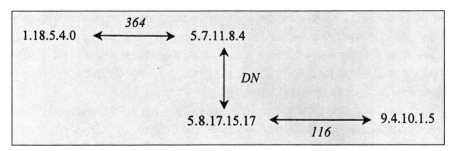

FIGURE 4.2: *Numerology concerning the placement of U K'ix Kan's personal history in the Long Count*

of all, 15,561 = 19 × 819, but he constructed the original interval out of 32 × 15,561 (3 × 10 × 15,561 + 2 × 15,561). Since 32 is divisible by 4, he knew that 497,952 would be divisible by 364 as would 1,092, so even though his overall interval is not divisible by 378 or 399, he would have found that it is divisible by 364 (see Table 4.2).

Along with the connection to Unen K'awiil's birth on the primordial side, Palenque historians would have found another relevant numerological link for the earlier pair of dates. In historic times U K'ix Kan's accession was connected to Kan B'ahlam I's birth by 116. One hundred sixteen is the period of Mercury, which was the celestial representation of K'awiil (see also Schlak 1996). Kan B'ahlam I was of obvious import to Palenque's historians since he was the namesake of their commissioner, Kan B'ahlam (II), son of Janaab' Pakal. Furthermore, Kan B'ahlam I's importance did not go unrecognized in the basic narrative of the history, since GI's tablet in the Triad Group culminated with his accession (on 9.6.18.5.12; see Figure 6.1).

If we step back and attempt to make sense of this numerology from a Maya perspective, we realize that the result makes astronumerological sense. The pair of dates chosen for the Long Count placement of U K'ix Kan's personal history reinforces the liminal position he held. The astronumerological links tied him to Unen K'awiil, a connection that allowed for the conjuring of royal ancestors, and the celestial representation of K'awiil (Mercury, 116) tied U K'ix Kan to the first member of the dynasty to have been named Kan B'ahlam. The other Long Count possibilities (5.10.4.3.4 and 5.11.10.10.17) were not connected to any other of the recorded dates using multiples of any of the numbers we have identified as being astronumerologically relevant. Kan B'ahlam's historians started out looking for a meaningful way to place a pair of Calendar Round dates in the Long Count, then they realized that only one set closest to the interval's halfway point allowed for the construction of an astronumerological puzzle.

This computational procedure was certainly more complex than simply utilizing individual tables for each of the periods of the planets, and on the first or second attempt to learn the procedure it probably did take longer. With practice, however, novice computers would have found the procedure substantially more efficient. Once an interval is divided by 819, the numbers being dealt with are much smaller; therefore, the overall scope of the individual planetary multiplication tables could be correspondingly much smaller. Given the number and types of computations necessary for placing one Calendar Round, the number 819 itself embodied an algorithm for constructing history relative to the periods of the planets.

This argument for the placement of U K'ix Kan's birth date, however, leaves us in the awkward position of suggesting that Kan B'ahlam's court historians were using fictitious Long Count dates for the birth date of one of the earliest rulers of the dynasty. Actually, such a practice is not unprecedented. Not far away (in time or space from Kan B'ahlam's reign) in early thirteenth-*k'atun* Dos Pilas, Itzamnaaj K'awiil erected a stela to commemorate his birth (Dos Pilas Stela 8). The Long Count date on this stela, 9.12.0.10.11, however, did not match the 13 Chuwen 19 K'ayab Calendar Round date it accompanied. Looking back at the history of Dos Pilas, we find that the Calendar Round date actually implied an earlier Long Count date (Houston 1993). This early date, though, occurred during the military skirmishes between B'alaj Chan K'awiil of Dos Pilas and his stepbrother, Nuun Ujol Chaak of Tikal, and that sent Nuun Ujol Chaak fleeing to Palenque for safe harbor (see Chapter 1). When Nuun Ujol Chaak returned to take vengeance on his kin, he drove B'alaj Chan K'awiil out of the city and set up a military occupation. Itzamnaaj K'awiil, it appears, did not want it known that he was born while his father was in exile, so he manipulated the inscribed date on Stela 8. Hence, the Calendar Round was preserved but the Long Count date manipulated in order to preserve (or construct) the prestige of the lineage (Houston 1993).

The numerological puzzle at Palenque is a more artistic version of this same phenomenon, which will be discussed further later in this chapter.

ASTRONUMEROLOGY AT WORK

Before we move deeper into the astronumerology of these tablets, we now find justification for the error describing the birth of the second ruler of Palenque, K'uk' B'ahlam, which Schele and Mathews left unresolved. Although neither of the two Calendar Round dates recorded, 5 Kimi 14 K'ayab (8.18.0.13.6) and 1 K'an 2 K'ayab (8.19.15.3.4), have any numerological ties to any other dates in the tablets, the "erroneously" implied Long Count date does. Specifically, the text records 5 Kimi 14 K'ayab (8.18.0.13.6) and then a distance number of 1.2.5.14, yielding 8.19.3.1.0 5 Ajaw 18 K'ayab. This last date, in fact, is connected by 9 × 379 × 378 to the acts of GI on 13.0.1.9.2 and to Janaab' Pakal's accession by 364; it is also connected by $(11^2 \times)$ 819 to the main conjuring ceremony of Kan B'ahlam on 9.12.18.5.19. This point is very important since it is only by inserting an "erroneous" date that the second *ajaw*, K'uk' B'ahlam, could be astronumerologically linked to the rest of the text. More importantly, only by referring to the numerology encoded within the 819-day count do we encounter an explanation for this computational "error."

In fact, each of the errors in the texts identified by Lounsbury, Schele, and Mathews (Schele and Mathews 1991) turns out to be a gateway into a numerological riddle (Aldana 2001b:176; 2004a). Floyd Lounsbury partially cracked one of these riddles in 1976. Unsatisfied with attributing computational incongruity in the Triad Group texts to scribal error, Lounsbury sought underlying reasons. Within the middle temple of the Triad Group, the Initial Series contains an 819-day count. The Calendar Round recorded for the 819-day count is 1 Ik' 10 Tzek, corresponding to 1.6.14.11.2, but the distance number recorded implies the date 1.18.4.0.15 5 Men 13 Yax. The difference between the recorded date and the implied date is 11.9.7.13, or 82,593 days. What Lounsbury noticed was that 82,593 is 207 multiples of 399 — the latter being the canonic value for Jupiter's synodic period (Schele and Mathews 1991). The recording of 1 Ik' 10 Tzek and an incorrect distance number suggested to Lounsbury that this was no error. Rather, he believed that the author of the text intentionally incorporated Jupiter's period as part of the commemoration of a celestial event. Lounsbury associated this reconstructed Jupiter association with a hypothetically observed Jupiter-Saturn conjunction reproduced with the invocation of the GMT correlation (Schele and Mathews 1991:94; see also Aveni 2001:169).[11] With the tools described here, however, we can now begin to see how and why the Triad Group texts contained this little puzzle without resorting to a specific calendar correlation and so what may have been observable in a given night sky. In particular, we recognize that the error was created as one small piece of a puzzle constructed through the language of astronumerology.

Moreover, turning to the smallest temple in the Triad Group, the one dedicated to Unen K'awiil, we encounter the complementary half to Lounsbury's puzzle. Within the inscription in this structure there is another problem with the 819-day count for the Initial Series. Here the error is an obvious one: the distance number is added to the base date. As Schele and Mathews (1991:91) pointed out, "[a]ny scribe as any experienced epigrapher should have known to subtract the DN [distance number] instead of adding it." Although not containing another clue, this "error" appears to have been a flag for the other 819-day count in the inscriptions of this temple. The second count was of great importance for it corresponded to the house dedication of Unen K'awiil's temple.[12] This date provides the other half of the puzzle recovered by Lounsbury. Namely, Lounsbury found that 1.6.14.11.2 − 1.18.4.0.15 = 82,593 = 207 Jupiter rounds; we now recognize that the interval between this second date and the earlier date is 9.12.18.7.1 − 1.18.4.0.15 = 1,113,966 = 2,947 Saturn rounds.

The point here is that two "correct" 819-day count stations related to the same "erroneous" 819-day count date implicate Jupiter and Saturn—precisely those planets best captured by the workings of the count. In other words, the power of the 819-day count and the means of accessing the numerological subtext are both contained in these two puzzles that are themselves tied together by a common date. The implication is that the authors of the text reconstructed their dynastic history, using the 819-day count both as a tool and as a key for later historically educated nobles to unravel a parallel numerological text within recorded history.

Further evidence that astronumerology was the purpose of the 819-day count is embodied solely within the Calendar Round date 1 Ik' 10 Tzek. Lounsbury showed that this Calendar Round also corresponded to the station for Kan B'ahlam's ceremonies dedicating the Triad Group during historical times (Schele and Mathews 1991). The ceremony took place from 9.12.18.5.16 to 9.12.18.5.19, carrying an 819-day count station of 9.12.16.2.2 1 Ik' 10 Tzek. The date 9.12.16.2.2 actually is connected with three other dates using every other "important" number in our list. With –0.0.6.15.0, the 819-day station for Ix Muwaan Mat's birthday, the interval invokes 378 (and, of course, 819). With 9.12.11.4.10 — Janaab' Pakal's *ajaw* ceremony — 584 comes in; and with 2.1.0.14.2 — Ix Muwaan Mat's accession — we find 116. Moreover, the difference between 1.6.14.11.2 and 9.12.16.2.2 (the two implied dates for 1 Ik' 10 Tzek) embodies 260, 364, 365, 780, and 819, as the product of 365 and 3,276, that is, the *haab'* multiplied by the full 819-day count. Taking into account the textual passages generating these intervals, we thus have all important numbers connecting only four individuals: Kan B'ahlam, Ix Muwaan Mat, Janaab' Pakal, and GIII.

The specific reasons for tying the aforementioned individuals together will be discussed extensively in the next two chapters. First, however, it is worthwhile to consider the purpose of these "errors" with respect to hypotheses of deterministic histories. Scholars have criticized Maya hieroglyphic records as having been manipulated strictly for political ends.[13] Given the machinations described here, however, we do not have to consider astronumerological contrivance to be corroboration of such hypotheses. First, the dates manipulated (with the exception of the birth date of Itzamnaaj K'awiil, who was not from Palenque) were not major historical events. The shifting of the date does not change the narrative at all; it only provides for the possibility of a numerological subtext. Second, most of the dates involved in contrivance correspond to mythological times. These events very likely were parts of narrative traditions that did not depend on Long Count correlations for any legitimation. These events, too, must have been associated with free-floating Calendar Round dates such that, within bounds, they may have been assigned to one of many possible

125

Long Count dates. Third, there must have been enough recorded history for the historians at Palenque to be able to choose, among myriad dates, pairs that produced numerologically relevant intervals. These dates were the ones included in the stone tablets, but they are not meant to serve as complete or representative histories. Rather, the texts were crafted as an art form that included a mathematical component.

Therefore, deterministic history in no way strictly follows from this reconstruction of historical method. It may, however, leave the reader curious about who the historians and astronomers behind this monumental task may have been. If we follow the suggestions of other scholars, we may have an answer for this question, yielding the identities of some of the most powerful minds of Palenque history.

AUTHORS

As noted at the end of the last chapter, Janaab' Pakal's sarcophagus lid contains the clearest corroboration of the numerological message coded within the tablets of the Temple of Inscriptions. Here, Janaab' Pakal was depicted reborn from the maw of the Underworld in the garb of the Maize God, and from his body, just as from GI's, rose the world tree as the portal between worlds. But the sarcophagus itself is a complex icon depicting more than the triumph of Janaab' Pakal. Besides showing him as the resurrected Maize God, the sarcophagus depicted all of the important members of Janaab' Pakal's ancestry inscribed in portraiture around its perimeter (Robertson 1983:65–73; Schele and Mathews 1998:119–125). More to the point, each of these figures was depicted as being reborn, each figure is shown emerging from a crack in an earth glyph (see Figure 1.3). This set of rebirths reifies one of the messages embedded in the numerology of the Temple of Inscriptions: that Janaab' Pakal resurrected the lineage after it had been "lost" by Aj Ne' Ohl Mat.

So the message of the sarcophagus lid thus far revealed is not surprising given what we have learned about Janaab' Pakal and his descendents. What is surprising is that three other figures were also carved into the lid and that these men are named (see Figure 3.7). What could three men genealogically unrelated to the *ajaw* have done to merit commemoration on this most impressive of monuments? Part of the answer comes from the title these men bore. Two of these men are identified as *aj k'ujuun*, a title whose interpretation has recently been debated but has been read as "he of the sacred book" (Coe and Kerr 1998; Jackson and Stuart 2001). Moreover, Mark Zender (2004:189–191) recently has suggested that this title signified a priestly rank associated with a special education and may have been read as "worshipper." Regardless of the specific reading, the sarcophagus lid text appears to name *sajal* Yuhk Makab'te, *aj k'ujuun* Chak Chan, and *aj k'ujuun* Mut as nobility, and whether or not they were employed explicitly as scribes, they were probably versed in scribal knowledge (Coe and Kerr 1998).

Now, during the Early Classic period, before the reign of Janaab' Pakal, scribes were not allowed to leave their names on the works of art they created. All emphasis was placed on the ruler depicted or on the events to which s/he was related. As cities and their nobility grew larger, however, new traditions emerged within the scribal community. During the Late Classic period, artists were allowed to "sign" their names to the tablets and stelae they carved, reflecting the increased quantity of artistic production and the concurrent interest in the quality of artwork (M. Miller 1999:200–210; Reents-Budet 1994; Tate 1992). At El Peru, for example, eight different carvers inscribed their names into the face of Stela 31 (Coe and Kerr 1998:133). By this time it had also become common for artists to include their names in the texts of the ceramic vessels they painted (Coe and Kerr 1998; Reents-Budet 1994:36–72).

Perhaps most explicitly, the change is attested by a non-royal elite residential complex at Copán, Honduras. Here, there is no escaping the prominence to which scribes had risen. A pair of sculpted human figures adorns the façade of Structure 9N-82. Both of these figures hold out their hands, carrying a brush in one and a half conch in the other.[14] Within this structure was a long bench bearing an hieroglyphic inscription in which the scribe names himself as a member of the royal court (W. Fash 1991:120). Here, then, we encounter a case in which a scribe holds a position that permits him to commission his own hieroglyphic texts.

In each of the above cases we find that by the Late Classic, space was made for the artists to record their contribution to the final product.

Following this logic, Robertson (1983) and Schele and Mathews (1998) suggested that the *aj k'ujuuntahk* Chak Chan and Mut were the artists who produced the artwork of the sarcophagus chamber and lid. The names of these men, however, are not preceded by the *yu-*[bat]-*lu* or *u tzib* glyphic compounds, which would solidify such an inference (Coe and Kerr 1998; Coe and Van Stone 2001). Moreover, the portraits of these men, along with that of Yuhk Makab'te, were included on the sarcophagus lid along with their names—an honor unprecedented for artists working in stone. All three were depicted within half-quatrefoil openings, suggesting that they were still alive at the time of Janaab' Pakal's resurrection as the Maize God and so on the other side of the cosmological border after the ruler's death.

Zender has argued that while alive, Chak Chan and Mut were warrior-priests who accompanied Janaab' Pakal on the successful capture of Suutz Saat, recorded on panel fragments found in Temple XIV.[15] So perhaps this closeness is behind the depiction of the two of them on the sarcophagus lid. But we may also construct two independent arguments for identifying Yuhk Makab'te, Chak Chan, and Mut as the inventors/collaborators of astronumerology and the 819-day count. First, we note that their commemoration was purely honorary, because given the location of the record inside a royal tomb, very few people would have witnessed their placement in the company of the Palenque *ajawtahk*. Unlike their contemporary artist colleagues who were publicly acknowledged (e.g., by name on stelae), these men were privately acknowledged, albeit more elaborately. Such an honor would have been reserved for non-ruling elite who contributed far more than was usual.

Second, we may appeal to the other portraits on the sarcophagus lid. Indeed, if these men constructed the astronumerological story behind the Re-Creation of Palenque, the whole of the sarcophagus lid's message is consistent; besides Janaab' Pakal, everyone whose image can be found on the lid had a role in Janaab' Pakal's position of honor. In commemoration of their work and the critical role it played in the re-legitimation of the polity, we may posit that the portraits of Yuhk Makab'te, Chak Chan, and Mut were inscribed into the lid to join those of Palenque's great *ajawtahk*—each in effect "composing" Palenque's portal between worlds.

This resolution resonates with Robertson's and Schele and Mathews's proposals that the men carved on the lid had some part in producing the message encoded in the sarcophagus chamber. Having recognized the unique means of encoding this message, however, it becomes completely reasonable to suggest that Yuhk Makab'te's, Chak Chan's, and Mut's roles as the intellectual source of Nal-k'awiil-based history would be acknowledged in this unique manner.

We will see in the next chapter that their efforts were not confined to elaborating the commemoration of Janaab' Pakal's feats and computing the early history of Palenque. Under the direction of Kan B'ahlam II, these inventors of astronumerology participated in the development of a much larger political and religious programme.

NOTES

1. Lounsbury (1978) attributed the first instance of the 819-day count to a time shortly before Kan B'ahlam's reign. We now know through a reading of the text that this tablet (the Palace Tablet treated later) was written some decades after Kan B'ahlam took office and that the instance of the 819-day count, like those in the Triad Group, was in retrospection. The text actually was commissioned by K'an Joy Chitam, Kan B'ahlam's younger brother. A second text carries an 819-day count for 9.11.15.11.11.

2. Cardinality is still a tentative interpretation. John Watanabe (1983), for example, has shown that modern Mayan languages linguistically maintain north and south as subordinate to a primary east-west direction.

3. See, for example, the ritual circuit described for the Wayeb rites (Chase 1989).

4. See, for example, the *Diccionario Maya* (Barrera Vásquez 1995:551); also, the cognate in Ch'orti' is *nar* (Proyecto Lingüístico Francisco Marroquín 1996:150).

5. Possibly corresponding to Glyphs G and F of the "Supplementary Series" (see Lounsbury 1978:767; Satterthwaite 1965; Thompson 1960).

6. Modern astronomers and the archaeoastronomical literature refer to this event as "heliacal rise."

7. Zero was represented by a shell in the Maya numerical system and was probably physically represented by one when performing calculations. For methods of computations using seeds, see Calderón (1966) and also B. Tedlock (1982).

8. This expectation analogizes conceptually to the epicycles of medieval Islamic and Christian astronomies. East of the Atlantic, the assumption of the

celestial bodies' perfection restricted their movement to uniform circular motion. Accommodation was then made using circles traveling on circles in order to compensate for imperfect commensuration. In the Western Hemisphere, the assumption was not of circular motion geometrically but arithmetically. The planets were restricted to integer cycles and the deviations were compensated for using the 260-day sacred count. We will return to this point later in this chapter.

9. Susan Milbrath (2002:127) notes that the 819-day count "is known to refer to Jupiter and Saturn." The notable planetary exception here is Venus. Sharing the factor of 73 with 365, however, Venus was easily captured in relation to *haab'* computations. What is interesting is that this relationship shows that numerologically the sun and Venus were kin—precisely what the numerology reveals within the mythology.

10. The number 819 is a more efficient base than 3,276 is relative to the specific periods of the planets.

11. See Chapter 5, note 8.

12. On house dedications, see Stuart (1998).

13. See, for example, Marcus (1993). As reviewed in Chapter 1, such histories should not be considered less valid than purportedly "objective" histories. Moreover, to attempt to separate "history" from "myth" or "propaganda" is to misunderstand all three (Chakrabarty 1992; Derrida 1997:10–18; Smith 1999:1–41).

14. Conches were cut in half to produce wells that would hold paint.

15. Zender (2004) includes a drawing of the text, which can be transcribed as *17 Pohp chu?-ka-ja* SUUTZ *sa-ti u* KAB'*-ji* K'INICH JANAAB' *pa-ka-la yi-ta-ji* CHAK CHAN-*na aj-*K'UJ-*na ?-*MUT? *aj-*K'UJ-? If the initial verb is read as *chukaj,* the text describes a capturing by Janaab' Pakal accompanied by the two *aj k'ujuuntahk.*

CHAPTER FIVE

THE PUBLIC FACE OF RE-CREATION

We have already seen one motivation for the tablets in the Temple of Inscriptions, commissioned as they were to adorn the temple atop the funerary monument of a great leader. Yet within the texts of the Temple of Inscriptions' third tablet we have also noted a telling anomaly — one that reveals a different sort of motivation. The third tablet is very different in character from the first two. Although the first tablet contains a break in normalcy with the record of the battle, the third tablet's break leads to a jumble of historical records without clear theme or consistent chronology. Looking at the distribution of astronumerological references within these tablets, we realize that the erratic chronology of the third tablet is responsible for all of the astronumerological subtext (see

Figure 2.3). This different format is precisely the situation one might expect if the first two tablets were composed before astronumerology was introduced (or invented). In order to integrate astronomical periods into the intervals between dates, then, the third tablet was forced to take on an eclectic narrative (Aldana 2001b:158; 2004a).

If indeed these changes indicate a separate composition, then the third tablet is very suggestive regarding who may have been responsible for it. The last passage of this tablet tells of Janaab' Pakal's death and of the accession of his son, Kan B'ahlam II. We thus are presented with the real possibility that Janaab' Pakal did not oversee the composition of this final tablet (Gillespie 2001; Robertson 1983:54; 1991:8; Schele and Mathews 1998:108). Indeed, the funerary monument itself was not completed before Janaab' Pakal's death. Archaeological investigation has shown that the structure was built in two phases (Schele 1981; Schele and Freidel 1990). In the first, a small structure similar in design to the Templo Olvidado was created as a crypt for the sarcophagus that would hold the *ajaw's* body. Once his corpse was placed within it, a pyramidal mound, crowned by a small temple, was built around this crypt.

Since the overall structure had to be left incomplete until his body could be placed within, several scholars have suggested that Janaab' Pakal also left one of the tablets blank for his son and heir to compose upon his "entering the road" (Gillespie 2001; Robertson 1983:54; Schele and Mathews 1998:108). The difference in character of this tablet from the other two strongly suggests a second author. In this chapter, we will investigate Kan B'ahlam's architectural patronage in order to see how it resonates with the message of the third tablet. The extended scope of this message sets the overall context for the next chapter in which we take up a close reading of the hieroglyphic inscriptions that Kan B'ahlam patronized. The unity of the underlying vision and its contemporaneity with the first records of the 819-day count suggests that Kan B'ahlam sought to send a message on various levels to the multiple communities of which he was an integral part.

KAN B'AHLAM'S ARCHITECTURAL PROGRAM

We have seen that Janaab' Pakal's reign was wildly successful and also very long. Kan B'ahlam was born to Ix Tz'aak Ajaw by Janaab' Pakal when the father was thirty-two years old. Kan B'ahlam was then designated as heir to the throne at only six years of age. Yet at eighty, Janaab' Pakal had still not passed the *ajawlel* on to his son. The Middle Tablet of the Temple of Inscriptions suggests that this delay in transferring power resulted from the ritual restoration needs of the dynasty, but it may also have resulted from the greater political context in which the polity was immersed.

As noted above, K'inich Janaab' Pakal had proven himself time and again during his reign in matters martial as well as political. Yet in Maya civilization, the success of an individual *ajaw* did not ensure the protracted success of the polity. In fact, the citizens of Palenque all too recently had witnessed evidence for justifiable concern that things might not be so stable upon their great *ajaw*'s passing. On 9.11.6.16.7 3 Manik 0 Ch'en, Nuun Ujol Chaak was forced to find harbor at Janaab' Pakal's city (West Tablet, Temple of Inscriptions; see Aldana 2005a). As related in Chapter 1, Nuun Ujol Chaak had been betrayed by a half brother who defected to a nearby city and then came back to attack him. A battle on 9.11.4.5.14 6 Ix 2 K'ayab had Nuun Ujol Chaak on the lam (Dos Pilas Hieroglyphic Stairway 2, East, Step I).

The half brother, we have seen, teamed up with the nobility of Kalak'mul. And herein lies the source of political instability. By this time, the *ajawtahk* of Kalak'mul had become the most powerful of all Maya polities. They commanded armies of smaller cities, leading to ubiquitous records throughout the Maya region of battles conducted *ukab'ijiiy Yuknom*, "under the auspices of the Kalak'mul *ajaw*" (Aldana 2004b; Martin and Grube 1995). The Kalak'mul *ajaw*, it seems, went so far as to exploit conflict within a single dynastic lineage in order to maintain the suppression of Tikal and continued dominance. Thus, even though the ruler of Tikal, Nuun Ujol Chaak, was returned to the throne through Janaab' Pakal's assistance and won a battle or two against B'alaj Chan K'awiil, in the end Nuun Ujol Chaak lost the war (Martin and Grube 2000:42).

With the ever-present threat of Kalak'mul's allies and without the return of Tikal to the international scene, Palenque's place in the Maya world must have appeared precarious. Perhaps this concern kept Janaab' Pakal in power into his eighties despite the fact that his son could have taken over much earlier.

Thus, during the extended rule of his father, Kan B'ahlam had plenty of time to develop a strategy for inspiring loyalty among the nobility and commoners alike and for expanding the cultural renaissance his father had patronized. Kan B'ahlam would not have been alone in the Maya world had he hoped simply to inspire confidence through an expanded building program incorporating the monumental glorification of the dynasty. In fact, both of his main allies, Jasaw Chan K'awiil at Tikal (son of Nuun Ujol Chaak) and Waxaklajuun Ub'aah K'awiil at Copán, had done the same—the former with a twin pyramid complex in the plaza directly in front of the main acropolis (Harrison 1999:126–130; C. Jones 1991:119; Martin and Grube 2000:47) and the latter with the commencement of an hieroglyphic stairway just southeast of his primary ballcourt (Stuart 1996). (See Figure 5.1.)

Indeed, Kan B'ahlam's first acts as ruler appear scripted. His first effort was to demonstrate Palenque's prominence by leveling an attack on nearby Tonina (Martin and Grube 2000:170)—an attack that would have severe long-term repercussions, as we will see later. Now, however, basking in his own military glory and that remaining from his father's reign, Kan B'ahlam was free to commence a building program that was sufficiently complex to have been the fruit of more than a decade of intellectual effort. In preparation for this new construction, on 9.12.11.12.10 8 Ok 3 K'ayab, the day he acceded to the throne, Kan B'ahlam dedicated his father's funerary monument.

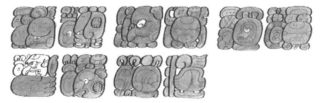

On 8 Ok 3 K'ayab, he ties the white headband on himself, K'inich Kan B'ahlam K'ujul B'aakal Ajaw. He gives the precious one [Janaab' Pakal] [to] Nine Tree House. It is the name of the burial of K'inich Janaab' Pakal K'ujul B'aakal Ajaw. (T8–T12)

With that ceremony, Kan B'ahlam completed his duties to his deceased father's body; his attention now turned to setting Janaab' Pakal's soul to work along the lines necessary to maintain power.

FIGURE 5.1: *Temple I of Tikal. Much of Jasaw Chan K'awiil's history is recorded within this monument's hieroglyphic inscriptions; his body used to lie underneath it. (Photograph by Jesse Aldana.)*

The multi-level scheme that Kan B'ahlam and his advisors hatched was in no way an exercise in humility. Kan B'ahlam intended to make clear to both noble and commoner that Creation had recurred at Palenque and that the message encoded in the West Tablet of the Temple of Inscriptions could be elaborated for full public view. His main construction effort went into creating a message to the west of Janaab' Pakal's funerary monument, nestled at the base of the hill named K'uk' Lakam Witz. Here, among the hills that overlooked the great plains leading to the Gulf Coast, Kan B'ahlam commissioned three temples in symbolic layout. The layout followed a pattern already common in the architectural record for hundreds of years: the three temples were arranged in the shape of a Mesoamerican hearth.[1] In Maya households, three large stones were placed in triangular fashion to contain a cooking fire and on which to place a comal or other cooking vessel. The obvious message, therefore, was that Kan B'ahlam's three temples would form the center of the Palenque polity, just as the hearth served as the center of every Maya home.

The metaphor of the hearth also set up an allusion to Creation, calling forth one of the most important acts transpiring at the beginning of the Maya era: the setting of the three cosmic hearthstones (Quirigua Stela C). Attested by inscriptions across the Maya region, the placement of three cosmic throne stones by the gods constituted the primary event occurring on 13.0.0.0.0 4 Ajaw 8 Kumk'u (approximately 3,000 years before historical Maya time). Located in Quirigua's main plaza, Stela C records that

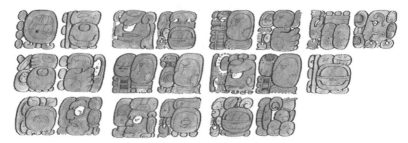

[o]n 4 Ajaw 8 Kumk'u the image of the three stone-bindings was sighted.[2] The Jaguar Paddler and Stingray Paddler plant the Jaguar Throne Stone at the Five Sky House. He [undeciphered] plants the Serpent Throne Stone at the earth-cave (?). Then it happened,

Itzamnaaj bound the Water lily Throne Stone at the k'i-sky. It is the yax-hearth-place.[3] The thirteenth bak'tun ended under the authority of the 6 Sky Ajaw. (B5–B15)

The public placement of the monument bearing this text at Quirigua is important. Stephen Houston and David Stuart (1992; also Stuart 1996) have suggested that priests read from stelae for public rituals. In such case, we would have corroboration that the Creation story was part of commoner knowledge as well as the ritual knowledge possessed by the nobility and recorded in their hieroglyphic books.

Also, modern and colonial ethnoastronomy (and some archaeo-astronomy) points to the cMd constellation of Orion as containing the celestial representation of the cosmic hearth (Aveni 2001:37). If that were its Classic period representation, nighttime observations would facilitate the maintenance of this story among commoners. Storytellers could point to the image of the first hearth in the sky as they recounted myths to familial audiences sipping atole in household patios. Such stories also would likely have included reference to other major events transpiring at the mythic thirteenth *bak'tun* end.

As the stones for the first hearth were set by the Paddler Gods, Itzamnaaj, and their counterpart with the Serpent Throne Stone, an important ceremony was taking place in the Underworld. Two ceramic drinking vessels from Naranjo provide this account through painted scene and hieroglyphic text. The first vessel, the cylindrical one known as the Vase of the Seven Gods (Figure 5.2), carries a descriptive text.

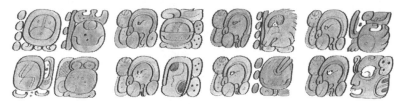

4 Ajaw 8 Kumk'u were put in order, Ek U Tan k'uj, the Sky place god, the earthly god, Bolon Okte k'uj, the three-? k'uj, Witech k'uj, the Jaguar God of the Underworld.

The text states that several Underworld gods were put in order on the very day that the cosmic hearth was being laid.

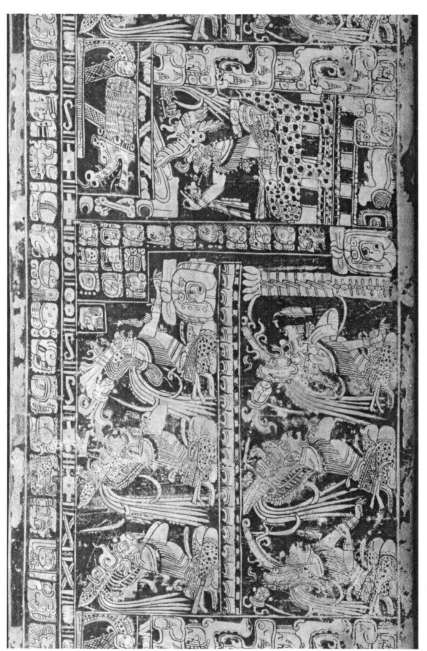

FIGURE 5.2: *Detail from the Vase of the Seven Gods (Kerr photo 2796)*

Just what this ordering entailed is elucidated by the iconography of the scene. On this vessel, two rows of three gods sit facing God L, lord of the Underworld.[4] Each row of three presents a bundle to God L as tribute. In other contexts, this type of bundle is most often marked with an *ikatz* glyph, which is translated as "burden" or "charge" (as is the bundle partially hidden behind God L). Here, however, the bundles being offered are labeled with a glyph representing war.[5] The implicit message is that by the day of Creation, the gods established order in the Underworld through military endeavor (Aldana 2001b:110–117).

Thus, Kan B'ahlam's placement of three stone temples in triangular fashion dedicated to the patron gods of Palenque called to mind the Creation of the cosmic hearth and the activities in the Underworld, in other words, the establishment of a new cosmic order. We will see later iconographic corroboration that the appeal was even so deep as to draw analogy between Janaab' Pakal's military rise to prosperity and the military tribute given to God L.

Beyond the architectural layout, hieroglyphic texts on their façades named the three temples as the *pib naahoob'* (sweatbaths) of the gods (Houston 1996). Stephen Houston (1996) has argued that these were metaphorical sweatbaths because the architecture would not have permitted them to serve as functional sweatbaths, and no archaeological evidence remains to contradict this inference. We will see later the potential use of a metaphorical sweatbath, but first we will contend with the concept of an "ownership" of these three structures by gods. Specifically, Kan B'ahlam's Triad Group was dedicated to the patron gods of the polity, who also happened to be three of the most important players during the Creation era. As the inscriptions tell us, the largest temple was dedicated to GI, the smallest to Unen K'awiil (known as GII before hieroglyphic decipherment), and the third to the god known as GIII (see Figure 5.3).

These three gods generated a great deal of discussion early on during the decipherment of the hieroglyphic script. The specific hieroglyphic contexts behind the various interpretations will be treated in the next chapter. Here, we will take up the commoner's perception of the Triad Group, or perhaps more accurately we will restrict interpretations here to those observations available to the commoners of Kan B'ahlam's reign. Of course many of these commoners provided the

FIGURE 5.3: *Abbreviated names of the gods who owned the sweat-baths in Kan B'ahlam's Triad Group: GI, GII, and GIII*

"unskilled labor" necessary to get the architectural project started and, in the process, they probably learned something more of the inspiration behind their toils. This knowledge could have crept out into the larger commoner social sphere, thereby providing the entire polity with a better understanding than we can reconstruct here. Nevertheless, sufficient data have survived the ravages of time to present some interesting perspectives on the three temples and their supernatural patrons.

Independent astronomically directed investigation has shown that the temple dedicated to GI bears a special relationship with the sun. First, we find that Kan B'ahlam conducted the dedication ceremony of the Triad Group on one of the solar stations, the autumnal equinox (Aldana 2001a). Next, and much more grandiose, Neal Anderson and Moises Morales (1981) have shown that Kan B'ahlam paid special attention to the spatial relationship between Janaab' Pakal's funerary monument and GI's temple. The alignment between the two structures sent rays of setting sunlight through two windows in Janaab' Pakal's funerary monument on the summer solstice. These rays then illuminated the only known carved stela from Palenque, a statue of Kan B'ahlam standing on the stairway of GI's temple (Anderson and Morales 1981; Robertson 1991). Through his placement of GI's temple, then, Kan B'ahlam demonstrated to a public audience that the Sun approved of the transfer of power from Janaab' Pakal to him through the recurrent illumination of his effigy on the steps to the Sun's own temple.[6]

Moving through Kan B'ahlam's Triad Group, the second temple was dedicated to GIII, a deity whose very long name includes the *k'in* ("sun") head variant (see Figure 5.4). For this reason, some scholars argued against Floyd Lounsbury's interpretation, suggesting that GIII, and not GI, corresponded to the sun (Robertson 1991:16–19). Follow-

FIGURE 5.4: *Full name of GIII*

ing Lounsbury's interpretation, however, GIII may be identified as the "jaguar sun," making him the moon. Such an interpretation resonates with Dennis Tedlock's work (1985:46) on the *Popol Vuh,* which elicited ethnographic evidence for the full moon as the "night sun." Although we will find resolution in the next chapter, for the ancient Maya commoner viewing the temple any further evidence regarding the identity of its owner is lacking.

Finally, the third temple was dedicated to a youthful representation of the god known as K'awiil. As noted in Chapter 3, K'awiil has been shown to have been no ordinary Creation-era deity but instead an anthropomorphized representation of royal blood (Stuart 1995a). What is interesting about the representation of K'awiil at Palenque — both public and private — is that he is depicted as an infant (Robertson 1983:37–40). On the face of the Temple of Inscriptions, four tablets separated the three doorways at the top of the structure. On these tablets, four figures (or perhaps the same figure in four different places) are shown holding a recently born K'awiil (Figure 5.5).[7] This was no ordinary child, however, as in each depiction one leg transforms into a serpent just below the knee. Also, on some of the pillars, we recognize a smoking celt in the child's forehead. This iconography follows standard Classic Maya representations of K'awiil (see Figure 5.6).

Why, though, would K'awiil have been so young at Palenque? The answer may now be obvious. As explained in Chapter 3, Janaab' Pakal had to rescue the dynasty's religious charter once it had been lost by Aj Ne' Ohl Mat. In doing so, the dynastic connection had to be born anew and, with it, the royal bloodline. A young K'awiil, then, represented

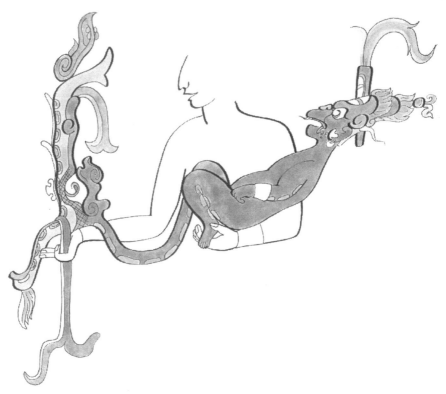

FIGURE 5.5: *K'awiil as an infant at B'aakal*

the new charter and renewed bloodline recovered by Janaab' Pakal after the military defeat by the army of Kalak'mul.

So on a very general level, the hearthstone layout of the temples evoked an association with Creation. But the architectural metaphor went even deeper in capturing this conceptualization, because the relative placement of each temple emphasized the cosmic aspect of their conceptualization. Specifically, the three temples were dedicated to gods with domains in the three cosmic realms: GI in the celestial realm, GIII in the Underworld, and Unen K'awiil as the royal representation of the earthly realm. Kan B'ahlam had these temples built to further reflect these associations. From the plaza at the center of the architectural hearth, one sees the sky behind the temple of GI, Janaab' Pakal's funerary monument behind the temple of GIII, and the steep hill K'uk' Lakam Witz behind K'awiil's temple (Baudez 1996:123). Moreover,

FIGURE 5.6: *K'awiil with serpent foot (after Kerr photograph 702)*

the relative heights of each temple reflected their cosmic associations. GI's temple was the tallest because of its affiliation with the sky; GIII's the lowest, reflecting its connection to the Underworld; and GII's sat between as mediator. These observable characteristics, along with their arrangement as a cosmic hearth and their explicit dedication to the gods of Creation, signaled to Palenque's citizens and visitors that Kan B'ahlam was enacting an architectural Re-Creation.

There is yet another message in the architectural analogy presented here, although at this point we cannot be sure of which members of Palenque's various sociological levels would have had access to it. In 1996 Stephen Houston updated the readings of some portions of the Triad Group inscriptions, thus revising an important portion of Schele and Freidel's 1990 interpretation of Palenque history. Houston focused on a set of phrases that Schele and Freidel had interpreted as making reference to a celestial event occurring in the sky on the night of the date recorded.[8] He recognized that the key glyphic compound should actually be read as *u chitinil*, corroborating other related passages that referred to *u pibnajil* (Houston 1996). These two terms, he noted, were used to refer to sweatbaths. Moreover, the *u-* prefix and *-il* suffix marked these sweatbaths as having been possessed (or owned) by the gods of Kan B'ahlam, not by Kan B'ahlam himself (Houston 1996:137).

Although this revision again removes the explicit astronomical reference from an hieroglyphic inscription, Houston's intent was to demonstrate that there was a logic to calling these structures of the Triad Group "sweatbaths." Houston insightfully draws on architectural, ethnohistoric, and ethnographic data to support the claim but also appears to be influenced by an intent to distance his reading from Schele and Freidel's interpretation such that a ready implication is dismissed. Namely, Houston (1996:135) recognizes that the Triad Group inscriptions explicitly record the births of the three patron gods at Matawiil through the action of Ix Muwaan Mat.[9] Houston (1996:138–144) also provides a preponderance of evidence that sweatbaths were used throughout Mesoamerica to facilitate the birthing process. What he leaves out, though, are the profuse records that give Kan B'ahlam's (and Janaab' Pakal's) relationship to the patron gods with the same glyphic compound expressing the relationship between mother and child: *u juntan*.

Coming together, these data suggest parsimoniously that Ix Muwaan Mat was the mother of the three gods (albeit perhaps not in a strictly human way given that she was a primordial deity). Further, the textual implication is that Kan B'ahlam as *ajaw* birthed the patron gods during his conjuring ceremonies. Houston (1996:135, 145), however, argues explicitly against both of these possible interpretations, preferring to read Ix Muwaan Mat's role more abstractly (and questioning her femaleness) and so placing Kan B'ahlam's role more in line with modern ethnographic records. But if the sweatbaths were metaphorical in the sense that the structures could not have functioned as physical sweatbaths, why can we not consider Kan B'ahlam's conjurings as metaphorical births of the patron gods? It may go against modern cMd constructions of gender, but that conflict does not exclude the possibility from ancient Maya experiences. Moreover, this interpretation leaves open the level of specificity necessary within the metaphor so that these conjurings may be seen as residing within a range of possible practices. It may be that we can interpret such conjurings simply as intellectual conversations with ancestors. Alternately, we might introduce a hallucinogenic component to such "conjurings" in concert with interpretations of House E of the Palace Complex. Although we cannot strictly rule out speculation at either extreme, the metaphorical/symbolic use of the sweatbath provides the justification for a more complicated understanding of Classic Maya ritual.

This discussion brings up the question of the extent to which any interpretation of an *ajaw*'s conjuring would have been known to the Palenque populace at large. Schele and Freidel (1990) suggest very public, theatrical roles for elite rituals, but royal ritual may just as well have been a private event. If, for example, we follow Patricia McAnany's (1995:53) suggestion that Classic Maya state religion is an elaboration of household ritual, virtually all ritual may have been relatively private with the differences in practice attributable to embellishments made possible through the nobility's greater access to resources. The point is that neither the extant archaeological nor textual evidence yet speaks to the public/private nature of elite ritual, so the level of recognition that the commoners would have had regarding the activities in these metaphorical sweatbaths is left in question. Accordingly, the degree of observation of the appeal to a Re-Creation by the Classic Maya commoner remains ambiguous.

ARTISTIC THEMES AT B'AAKAL

There is still another level to Kan B'ahlam's message visible in the art he and his brother patronized. Noble visitors to Palenque would have noticed that the city was anomalous in the Maya world. Besides its drastically unorthodox tower, patronized by Kan B'ahlam's brother K'an Joy Chitam, Palenque was home to a form of artistic expression that was different from cities to the east. Absent from Maya monumental construction were the rectangular stone pillars, known as stelae, plentiful throughout the Maya region. Instead, the artists of Palenque focused their efforts on inscribing hieroglyphic texts and royal portraits into tablets mounted within and upon the outer façades of the city's temples and elite structures. The tablets of Janaab' Pakal's funerary temple fit into this tradition, as do the tablets of Kan B'ahlam's Triad Group.

In these reserved settings, the artists were permitted to record less rigid images of their patrons than those created by their contemporaries, which were placed in public plazas. Herein do we encounter the imagery patronized by Janaab' Pakal, Kan B'ahlam, and K'an Joy Chitam that corroborates the architectural motif of a mythological Creation. The imagery patronized by Janaab' Pakal was examined in Chapter 4; that by Kan B'ahlam will be treated extensively in the next chapter. Here, we consider the artistic message of Creation as it was patronized by K'an Joy Chitam, Kan B'ahlam's brother and successor.

First we return to House E of the Palace Complex where K'an Joy Chitam added a throne, tablet, and mural conspicuously to an inner wall. Known as the Oval Tablet, the tablet's centerpiece depicts Janaab' Pakal's receiving a headdress from his mother while seated on a double-headed jaguar throne (Figure 5.7). Two hieroglyphic texts adorn the tablet. The first is located near Janaab' Pakal's mother, Ix Sak K'uk', between her head and the feathers of the headdress she offers to her son. The glyph preceding her name includes a reference to GI. The text next to Janaab' Pakal begins with a reference to Jun Ajaw(?)[10] and then lists "K'inich Janaab' Pakal K'ujul B'aakal Ajaw." Since there is no date associated with the event, we cannot elaborate on the event's significance. Janaab' Pakal's casual attire, however, speaks to the possible private nature of the ceremony. Also, recalling that he became *ajaw* at twelve years of age, his size relative to Ix Sak K'uk' argues against this image being a depiction of his formal coronation (Gillespie 2001; cf. Schele and Freidel 1990:227; Schele and Miller 1986:114). Finally, Janaab' Pakal sits on a throne that is vastly different from the one sitting under the tablet, and since House E was probably not built until well into Janaab' Pakal's reign, this site was probably not the location of his coronation.[11]

The texts that survive on the altar and on the wall refer to K'an Joy Chitam's accession and, in another passage, to a conjuring (perhaps not performed by him) of the square-nosed deity. More suggestive of the intent of the bench's symbolism is that the figures on the

FIGURE 5.7: *Oval Tablet with throne and background (illustration by Merle Greene Robertson)*

throne's legs each carry a water lily decorated with a pattern of the Creation turtle's carapace. If we take the ovalness of the tablet (along with the painted stucco motif surrounding it) into account, we may see the tablet itself as a turtle's back. Since the Maize God was resurrected from the turtle's carapace (see Figure 5.8),[12] the references to GI and Jun Ajaw associate Janaab' Pakal with the Maize God, father of the Hero Twins.

Moving to the structure known as Temple XIV—a structure just north of GI's temple and east of GIII's temple—we confront another provocative image (Figure 5.9). Visible from the stairs leading up to the

147

FIGURE 5.8: *Resurrection Plate (Kerr photo 1582)*

temple was a tablet mounted on the back wall depicting Kan B'ahlam. He stands with one heel lifted off the ground in a pose signaling that he is dancing (Schele and Miller 1986:272). The platform on which he dances is laced with the iconography of the Underworld, and indeed the event cited in the text took place after Kan B'ahlam's death. To Kan B'ahlam's right, Ix Tz'aak Ajaw (his mother) offers him a representation of K'awiil—an artifact representing the same being received by Janaab' Pakal on the façade of the Temple of Inscriptions.

The text on the left of the tablet describes precisely the event depicted.

FIGURE 5.9: *Tablet from Temple XIV (illustration by Merle Greene Robertson)*

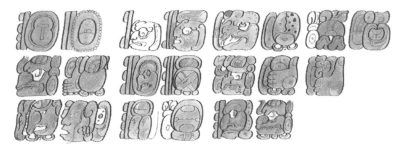

9 Ik' 10 Mol, it happened, the taking of k'awiil by the authority of the Moon Goddess ? ? 13 Ok 18 Wo 9 pij[-event] by White Bone Great Centipede, the *way* of K'awiil. Bolon Okte received it; it happened at the White ?-place. Then it was made/formed, the first taking of k'awiil.

The left side follows with a tremendous distance number.

149

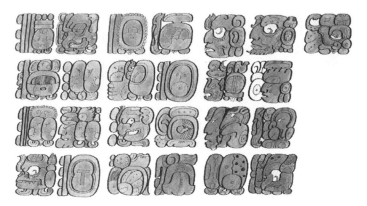

5.18.4.7.0.13.18 [932,166 years] since the first taking of k'awiil happened on 9 Ik' 10 Mol, on 9 Ajaw 3 K'ank'in he entered the cave of the Black Middle Place in the company of GI, GIII, the fiery White 2 House, and Jun Ajaw, the gods of the B'aakal Wayal K'inich Kan B'ahlam K'ujul B'aakal Ajaw.

The difference between text and image is that in the former, the Moon Goddess presides over the ceremony, but in the latter, Ix Tz'aak Ajaw presents K'awiil (Aldana 2001b; Schele and Miller 1986:272). Further, the being who receives the k'awiil idol in the left-hand text is Bolon Okte—a name that may refer to lineage and great spans of time[13]—whereas the image depicts Kan B'ahlam.[14] The inscription ends by telling us that three years after his death on 9.13.10.1.5, Kan B'ahlam entered a cave within the Underworld accompanied by GI, GIII, and Jun Ajaw (among others) to reenact the taking up of the royal bloodline. The direct parallel between text and image across time can be found in Table 5.1. The implication is strong: in ancient times, the Moon Goddess (the mother of GI) oversaw the passing of the royal bloodline; here, Ix Tz'aak Ajaw presented her son with the Classic period symbol of the royal bloodline, the K'awiil idol. Thus, Ix Tz'aak Ajaw was analogized to the Moon Goddess, and Kan B'ahlam to the progeny of the Moon Goddess, GI.

K'an Joy Chitam commissioned a third (even more public) tablet bearing a corroborative theme. On the exterior of the northern wall of the palace, the aptly named Palace Tablet was hung. This time, K'an Joy Chitam has moved on, after honoring his father and his brother, to show how he fit into the family's reigning rhetoric. Occupying only

TABLE 5.1: Parallel events across time depicted and recorded on the tablet in Temple XIV

	Left-hand text	Image	Right-hand text
Event	Receives k'awiil	Receives k'awiil	Enters the cave (with GI, GIII, and other gods)
Location	White ?-place	White ?-place	Black ?-place
Protagonist	Bolon Okte	Kan B'ahlam	Kan B'ahlam
Authority	Moon goddess	Ix Tz'aak Ajaw (Kan B'ahlam's mother)	Gods

a small portion of the tablet, the image at the top shows K'an Joy Chitam's receiving gifts from his parents, Janaab' Pakal and Ix Tz'aak Ajaw (Looper 2003:62; Robertson 1985b:figs. 259–284; Schele 1981:115). The allusion to mythological Creation here is very clear as the three figures sit on the thrones that were used to create the first primordial hearth: the Jaguar, Serpent, and Fish Throne Stones described on Quirigua's Stela C. Here, K'an Joy Chitam receives the headdress from Janaab' Pakal that was given him by his mother on the Oval Tablet. From his mother, K'an Joy Chitam receives the symbols of war: a flint and shield.

The text framing this image is quite long, making reference to the four major players in this Creation metaphor reification: Janaab' Pakal, Ix Tz'aak Ajaw, Kan B'ahlam, and, of course, K'an Joy Chitam. In the next chapter we will see some of the important points in this text as they shed light on our readings of Kan B'ahlam's artistic patronage. For now, we simply note that the inscription ends with a description of K'an Joy Chitam as guardian of the Lakam Ja' *chan-ch'en* — precisely the portal of communication reconstructed by Janaab' Pakal.

K'an Joy Chitam made clear through his artistic patronage that he was intimately familiar with the Creation metaphor that we have recovered from Janaab' Pakal's Temple of Inscriptions and also that he played an equally important role in maintaining that metaphor. Moreover, these images of him and his brother Kan B'ahlam were plainly visible to visiting nobility who could leisurely read them and so confirm the claim that Kan B'ahlam had fashioned architecturally for the commoners: that is, Kan B'ahlam and his family were reenacting Creation for the kingdom of B'aakal.

In iconography and architecture, then, a visitor to Palenque confronted a message of Re-Creation with Kan B'ahlam, his mother, his brother, and his father acting the parts of mythological figures. In fact, as reflected in the incised bones of Figure 3.5, this rhetoric was not out of the ordinary for Maya *ajawtahk* during this day and age. It seems that in Classic Maya culture, every *ajaw* served as the analogue of the *Popol Vuh*'s Junajpu, with his predecessor playing the role of Jun Junajpu. The important differences here were that Kan B'ahlam also had a younger brother who could play perfectly the role of the younger Hero Twin and that they had constructed an underlying intellectual language unique to Palenque — astronumerology.

Within the new temples of the Triad Group lay a number of extensive inscriptions. These texts, like the third tablet of Janaab' Pakal's funerary monument, recorded both mythological and historical events. Yet where Janaab' Pakal's inscriptions presented only a few clear astronumerological messages, the Triad Group's inscriptions contained an extensive astronumerological framework. It is to these inscriptions that we turn our attention in the next chapter.

NOTES

1. For more on the hearth, see Laporte and Fialko (1995) and Schele and Freidel (1990).

2. For an explanation of the "sighting" reading (i.e., as *jel* versus *jal*), see Aldana (2005a).

3. "Yax-hearth-place" is not a reading of the glyph; the three-stone logograph still has not been deciphered.

4. Many of the Maya deities are known by alphabetic designations. These names come from the work of Paul Schellhas (1904). For a recent treatment of God L, see Susan Gillespie and Rosemary Joyce (1998).

5. See Aldana (2005a) in which I have read the glyph as *ek'emey*, not as a formal decipherment but as a reading of the glyph's meaning.

6. Although I seem to be using a calendar correlation to associate a hieroglyphic date with a solar calendar, actually sufficient solar data has been recovered from the hieroglyphic inscriptions such that the observational solar year can be anchored to the Long Count without anchoring it to a specific calendar year (Aldana 2001a). The question, however, does arise as to why the temple would have been dedicated on the autumnal equinox when the statue was illuminated on the summer solstice. We might also inquire as to when

the architectural message was originally conceived. Janaab' Pakal's funerary monument was set according to the summer solstice alignment presumably long before Kan B'ahlam commissioned the Triad Group. It also matched the alignment of several other temples predating it. If we consider the solstitial alignment to have been traditional at Palenque, Kan B'ahlam would have commissioned his Triad Group to be built such that the steps of the largest temple would be spotlighted according to this alignment, thereby invoking the traditions of past rulers. But if this alignment was traditional, why did he dedicate his Triad Group on an autumnal equinox instead of a summer solstice? It may have been a practical matter of location, because the relative placement of the Temple of Inscriptions and K'uk' Lakam Witz, the mountain behind it, would not have permitted a solstitial alignment for GI's temple. Or perhaps the structures were not finished in time for a summer solstice commemoration, yet they would have had to be completed by the 9.13.0.0.0 *k'atun* end, so the equinox was the only option available. There also may have been an answer coming from celestial implication as both GI and GIII, the sun and the full moon, were being commemorated with temples in the Triad Group. A summer solstice would have placed undue emphasis on the sun, whereas an equinox balanced night and day. Without a confirmed calendar correlation, though, we are left to speculate.

7. This interpretation differs greatly from the proposal of Linda Schele and Peter Mathews (1998), who argue that four different *ajawtahk* hold the same baby and that the baby is Kan B'ahlam. As Merle Greene Robertson (1985a) noted, however, from what is left of the face and head, there is no evidence that the baby is not K'awiil. If the iconography's emphasis is on Janaab' Pakal, he may be depicted here in four different places, each time holding the reborn K'awiil. If, on the other hand, the emphasis is on K'awiil, then his being held by four different *ajawtahk* makes sense. A part of the message is consistent between these interpretations and that offered by Schele and Mathews. Linda Schele and David Freidel noticed that the young K'awiil is unconventionally depicted as having six toes. On some of the images of Kan B'ahlam, he is also shown as having six toes and six fingers (Schele and Freidel 1990:235–236). Because the six-finger depiction is sporadic, I do not accept their argument but the underlying message is consistent. The royal blood of the Palenque dynasty was reborn through Janaab' Pakal and was literally carried on in Kan B'ahlam's own blood.

8. Specifically, Schele and Freidel (1990:figure 6:15) read the phrase as a conjunction of GII and GIII: "6 years, 11 months, 4 days after he had been seated as [ajaw] and then GI, GII, GIII and their companion gods came into conjunction. Lord [Kan B'ahlam] enacted a ritual. In 1 year, 12 months, 4 days it will happen, the end of the 13th katun on March 17, 692. And then it came

to pass July 23, 690, and then they were in conjunction the gods, who are the cherished-ones of Lord [Kan B'ahlam], Divine Palenque Lord" (Schele and Freidel 1990:249). They then turned to Dieter Dütting and Anthony Aveni's work (1982), which invoked the GMT to reconstruct the night sky on the date given for this "conjunction." Here, they found an astronomical conjunction of three planets (actually four) and so claimed that the inscription was explicitly recording an astronomical event (Schele and Freidel 1990:256).

9. Houston (1996:135) states: "I believe this supernatural deserves more cautious interpretation, since the female head appears to function phoneti-cally, without necessarily recording the concept of Lady. Equally troublesome is the nature of the relationship between Lady Beastie [Ix Muwaan Mat] and other gods; it involves an esoteric expression, u-b'a-hi/u-CH'AB, that eludes ready interpretation. In short, Lady Beastie may have been neither a lady nor a mother." Regarding the phonetic interpretation of the prefix Ix, Houston gives no examples of such use for personae that were not female. As for the expres-sion, his later work with David Stuart (1992) revealed u b'aah to be read as either "one's person" or "one's image." Ch'ab is glossed by Martha Macri and Matthew Looper (2003) as "penance, offering." Thus, it does not seem so eso-teric to refer to birth (especially one by a primordial deity) as the image of the offering (or any other possible combination of these two translations). Indeed, it seems that Houston's statement is made as a conservative response to his citation of Schele and Freidel's identification of Ix Muwaan Mat as "the moth-er of the gods and the Creatrix in the Maya vision of the cosmos" (Houston 1996:135). The interpretation offered in this book sits somewhere in between these two extremes.

10. This glyph might be NAL, suggesting a connection to GI.

11. Palenque's Tablet of 96 Glyphs tells us that after 9.11.0.0.0, other aja-wtahk were enthroned in the Sak Nuk Naj. Therefore, if that turns out to be the name for House E, their enthronement probably occurred there because of the religious importance of the structure, not because Janaab' Pakal was enthroned there (since he could not have been).

12. See, for example, the Resurrection Plate (Kerr photo 1582; Figure 5.8).

13. J.E.S. Thompson (1960:56) translates Bolon Yokte as "9 Strides" and suggests that s/he may be related to Bolon Tzacab of the Chilam Balam of Chumayel. Ralph Roys (1967:99) favors the meaning "nine generations" or "eternal."

14. An interesting secondary point is that here the White Bone Great Cen-tipede—associated with the Milky Way—is named as the way of K'awiil. Re-calling that K'awiil himself is a representation of royal blood, here we find corroboration of the aforementioned relationship between the Milky Way and accession into the ajawlel.

CHAPTER SIX

RE-CREATION THROUGH
K'AWIILIAN ASTRONOMY

The inscriptions from Kan B'ahlam's Triad Group have been mined by modern scholarship for several different purposes. During the early eighteenth century, they were reproduced as evidence of a glorious "lost" civilization. During the twentieth century, John Teeple was able to tease out elements of Maya lunar astronomy from these tablets. And most recently, they have been a primary source in the restoration of the Palenque dynasty. So far, though, none of these studies has looked at the tablets as whole documents revealing the nuances of Classic Maya political and elite religious thought. In this chapter, we do just that in order to see both that the inscriptions betray a *longue-durée* Maya conceptualization of Creation and more importantly that the astronumerology we have recovered held a very practical function in the composition of official history.

Each of the temples in the Triad Group was designed to follow the same architectural layout: an entrance led to small rooms on either side of a central chamber (Robertson 1991:9–12). Our interest at this point is not so much in the ritual space defined by this architecture but in the ample space it provided for housing private inscriptions. Yuhk Makab'te, Chak Chan, and Mut composed texts and imagery to frame the entrances of the temples and the interior walls. Then, in each temple, they included one main tablet within the inner sanctum. These three inner sanctum tablets were each divided into three sections: the beginning of a hieroglyphic text on the left, an image of Kan B'ahlam involved in a ceremony in the center, and a continuation of the hieroglyphic text on the right. In each case, image and text were germane to the deity to whom the temple was dedicated; therefore, GI's temple held a celestial affiliation, GIII's temple was tied to the Underworld, and Unen K'awiil's temple represented the middle realm. Since these three realms carry along the numerological affiliations of 13, 9, and 7, respectively, the 819-day count is strongly implied. Seemingly to ensure that this connection did not go unnoticed, Yuhk Makab'te, Chak Chan, and Mut began each tablet inscription with an Initial Series date that included an 819-day count. We have already seen that these records formed the source of some numerological puzzles in the tablets, but there is more to be unpacked.

In this chapter, we will treat each tablet chronologically (according to the Initial Series date of each), extracting both the rhetorical intent and the astronumerological puzzles found therein.

GI

In GI's temple, the main image shows Kan B'ahlam presenting an idol to a celestial bird who sits atop a World Tree. The bird looks down from its perch with one claw suspended in the air, as though contemplating the possibility of snatching the idol away. Both the bird and the World Tree should be familiar as they bear extreme likeness to those depicted on Janaab' Pakal's sarcophagus lid (compare Figures 3.7 and 6.1). Allowing for stylistic differences between the artists ren-

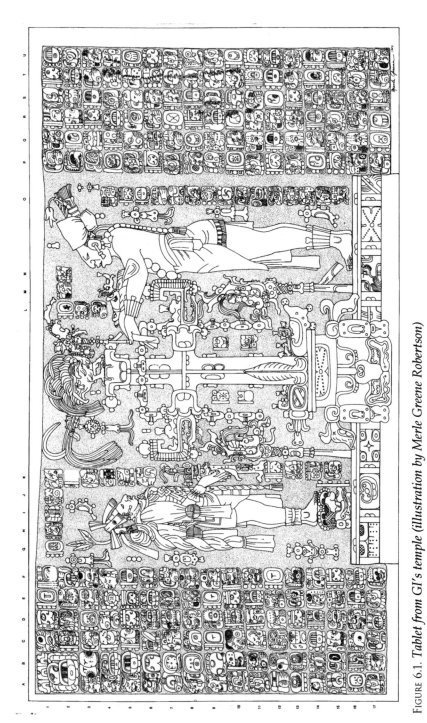

FIGURE 6.1. *Tablet from GI's temple (illustration by Merle Greene Robertson)*

dering the two images, the birds are identical. The World Trees are somewhat different, but both rise from the same animated bowl, both are draped with segmented double-headed serpents, and both have square-nosed, bearded heads protruding from the "branches" coming out each side.[1]

Besides the similarity in iconography, there are other reasons to associate the ritual activity depicted here with Janaab' Pakal and specifically his recovery of the dynastic charter. First, one of the four glyphs adjacent to the World Tree — the one with *te* ("tree" or "branch") as part of its name — is the same glyph that names one of the beings reborn under Janaab' Pakal's supervision for the 9.11.0.0.0 *k'atun* end, recorded in the Middle Tablet of the Temple of Inscriptions. The Middle Tablet also tells us that the animated bowl from which the World Tree rises is the headdress that belongs (and that Janaab' Pakal gave) to GI once the tree was reborn. Finally, throughout the interstices between figures and text on the tablet in GI's temple, we find floating images akin to those decorating the façade of House E of the Palace Complex. Scholars have associated these images with hallucinogenic-plant-induced visions, which in turn have been associated with conjuring rituals. We will see in Kan B'ahlam's texts that conjuring constituted an extremely important theme.

The inscriptions on the outside of this temple name it as the sweatbath of GI, as we saw in the last chapter. But the text on the main tablet actually starts with a consideration of someone other than GI: his mother. Our treatment of this hieroglyphic inscription reveals the rationale for her central place in the narrative along with resonances between this text and other Maya literature.

The inscription begins with a date that scholars consider as part of a previous "era." The implicit periodization comes from the way in which the Maya worked with the Long Count calendar. All of the historical events transpiring during the Classic period occurred during the ninth, tenth, or eleventh *bak'tuns*.[2] This system implies that there was a first *bak'tun* during which the Long Count would have begun with a zero register, that is, 0.0.1.9.2. Although we have no such explicit records, we do have records stating that the *bak'tun* preceding the first one was the thirteenth *bak'tun,* such that what we would expect to be 0.0.0.0.0 4 Ajaw 8 Kumk'u was written as "4 Ajaw 8 Kumk'u the completion of the thirteenth bak'tun." This thirteenth *bak'tun,* therefore, constituted some kind of fundamental change—one that we refer to in shorthand as "Creation."[3]

So the first date on the tablet in GI's temple comes from before Creation during the thirteenth *bak'tun*: 12.19.13.4.0 8 Ajaw 18 Tzek.[4] This date corresponds to the birth of Ix Muwaan Mat, the primordial figure we met in Chapters 1 and 5, who "births" the patron gods of Palenque. According to the tablet's text, her birth occurs only twenty days after the 819-day count station, which is recorded as 1 Ajaw 18 Zotz'. A very short passage follows the birth date before we encounter the completion of the thirteenth *bak'tun.*

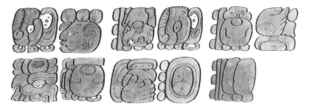

Ix Muwaan Mat was born. Eight years (8.5.0) after her birth, she binds the deer hoof [13.0.1.9.0].[5] [Then] on 4 Ajaw 8 Kumk'u it ends, 13 bak'tuns. (A17–C5)

At this point, the text shifts attention to another primordial figure.

A year and a half (1.9.2) after the sighting of the image at the k'i-chan of the First Hearth Place, GI entered the sky. On 9 Ik' 20 Mol he dedicates the 6 Sky Ajaw place, 8-GI-structure. It is the name of the house of the north. (D5–C13)

The sighting of the First Hearth Place was reviewed in Chapter 5. Here we find that 542 days later—and only two days after Ix Muwaan Mat's deer hoof event—GI enters the sky to set up the house of the north, which is located at the 6 Sky Ajaw place. The 6 Sky Ajaw, we saw, was the authority through whom the hearthstones were set.

In the next passage, we encounter the section of ambiguous text that caused significant controversy when it was first being deciphered.[6]

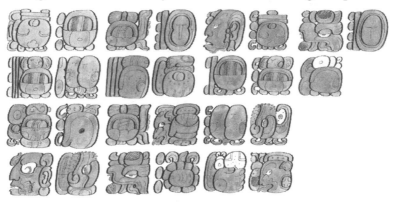

Over 750 years (1.18.3.12.0) after the Six Sky GI was [something-ed], then he arrives at Matawiil. On 9 Ik' 15 Kej he is born at Matawiil. It is the image of the penance of Ix Muwaan Mat. [Then] over 800 years (2.1.7.11.2) after she was born, she tied the white headband on herself, Ix Muwaan Mat. It is 9 Ik' 0 Sak. (D13–F9)

The text states that GI was acting on the day of Creation and entering the sky thereafter, only to be "born" over 700 years later at a place known as Matawiil. The solution that Floyd Lounsbury proposed, and that we will adhere to here, is that these are two different figures, one who is a principal figure in the acts of Creation, who we will call GI$_{father}$, and another who is born by Ix Muwaan Mat some time after Creation, GI$_{son}$ (Lounsbury 1980; see also Robertson 1991:16–19). Here, Lounsbury was following the pattern found in the *Popol Vuh* wherein father and elder son shared most of the same name: Jun Junajpu and Junajpu. So we can read the quote above as follows: "Over 750 years after GI$_{father}$ is something-ed, then GI$_{son}$ arrives at Matawiil. On 9 Ik' 15 Kej GI$_{son}$ is born at Matawiil." Or we can shift the ambiguity downstream such that GI$_{father}$ arrives at Matawiil in time for the birth of GI$_{son}$. We will gain support for the first interpretation when we examine the next tablet, but either way it appears that the author of the text chose to save space by including only one name, assuming that the reader would know that both father and son shared it.

After noting Ix Muwaan Mat's accession near the end of the left-hand inscription, the narrative jumps ahead over 1,300 years (3.6.10.12.2) later to record U K'ix Kan's birth and the tying of the white headband on himself by U K'ix Kan K'ujul Mat Ajaw. Here we encounter the awkward historical passage we treated in Chapter 4 that implies one or more *ajawtahk* of extreme longevity. Shifting to the inscription on the right-hand side of the tablet, the narrative moves through successive rulers of Palenque from B'ahlam K'uk' through Kan B'ahlam I, noting the births and white headband accessions of each. The tablet ends with Kan B'ahlam II's namesake's accession: *i k'al sak ju'un tu b'aah*, "then he tied the white headband on himself, Kan B'ahlam."

There is no question that the intent here is to spell out the credentials of the Palenque *ajawtahk*, linking them to the primordial deities (Robertson 1991:29–32; Schele and Freidel 1990:245–253). The emphasis, however, is not on the specific genealogical composition of the lineage but rather on the *type* of composition we are seeing. Specifically, the rhetorical emphasis in the text is on the white headband ceremony. We know from myriad other sources throughout the Maya region that the white headband ceremony is what installed an *ajaw* into office, but as the texts of the Temple of Inscriptions reveal, the Palenque *ajawtahk* lost this privilege through military defeat and it had to be regained by Janaab' Pakal's work. Here, the inscription is telling us that the first figure associated with Palenque to earn the right to tie the white headband on herself was Ix Muwaan Mat, and that she did so some fifty-five years after giving birth to GI_{son}.

If we go back to the Palace Tablet, we gain further insight into the rhetoric of the white headband. The reader will recall that K'an Joy Chitam commissioned the Palace Tablet, which showed him sitting on the Fish Throne Stone of Creation. The text on this tablet resonates with the text in GI's temple. It begins with an Initial Series date corresponding to K'an Joy Chitam's birth. After a statement of his parentage (as Janaab' Pakal and Ix Tz'aak Ajaw's son), the next record is of his deer hoof event in the presence of Palenque's patron gods. Next, just as the tablet in GI's temple moves from Ix Muwaan Mat's deer hoof event to the activities of other figures, the Palace Tablet moves on to record ceremonies performed by Janaab' Pakal and Kan B'ahlam during K'an Joy Chitam's life. The end of the tablet returns to K'an Joy Chitam's tying on himself of the white headband. The implication is that the deer hoof event designates one as heir but places them in the background until the opportunity arises for them to don the white headband.

With this reading, GI_{son}'s tablet starts with Ix Muwaan Mat's birth and heir designation but then moves on to record the other important activities that had to transpire before she would be able to take on the responsibility of the white headband. These intermediate events included the Creation activities of GI_{father} and the birth of GI_{son}. Thereafter, the early *ajawtahk* of Palenque all acceded to the throne with the same white headband.

Putting aside the astronumerology for now, beyond the rhetoric of the narrative Kan B'ahlam included an underlying celestial message on the left side of the inscription. The recognition of this message, however, is dependent on the celestial affiliations of the mythological actors. Some of these affiliations already have been suggested, but further corroborative evidence comes from a comparison of the observational characters of Venus and the sun relative to the Classic and Postclassic K'iche stories relating the Hero Twins to their father.

Both the *Popol Vuh* and the imagery of Classic period ceramic vessels tell us that Jun Junajpu held two positions with respect to his sons. Genealogically, of course, he came before his sons, but in a sense he also comes after his sons as they resurrect him as the Maize God. The same relationship exists between the sun and Chak Ek' (Venus). Because Venus is an interior planet (relative to the Earth), it may be observed in two positions relative to the sun. First, the planet can be seen rising in the east just before dawn; then after a period of obscurity, Venus follows the setting sun in the west. So first Chak Ek' precedes the sun, then it disappears, then the planet follows the sun. Observationally, therefore, Chak Ek' and the sun match Jun Junajpu and Junajpu of the *Popol Vuh,* and so here, GI_{father} and GI_{son}.

Corroborating this observable affiliation (as we have seen in Chapter 3 and as we will see in the following pages), the father GI is consistently associated astronumerologically with the number 584, tying him to Chak Ek' (Aldana 2001b:56, 161; with the caveat mentioned in Chapter 2, see D. Tedlock 1992). Historiographically considered, the latter is also the oldest of associations since the Venus Table in the Dresden Codex is anchored on the date 1 Ajaw, the Yucatec equivalent of the K'iche 1 Junajpu or Jun Junajpu.

When we take into consideration the celestial affiliations of these primordial figures, we therefore confront a resonance between Kan B'ahlam's inscription and the text of the sixteenth-century *Popol Vuh*. The inscription states that shortly after the sighting of the First Hearth Place, GI_{father} entered the sky. Recalling the affiliation of GI_{father} with Venus and accepting Lounsbury's proposal affiliating GI_{son} with the sun, the text presents Venus entering the sky just before the sun is born. This situation is similar to the beginning of Part IV of the *Popol Vuh*. In the sixteenth-century version, humans have been created by the gods, but they wait in darkness, wandering about the primordial world among the deities. These first humans know that they are to wait for Venus to enter the sky, as Venus's appearance will be a sign that the sun soon will follow.

> And here is the dawning and showing of the sun, moon, and stars. And Jaguar Quitze, Jaguar Night, Mahucutah, and True Jaguar were overjoyed when they saw the daybringer [Venus]. It came up first. It looked brilliant when it came up, since it was ahead of the sun.
>
> After that they unwrapped their copal incense, which came from the east, and there was triumph in their hearts when they unwrapped it. They gave their heartfelt thanks with three kinds at once. . . .
>
> There were countless peoples, but there was just one dawn for all tribes.
>
> And then the face of the earth was dried out by the sun. The sun was like a person when he revealed himself. His face was hot, so he dried out the face of the earth. Before the sun came up it was soggy, and the face of the earth was muddy before the sun came up. And when the sun had risen just a short distance he was like a person and his heat was unbearable. Since he revealed himself only when he was born, it is only his reflection that now remains. (D. Tedlock 1985:181–182)

Although the actions of GI_{father} and the birth of GI_{son} are separated significantly in time in Kan B'ahlam's account and although the creation of humans is still temporally distant, in the first part of the hieroglyphic inscription GI_{father} and GI_{son} are acting out the same pattern that the first humans will witness once they have been created.

The parallel between the two versions of Maya mythology is stronger when we come to the first members of the Palenque dynasty. The

implication—as we (and Schele and Mathews [1991]) have reconstructed the dates—is that U K'ix Kan was born in ancient times and
then lived and ruled for a tremendous amount of time. After him,
K'uk' B'ahlam lived a normal mortal life in historic times, as did all of
his recorded successors. Similarly, in the *Popol Vuh*, the first humans
were created without mothers or fathers:

> After that, they put it into words:
>
>> The making, the modeling of our first mother-father,
>> With yellow corn, white corn alone for the flesh,
>> Food alone for the human legs and arms,
>> For our first fathers, the four human works.
>> It was staples alone that made up their flesh.
>> These are the names of the first people who were made and
>>> modeled.
>> This is the first person: Jaguar Quitze.
>> And now the second: Jaguar Night.
>> And now the third: Mahucutah.
>> And the fourth: True Jaguar.
>
> And these are the names of our first mother-fathers. They were
> simply made and modeled, it is said; they had no mother and no
> father. We have named the men by themselves. No woman gave
> birth to them, nor were they begotten by the builder, sculptor,
> Bearer, Begetter. By sacrifice alone, by their *nawals* alone, they were
> made, they were modeled by the Maker, Modeler, Bearer, Begetter,
> Sovereign Plumed Serpent. And when they came to fruition, they
> came out human. . . .
> They then came out of Tulan Zuyua, to return to their rightful
> home (the Maya region). (D. Tedlock 1985:164–165)

There is a strong parallel to the hieroglyphic text here in that the patron
deities are born of a primordial mother, but U K'ix Kan comes out of
nowhere. He comes into being without genealogical context and then
lives a very long life before K'uk' B'ahlam is born. Similarly, in the
Popol Vuh, after an extremely long life of wandering and waiting for
the sun and after the dawning, the four original humans established
their lineages as primary and then "disappeared." With their disappearance, though, they left behind "bundles" and instructions for how
these bundles should be revered and given burned offerings.

It makes sense, therefore, to see U K'ix Kan as one of the original humans who generated the dynasty that would eventually produce the Palenque *ajawtahk*. It also, then, makes sense of an anomaly in the imagery of GI$_{son}$'s tablet (along with the others of the Triad Group). Namely, the smaller figure in each tablet is depicted wearing garments that are completely foreign to and unsuitable for life in or around Palenque (Robertson 1991:27–28). In the abundance of cloth (that would be stifling anywhere near the plains of Tabasco), though, we find an iconographic clue to its foreign source. On each tablet, the smaller figure wears a circular weave identical to a motif that George Kubler has associated with Teotihuacan (Robertson 1991:28). If the Palenque *ajawtahk* followed the sixteenth-century K'iche in finding their origins associated with the Basin of Mexico, we might find reason for the cold-weather clothing worn by this smaller figure (cf. Stuart 2000a). Not necessarily in contradiction, we might also see the excessive cloth as that which would have wrapped a mummy bundle. We know from the *Popol Vuh* that the original humans were revered as mummy bundles upon their demise, so it may be that this image is intended to depict Kan B'ahlam acting in concert with U K'ix Kan in the Underworld through the latter's mummy bundle.[7] Possible corroboration comes from the iconography of the tablet just outside the inner sanctuary. As Linda Schele noted long ago, Kan B'ahlam is shown here wearing the name of U K'ix Kan as a headdress (Schele and Miller 1986:114).

Although rich in context, the latter points are secondary to the message of the inscription as a whole. When considered in its entirety, the inscription is demonstrating the legitimacy of the white headband accession at Palenque as it was established by Ix Muwaan Mat. Furthermore, this placement of Ix Muwaan Mat relative to the Palenque *ajawtahk* clarifies the dynastic sequence leading up to Janaab' Pakal's reign as discussed in Chapter 1. Namely, Ix Muwaan Mat's role as the legitimizer of the white headband for Palenque justifies her having to take over the duties of the K'ujul B'aakal Ajaw after the city had been defeated by the *ajaw* of Kalak'mul and before Janaab' Pakal could come into power. Thus, we no longer need an appeal to metaphor in order to understand the apparent ambiguity in the East Tablet of the Temple of the Inscriptions. If we allow for the agency of a deity in a Classic Maya history, there is no ambiguity, and we do not have to look to Janaab' Pakal's mother to fill a conjectural role.

We now turn to the astronumerological under-girding of GI_{son}'s tablet. We have already seen much of this astronumerology, since this tablet provides the information for the earliest rulers of Palenque and its sister site Matawiil. The puzzle built around U K'ix Kan's liminality, discussed in Chapter 4, provided a celestially relevant Long Count position for the historical placement of U K'ix Kan's reign. We also saw that the "error" in the passage dedicated to K'uk' B'ahlam was actually a means to astronumerologically tie his tenure to the rest of the text.

Yet Kan B'ahlam included other puzzles within GI's tablet: one built on a computational clue and the other constructed around a play on words. The first corresponds to another error identified by Lounsbury, Schele, and Mathews (Schele and Mathews 1991). The beginning of the tablet, as we saw above, gives Ix Muwaan Mat's birth date (12.19.13.4.0 8 Ajaw 18 Tzek) along with the corresponding Nal-k'awiil station exactly twenty days before (1 Ajaw 18 Zotz'). The passage that then gives her taking of the white headband states that her accession occurred 297,942 days (2.1.7.11.2) later on 9 Ik' 0 Sak. The problem is that adding this distance number to the date of her birth gives the date 2.1.0.15.2 3 Ik' 0 Sak, yielding the right day sign and *haab'* but the wrong *chol qiij* coefficient. If this discrepancy was simply the result of an inattentive mistake and the distance number was anchored on the Nal-k'awiil station for the birth date instead of the birth date itself, the result would be 2.1.0.14.2 9 Ik' 0 Yax, yielding the right *chol qiij* and *haab'* coefficients but the wrong month. The closest 9 Ik' 0 Sak date to either of these "incorrect" dates in the Long Count would have been 2.0.0.10.2 9 Ik' 0 Sak. But we know from the next distance number leading to the birth of U K'ix Kan that the intended birth date for Ix Muwaan Mat was 2.1.0.14.2 9 Ik' 0 Yax.

The connections among this set of numbers are astronumerological (Aldana 2001b:177–179; 2004a; Figure 6.2) As noted in Chapter 3, Floyd Lounsbury recognized that Ix Muwaan Mat's and Janaab' Pakal's births were contrived to include 260, 364, 780, and 3,276 as factors of the interval between them (Lounsbury 1978:804–808; Schele and Freidel 1990). Lounsbury (1978:773) also showed elsewhere that 364 was an important number facilitating computations over long stretches of

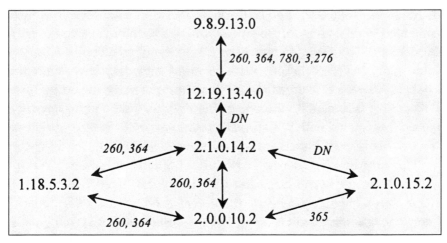

FIGURE 6.2. *Numerology framing the "error" in Ix Muwaan Mat's accession date*

time; perhaps it served as an earlier version of the Nal-k'awiil base. So 260 and 364 along with 3,276 were fundamental in this computation, but 260 and 364 were extended to construct a small puzzle. The intervals between Kan B'ahlam's mythical analogue, GI$_{son}$, and each of the dates given for Ix Muwaan Mat's accession (2.1.0.14.2, the implied date, 2.1.0.15.2, and the "erroneously" recorded Calendar Round of 2.0.0.10.2) were multiples of both 260 and 364. The 260, of course, was necessary in order to maintain the same *chol qiij* date of 9 Ik'. The number 364 was used in order to facilitate computations and because it was close enough to the tropical year to imply the sun's presence. This association makes complete sense since the birth date included was that of GI$_{son}$, the deity who we have identified as having an astrological affiliation with the sun.

Rhetorically then, the text connects Ix Muwaan Mat's accession to the birth of her first son; numerologically, her accession is connected to this birth by 364 and to an "errant" Calendar Round by 365. With these recognitions we find the rationale behind the first computational anomaly: the sun was being numerologically invoked by 364 and 365 to be present in the inscription of GI$_{son}$'s birth at Matawiil.

An extension of this puzzle alludes to the story already told of Kan B'ahlam's desire to ensure that his work would be seen as an extension of his father's success. The birth of Ix Muwaan Mat, therefore, was contrived to relate not only to Janaab' Pakal's birth but also to the critical defeat of Lakam Ja' by the *ajaw* of Kalak'mul (see Figure 6.3). The same planetary associations were brought into play here, with the interval between Ix Muwaan Mat's birth and the battle including Jupiter's period (associated with one of the Paddler Gods) and Mercury's period (associated with K'awiil). The latter was entirely appropriate as we will see later in K'awiil's association with conjuring.

Cleverly, another Mercurian period is built into this puzzle. A multiple of Mercury's synodic period also linked the "death" of Ix Tz'aak Ajaw, Kan B'ahlam's mother, to the defeat of Lakam Ja'. I flag "death" here, since the term used is *ok b'ij*, "to enter the road." It is well known that the Maya used this term to refer to some aspect of death, but its metaphorical nature may have allowed for some leeway in anchoring to a specific date. After all, the *chol qiij* date on which she entered the road was 5 Etz'nab, or 5 Flint—a day associated with death—and the *chol qiij* of Janaab' Pakal's *ok b'ij* was 4 Ok, or 4 "Entering." It may well be, therefore, that the Classic Maya practiced death commemorations in the same way that the Aztec enacted naming ceremonies. That is, a child's naming ceremony could occur on any of those days within the same thirteen-day cycle as the child's "actual" birth (Boone 2000:48). With some flexibility as to its specific calendric assignment, therefore, the historians appear to have contrived the date of Ix Tz'aak Ajaw's "death" to add to the puzzle already begun.

The link to Ix Tz'aak Ajaw betrays a rhetorical intent as well. Ix Tz'aak Ajaw's death was linked not only to the defeat of Lakam Ja' by 116 but also to the errant accession of Ix Muwaan Mat by that same number. Ix Tz'aak Ajaw means, literally, "female ordering (of) lord[s]," and Ix Tzak Ajaw (with an unglottalized *tz*) means "female conjuring (of) lord." The second phrase was implied since 116 was the canonic period for Mercury—the celestial image of K'awiil—and by the link to Ix Muwaan Mat. Furthermore, both nominal phrases could have been used as descriptions of the primordial figure, Ix Muwaan Mat. For the former, she literally ordered the lords of the sky by bearing the day Sun, then the night Sun (the full moon), and finally K'awiil. And the act of birthing was frequently associated with conjuring rites. Hence, we confront the solution to the second puzzle: Ix Tz'aak Ajaw was

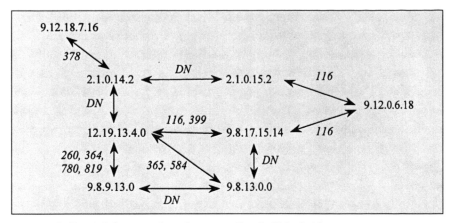

FIGURE 6.3. *Extended numerology incorporating Ix Tz'aak Ajaw*

analogized to Ix Muwaan Mat through the canonic period of Mercury, a semantic pun, and the chopping down of Lakam Ja'.

Ix Tz'aak Ajaw's connection to his mother through an errant Long Count date may have been enough to imply Kan B'ahlam's presence in the reconstruction of Palenque's religious charter, but Kan B'ahlam apparently would not settle for implication. Instead, he included one last computational puzzle on GI's tablet in the small text running along Kan B'ahlam's back. Here, the main dedication of Kan B'ahlam's Triad Group is implied by distance number to have begun on 9.12.18.7.16 3 Kib 14 Yax rather than 9.12.18.5.16 2 Kib 14 Mol. The forty-day difference ensures that the *haab'* coefficient and the day sign of the *chol qiij* remain unchanged. But the shift allowed for one more link: the interval between this errant date for Kan B'ahlam's ceremony and Ix Muwaan Mat's accession carries 378 as a factor. With this last numerological connection, Kan B'ahlam had reconstructed the astronumerological metaphor built into the history of the Temple of Inscriptions' tablets. Once again, he had tied the fall of Lakam Ja' to the events of Janaab' Pakal, using the periods of Venus, Jupiter, and Saturn to build a numerological canoe that would rebirth the religious charter of the polity. But this time he extended the metaphor to include his mother and himself. Perhaps as a clue parallel to the one in the West Tablet of the Temple of Inscriptions, Kan B'ahlam built himself into the puzzle through an "erroneous" Long Count date.

Within GI's tablet, then, we find that text and iconography combined with astronumerology all reinforce the same messages. The inscription emphasizes the white headband ceremony obtained by Ix Muwaan Mat as fundamental to the religious and political charter of Palenque. The astronumerology highlights Ix Muwaan Mat's white headband ceremony with a puzzle built around 260, 364, and a connection to Janaab' Pakal's birth. The iconography of the tablet depicts the World Tree that Janaab' Pakal had resurrected in his role as the Maize God for his polity. Accordingly, the astronumerology reconstructs the puzzle that puts Janaab' Pakal in a numerological canoe, so that his heir would have the opportunity to maintain that World Tree. As we saw in Chapter 5, the functional nature of the 819-day count was demonstrated in the placement of the Long Count dates associated with U K'ix Kan and K'uk' B'ahlam; here we see the esoteric use to which it was put.

GIII

Chronologically according to birth records, the next tablet to be treated is in GIII's temple. As previously mentioned, the architectural layout of the temple is the same as that for GI, with the main tablet housed in a small interior room. Upon entering this room, however, a visitor is greeted by a *tok'-pakal* compound, an image of war. The *pakal* ("shield") at the tablet's center bears the face of the Jaguar God of the Underworld, who meets the viewer's gaze. Two elaborate spears, with points hafted to skeletal snake jaws, cross behind the shield to support it (see Figure 6.4). The spears rest on a composite throne made up of the three Creation throne stones. The head of the Jaguar Throne Stone parallels the face on the shield, also looking out of the tablet, while the other two heads face either side. This composite throne rests on the shoulders of two seated male figures: God L, lord of the Underworld on the left, and an old celestial deity on the right. Kan B'ahlam stands on the right, presenting a K'awiil idol to this war construct, and the smaller figure presents a war idol.

The imagery here speaks to two iconographic contexts we have already seen. First, the Jaguar God of the Underworld, war, and the three hearthstone thrones recall the events transpiring on 13.0.0.0.0

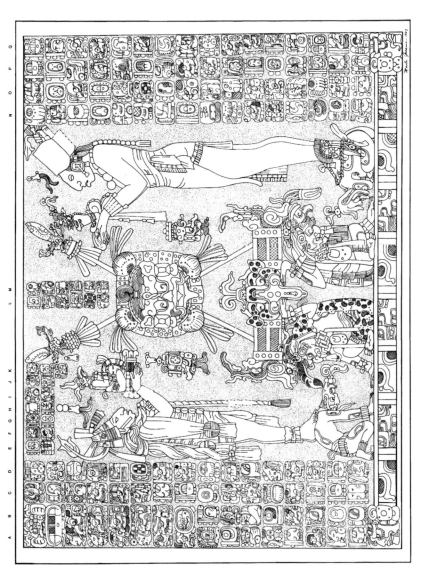

FIGURE 6.4. *GIII's tablet (illustration by Merle Greene Robertson)*

4 Ajaw 8 Kumk'u, as we saw in Chapter 5. This emphasis on an Underworld theme in GIII's temple argues against proposals that GIII is represented celestially as the sun (Robertson 1991:16–19). Likewise, the band at the bottom of the tablet bears heads at either end that resemble the K'in deity but are missing key elements. Specifically, as K'in, a "sun" icon is placed on the cheek and/or forehead of the glyphic face. Here, however, the sun icons are replaced with markers of "reflectivity." These clues combine with textual evidence presented later to corroborate Lounsbury's original hypothesis that GIII was affiliated with the full moon, whereas GI_{son} was associated with the sun.

Second, the combination of the Creation throne stones and the implements of war remind us of the scene commissioned by K'an Joy Chitam on the Palace Tablet. There, the younger brother sat on one of the separated throne stones, receiving a shield and spear point from his mother, who was seated on a different throne stone. This parallel demonstrates that not only did the two brothers maintain the same affiliation between events occurring on the day of Creation but they also maintained a larger common metaphor. Namely, we have seen that Janaab' Pakal was analogized to GI_{father} as Venus and as the father of the Hero Twins. Similarly, Ix Tz'aak Ajaw, the brothers' mother, was analogized to the mother of the Hero Twins and the waxing moon. These tablets confirm that Kan B'ahlam was taking the role of the elder Hero Twin and the sun and K'an Joy Chitam assumed that of the younger Hero Twin and the full moon. We also will find that these affiliations are corroborated by the astronumerology in the tablets.

Turning our attention to the inscription, we confront the same Underworld theme. The left side of the inscription follows GI's tablet, beginning with a birth record that is anchored to an 819-day count. This birth record, however, is that of GIII, which serves to disambiguate the chain of events tied to GI's birth. It reads: "13 Kimi 19 Kej GIII is born.[8] Seven hundred fifty-four years (6.3.5.18.1) after the 6 Sky is something-ed, then he arrives at Matawiil. It is the image of the penance of Ix Muwaan Mat K'ujul Matawiil Ajaw." Here, birth is equated with an arrival at Matawiil and, in both cases, these arrivals are brought about by the penance of Ix Muwaan Mat.

Also of interest are several references to the lower realm in GIII's extremely long name, which takes up eleven glyph blocks and com-

TABLE 6.1: Sun references in the full name of GIII

Hieroglyphic Name	Translation	Underworld Affiliation
K'inich Way	Brilliant, Resplendent Nagual	*Nagual* = spirit companion
K'intan B'ahlam-?	Sun-fronted Jaguar-?	Sun-fronted Jaguar as a *nagual*
Sak B'aak Noj Chaapat	White Bone Great Centipede	Name of serpent-maw entrance to the Underworld

prises six phrases (see Figure 5.4 and Table 6.1). References to the sun show up in his name but as modifiers to subjects belonging to the Underworld. As we have seen, the "night sun," or the image of the sun as it passes through the Underworld, is the full moon.

Unlike the inscription housed in GI's temple, however, the text here moves directly to historic times. Anchoring a distance number to the day on which the First Hearth Place was sighted (13.0.0.0.0 4 Ajaw 8 Kumk'u), the reader is led to a series of days on which Kan B'ahlam enacted the ceremonies depicted on the tablets. The inscription tells us that on 9.12.18.5.16 2 Kib 14 Mol, Kan B'ahlam dedicated the temple to GIII.

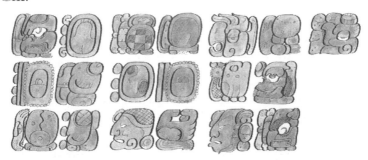

Then on 2 Kib 14 Mol he set fire to the dreaming place of GIII. On the next day, 3 Kaban 15 Mol, he dedicated the West K'uk' Structure for the house of the ch'ajom B'aakal Wayal K'inich Kan B'ahlam K'ujul Mat Ajaw. (O3–12)

The "burning of the dreaming place" has been interpreted as the "firing" of a sweatbath, although, as previously noted, there is no evidence that these temples functioned as such (Houston 1996). Regardless, the text refers to the "West K'uk' Structure," probably in reference

173

to GIII's temple as it is the western member of the Triad Group, which as a whole butted up against K'uk' Lakam Witz'.

The next passage is very interesting because it makes explicit reference to a conjuring portal.

It is the third [time]. He [Kan B'ahlam] conjures k'uj. The Lakam Ja' chan-ch'en is formed [at] ?-K'uk' Lakam Witz. (N13–N16)

As discussed in Chapter 3, Janaab' Pakal reopened the portal for Palenque that allowed for renewed communication between worlds. Here, Kan B'ahlam appears to be making a distinction between a portal at Palenque and *the* portal of Lakam Ja'. Recall that the whole mess began for Palenque when Lakam Ja' had been "chopped down." If, as the text here tells us, Lakam Ja' were the principal *chan-ch'en* for Palenque, Kan B'ahlam is claiming to have created it with his conjurings in the Triad Group. Kan B'ahlam, then, is picking up precisely where his father left off but here through a public portrayal of a Re-Creation.

We will see that to this point, this inscription is virtually identical to the one in the temple of Unen K'awiil (GII). The last two columns on each of these tablets, though, bring back the focus of the narrative to the nature of the deity to whom the sweatbath belongs, as in this case they refer to Palenque's relationship with the Underworld.

In this last section, the recurrent term guiding the discussion is the one found at Q3, P8, Q13, and Q16. The reading of the main element as *ok* is not in question—in fact, we saw it above in the name Bolon Okte. The interpretation here, though, incurs some ambiguity. In two of the four cases in which it shows up here on GIII's tablet, the glyph is preceded by the verb *k'alwan,* or "becoming bound/fastened." Conventionally, this compound has been read as an entering into a royal lineage as a designated heir (Schele and Freidel 1990:251). This reading makes some sense given the genealogical interpretation of Bolon Okte's name. The interesting wrinkle in the passage on GIII's tablet is that the second usage of the compound provides additional interpretive data.

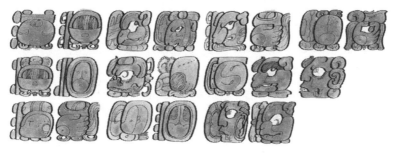

Over 140 years (7.6.12.3) after 12 Ajaw 8 Kej K'an Joy Chitam I
became bound/enclosed in the [okel] at Toktan. Then on 9 Ak'bal
6 Xul, the first [okte] of the Sun and K'inich Kan B'ahlam became
enclosed/bound in the presence of GI. (O16–Q10)

Rhetorically, the connection here to the ceremony of K'an Joy Chitam
(i.e., the first ruler with this name, not Kan B'ahlam's brother) goes
unspecified. It may be that locals regarded his action as a particularly significant one, such that it would not require explicit elaboration. Regardless, the next passage is important because it describes the
enclosing of the fifth *okte* of the Sun and Kan B'ahlam. The date was
certainly an appropriately chosen one for engagement with the Underworld, as the corresponding *chol qiij* is 9 Ak'bal, or 9 Darkness. What
transpired on that day may seem simply an esoteric ritual until we
have a look at the dates recorded in the passage that follows.

This was six years (6.2.18) after his birth on 2 Kimi 19 Zotz', when
he [okaj]. Then after another year (1.8.12) on 13 Ajaw 18 K'ank'in, on
the lajuntun, he descended into the [okel]. (P11–Q16)

In particular, we recognize in the summary of dates presented in Table
6.2 that without additional information, the numbers do not fit. The first
distance number fits between K'an Joy Chitam's and Kan B'ahlam's
events, but the next two require some "massaging." Specifically, the
text notes that "he *okaj*" the day after the preceding passage claims that
he enclosed the *okte*. Also, the last passage states that 532 days later, it

TABLE 6.2: Sequence of dates in the last two columns of GIII's tablet

Date Sequence	Textual Association
9.3.1.15.0 12 Ajaw 8 Kej	K'an Joy Chitam I becomes bound in the *okel*
+ 7.6.12.3	Distance number
9.10.8.9.3 9 Ak'bal 6 Xul	First *okte* of the Sun and Kan B'ahlam with GI
9.10.2.6.6 2 Kimi 19 Zotz'	Kan B'ahlam's birth
+ 6.2.18	Distance number
9.10.8.9.4 10 K'an 7 Xul	"then he *okaj*"
+ 1.8.12	Distance number
9.10.10.0.0 13 Ajaw 18 K'ank'in	*Lajuntun*; descent into the *okel*

was the *lajuntun*, 9.10.10.0.0 13 Ajaw 18 K'ank'in, but if we subtract 532 days (1.8.12) from the *lajuntun*, we get 9.10.8.9.8 1 Lamat 11 Xul.

The key here is to recognize that the missing days are accounted for metaphorically. Moving forward from K'an Joy Chitam I's "enclosing" to Kan B'ahlam II's youth event leaves us with a gap of five days relative to the distance number that leads to the 9.10.10.0.0 period end. But these five "missing" days may be signaled by the implicit sequence starting on 9 Ak'bal 6 Xul. That is, the first binding of the *okte* by the sun, Kan B'ahlam, and GI appears to correspond to the passage of a day qua a sunset, or, equivalently, a trip of the sun into (and through) the Underworld. The distance number going back to his birth then notes that Kan B'ahlam *okaj* again on the next day, 9.10.8.9.4 10 K'an 7 Xul. It may be, then, that he had to perform this ritual five times over five days such that the process ended on 9.10.8.9.8 1 Lamat 11 Xul. Then the distance numbers would match the given dates. As they used the same phrase to describe the "passage of time" and the actions of the rulers-elect, we gain insight into the ritual requirements of heir designation. The ceremony in question here required the ruler-elect to enclose/bind an *okel*, analogous to the sun being "swallowed up" by the Underworld at sunset. Perhaps this ceremony paralleled the Hero Twins' successful journey through the Underworld before rising out with the sun the following morning. The upshot, then, is that Kan B'ahlam's ceremony in his youth, and that of K'an Joy Chitam I 140 years before, mimicked the activity of the sun's daily movement.

Overall, then, Kan B'ahlam's intent with this tablet was to record the reconstruction of the Lakam Ja' *chan-ch'en* portal through his building of the Triad Group. On this tablet, Kan B'ahlam linked this construction to his first experiences in the Underworld, which transpired over the course of a five-night ceremony during his youth. In this way, the last two columns of the tablet reflect the emphasis on the Underworld of the imagery in the tablet's center.

Regarding the astronumerology on GIII's tablet, the first instance is quite compact. The Initial Series date on the tablet gives GIII's birth as 1.18.5.3.6 13 Kimi 19 Kej, which is only four days after the birth of his brother, GI (1.18.5.3.2 9 Ik' 15 Kej). Merle Greene Robertson (1991:16–17) commented that this range is a considerable amount of time considering that GI and GIII were twins (as in the Hero Twins), but that since this was primordial time (before the dawning of the sun), "four days is not too long." Numerologically, however, the number 4 is ideal for representing such a relationship between the two. When written as a head variant, the number 4 was depicted with a portrait of the sun, as exemplified in the winal position for the Initial Series dates of GI's and Unen K'awiil's tablets (see Figures 4.1 and 6.1). Four makes sense astronomically because of the sun's four "stations" (i.e., counting the solstices and equinoxes) as well as the four directions that it defines (east as the region where the sun rises, west where the sun sets, south as the left hand of the sun, and north as the right hand of the sun; Watanabe 1983). Combining this information with the facts that GI_{son} was born on the day Ik', and GIII on the day Kimi, we recognize the solution. Since *Ik'* was a term connotative of breath and the soul, we now have GI_{son} as the soul of the sun and GIII as the death of the sun qua the Sun in the Underworld (the Jaguar God of the Underworld). Indeed, then, the brothers were twins in that they were both aspects of the sun.

The second puzzle within GIII's tablet we have already seen in Chapter 5. This puzzle was the connection originally recovered by Lounsbury between the implied and recorded Long Count dates for the Calendar Round 1 Ik' 10 Tzek. The end result demonstrated an incorporation of Jupiter cycles as a complement to the Saturn cycles built into K'awiil's tablet.

The most extensive numerology on this tablet, then, has to do specifically with Kan B'ahlam's "pre-accession" rights. We have seen here that Kan B'ahlam went through a five-day ceremony when he was six

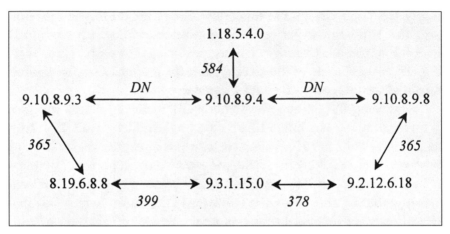

FIGURE 6.5. *Numerology in GIII's tablet*

years old. We also noted the oddity that different days over the course of this ceremony were used as anchors for textual moves through the text. But the specific dates that Kan B'ahlam used facilitated the inclusion of another version of the same astronumerological story told in GI's tablet and in the Temple of Inscriptions' tablets (see Figure 6.5). Using two dates from earlier *ajawtahk* as bridges, Kan B'ahlam reconstructed the numerology of the canoe metaphor between his own "preaccession" rites and those of K'an Joy Chitam I. First, the number 365 links the first day of the ceremony to the birth of the second *ajaw* in the Palenque dynasty and the last day of the ceremony to the accession of the third *ajaw*. Both of these events were then linked to the 9.3.1.15.0 "pre-accession" rites of K'an Joy Chitam I by 399 and 378, respectively. The puzzle so far included the sun as GI_{son} and the two Paddler Gods. The last move was to include Venus as GI_{father} through the "extra" date given for Kan B'ahlam's ceremony. The interval between the birth of Unen K'awiil (the embodiment of dynastic blood) and the second day of the ceremony, 9.10.8.9.4, is a multiple of 584 days.

The important place given to K'an Joy Chitam I in the text and especially in the astronumerology suggests that this *ajaw* or the general time period of his reign must have held some particular importance to Kan B'ahlam. We find further evidence for this special relationship in Palenque's Temple XVII. The tablet hung within this temple portrays

Kan B'ahlam standing over a war captive—a record of his successful campaign against Tonina (Martin and Grube 2000:170). The text, however, begins with an event enacted by Butz'aj Sak Chi'ik, third *ajaw* of Palenque, around six years before K'an Joy Chitam I's "pre-accession" rites, on 9.2.15.9.2 9 Ik' 0 Mol. Butz'aj Sak Chi'ik's event takes place at Lakam Ja', so Kan B'ahlam may have been hoping to connect his narrative to this event but had found that astronumerologically K'an Joy Chitam's history worked better given the numbers available.

Once again, the astronumerology of the tablet resonates with the rhetorical impact of the text. On GIII's tablet, the emphasis is on the Underworld and Kan B'ahlam's first ventures into it. Likewise, the numbers focus on the five-day ceremony of Kan B'ahlam's youth and demonstrate that Kan B'ahlam carries on the lineage (K'awiil) through his father's recuperation of the religious charter of the city.

GII

Finally, we reach the third member of the Triad Group, the temple referred to as the sweatbath of Unen K'awiil (GII). As mentioned in Chapter 4, Kan B'ahlam's artists built a visual pun around a stalk of maize for the central image of the tablet. Here we can see that there is a strong resemblance between this imagery and that of the tablet in GI's temple. The maize plant takes on the role of the World Tree, but rather than rising out of GI's hat (the sacrificial bowl), this plant grows out of an animated symbol of fertility, the so-called K'an cross. The leafy, organic quality of the imagery makes it clear that this tablet is dedicated to the Middleworld, a maintained place of agricultural abundance.

Also like the World Tree on GI's tablet, the Nal-k'awiil is topped by a bird to whom Kan B'ahlam presents an idol. This bird bears a strong resemblance to the ones on GI's tablet and Janaab' Pakal's sarcophagus lid, but there are some telling differences, particularly in the face (compare Figures 3.7 and 4.1). Finally, the conflation of maize and royal blood reminds the viewer of the importance of the 819-day count.

As for the inscription, the history follows the pattern set in GIII's temple. First, Unen K'awiil's birth is explicitly recorded as the third of the births—utterly sensible since the first two occurred on 1.18.5.3.2 and 1.18.5.3.6 and this one occurred fourteen days after the latter, on 1.18.5.4.0 1 Ajaw 13 Mak. The *chol qiij* day sign of Ajaw is appropriate as K'awiil represents the blood of the local *ajawtahk*. In composing the text, though, the author had to contend with the fact that K'awiil's name is substantially shorter than GIII's name, so that there would be some extra room on the left side of the inscription. After Unen K'awiil's arrival at Matawiil, therefore, Kan B'ahlam included Ix Muwaan Mat's god-conjuring for the end of the second *bak'tun*. This subject also was entirely appropriate for the tablet since K'awiil is the enabler of conjuring. Moreover, the conjuring event was recorded as occurring at Yaxhaal Witz Sak-nik Nal Na ? K'anal. The first part of this location (Yaxhaal Witz Nal) is noted in the eyes of the mountain upon which Kan B'ahlam stands as he makes offerings to the Nal-k'awiil (Stuart, personal communication 1998). The second part, Na ? K'anal, is recorded as the name of K'awiil's temple on its façade. So, just as in the imagery of Temple XIV, here Kan B'ahlam acts in the same places as the primordial gods.

Next, like the tablet in GIII's temple, the text goes on to describe the "firing" of the sweatbaths of GI, Unen K'awiil, and GIII, as well as the formation of the Lakam Ja' *chan-ch'en* (L1–L16). The text also notes that the firing of the sweatbaths occurred at Lakam Ja' *chan-ch'en* through the Ch'en of the 6 Sky 183 Chaak K'ujul ? Ajaw, tying the location to GI's activity in the sixth sky. Finally, the last two columns look back to Kan B'ahlam's birth and accession, tying them both directly with his three-day conjuring and dedication of the Triad Group.

The last statement in Unen K'awiil's tablet wraps up the entire text of all three temples.

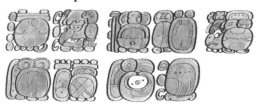

One year (1.12.4) later it will be 8 Ajaw 8 Wo. It is the thirteenth k'atun. So it happens on 2 Kib, then it is built/completed. It is the juntan of K'inich Kan B'ahlam K'ujul B'aakal Ajaw. (O13–O17)

Kan B'ahlam has tied on the white headband, he has (re-)built the *chan-ch'en* of Lakam Ja', and he now will complete a period end to seal his position in the dynasty as the *juntan* of the patron gods.

Read closely, the Triad Group reveals a coherent program patronized by Kan B'ahlam. As noted in the Introduction, this program was par-tially recorded in the imagery tying his Triad Group to his father's Temple of Inscriptions. The figures modeled in stucco within Janaab' Pakal's tomb carried K'awiil staffs and Jaguar God of the Underworld shields. We have just seen how both of these entities took prominent roles within Kan B'ahlam's patronage. The question in the Introduc-tion concerned the possible meaning of this iconographic continuity. Read relative to an exegesis of the 819-day count, we confront a rich message here.

The source of the first temple in the Triad Group does not seem to find iconographic representation in the stucco figures as there is no iconographic representation of either GI_{father} or GI_{son}. The reconstruc-tion described here, however, identifies GI_{father} and GI_{son} as the proto-typical ruling lineage. The implication, therefore, is that the nine stucco figures carrying K'awiil staffs and the Jaguar God of the Underworld shields represent the nine members of the Palenque dynasty preced-ing Janaab' Pakal—including Aj Ne' Ohl Mat. Schele and Mathews (1998:128–130) have found evidence in the headdresses for the names of two of these rulers, so this implication finds ready iconographic cor-roboration. More importantly, though, this instance of iconographic continuity captures the main message coded within the astronumerol-ogy patronized by Kan B'ahlam. Herein we see that Janaab' Pakal was able to re-legitimize the dynasty through military efforts and an appeal to Creation, whereas his son was able to elucidate Janaab' Pakal's suc-cess through the use of the 819-day count. Now we have uncovered an important impetus for Janaab' Pakal's and Kan B'ahlam's re-legitima-tion plans that is quite different from those proposed by Linda Schele and David Freidel.

I mentioned earlier, however, that local legitimation was only one part of Kan B'ahlam's agenda. The second part comes from the recog-nition that each temple gives us specific insights into a cosmological realm, but overall the triadic complex demonstrates a clear appeal to

Palenque as a Maya polity. That is, even though Palenque sat on the western edge of the Maya world, Kan B'ahlam wanted its citizens and visitors to know that Palenque subscribed to elite Maya ideology.

This part of the agenda is evidenced further through a larger appeal to Maya-ness constructed through an inter-polity context as seen in Palenque's Palace Tablet, which includes a loaded posthumous reference.

It happened on 5 Lamat 1 Mol. K'inich Janaab' Pakal K'ujul B'aakal Ajaw Kalomte tied the white headband on himself. (O17–R1)

Although his father never used the term for himself, here K'an Joy Chitam names him as a *kalomte*. As noted in Chapter 1, this title appears to have originated during the Early Classic in association with the arrival of Teotihuacano elites (see also Coggins 1993; Stuart 2000a) Aside from this record on the Palace Tablet, the only cities claiming to have a *kalomte* in residence as their ruler were Tikal and Copán. Both of these cities claimed dynastic lineages anchored by Teotihuacano inter-lopers. K'an Joy Chitam's assignment of his father to a lineage associated with Teotihuacan corroborates our inference that U K'ix Kan was the smaller figure shown on each Triad Group tablet as the myth-ical founder of the Palenque dynastic lineage. Part of this inference depended on the Teotihuacano iconography that this smaller figure wears. K'an Joy Chitam's posthumous attribution of the *kalomte* title to his father therefore suggests that he and his brother were working under the same agenda.

Moreover, K'an Joy Chitam's calling his father a *kalomte* suggests an explicit attempt at forming (or solidifying) a far-flung alliance since this record comes on the heels of another enigmatic record from Copán. There, scholars have long recognized an interesting phrase on Stela A that brings together the *ajawtahk* of four major Classic Maya cities: Tikal, Copán, Kalak'mul, and Palenque (Schele and Mathews 1998:160, figure 4.28). Along with the *kalomte* political structure and some interesting lunar astrology, I have linked this reference to a tem-porary pan-Maya alliance transpiring during K'an Joy Chitam's reign

(Aldana 2006a). Although a full explication would take us too far afield here, through these references it becomes clear that Kan B'ahlam's agenda was not a local one confined to genealogical rationalization. Furthermore, by considering rhetoric, historical context, and scientific endeavor, the 819-day count, combined with the decipherment of the hieroglyphic script, has provided the modern researcher with a window through which we can now begin a subtle interpretation of the deeds and thoughts of these Maya scribes.

NOTES

1. The latter "square-nosed" heads have been associated with flowers by Linda Schele and Mary Miller (1986:113)

2. When scholars refer to "Bak'tun 9," they are actually referring to "Bak'tun 10." J.E.S. Thompson (1960:149) explains: "It should be remembered that when we speak of a date, such as 9.15.10.0.0, belonging to, or falling in, Baktun 9, we are, almost without doubt, committing an error, for Baktun 9 had been completed over 300 years before that date and the count was already more than three-quarters of the way through Baktun 10. However, as the Maya did not record a *bak'tun* or any other period before it was completed, it has become customary among specialists on the Maya to speak of a date belonging to the *bak'tun* which had expired. It is as though one referred to 1920, 1948, and 1965 as dates in the nineteenth century. Nevertheless, the custom of referring to such dates as 9.15.10.0.0 as falling in Baktun 9 is so firmly established, not only among epigraphers, but among students of all branches of Maya archaeology, that to start speaking of such dates as falling in Baktun 10 would cause inextricable confusion; the correction of the error would cause more harm than its perpetuation." I disagree and so refer to 9.15.10.0.0 as falling in Baktun 10.

3. Numerologically, 13 and 9 are interesting numbers. The number 13 was considered the number of the sky, and 9 that of the Underworld, so the Maya interest in both the Underworld and the sky feels contrived.

4. Using notation from the much later Dresden Codex, we would write this as 6.14.$\underline{0}$ where the underscore represents a red circle around the 1–19 register, and the number can be considered a negative integer.

5. Originally, there was some ambiguity as to who was enacting the deer hoof event. Floyd Lounsbury (1976, 1980) suggested that the reference of eight years after a birth was not to the birth just noted but to a missing one corresponding to that of GI. As we will discuss later, however, the recovery of the altar in Temple XIX prevents this interpretation since it records GI's actions

some time before this purported birth. Moreover, later in this text, the pattern is corroborated wherein a distance number reaches back to Ix Muwaan Mat's birth in order to project ahead to the next event. The only viable conclusion left is that the 8.5.0 counts forward from Ix Muwaan Mat's birth to within two days of the next major event recorded (GI's entering the sky on 13.0.1.9.2) and then the text goes back to record the end of the thirteenth *bak'tun* before coming back to record GI's activity.

6. Most controversial was the identity of GI. Scholars seemed to find that the hieroglyphic name GI was actually used for two different mythical beings (Lounsbury 1980; Robertson 1991). This controversy will be discussed in more detail later.

7. Mummy bundles were also well documented in Central and Southern Mexico.

8. The SIH* iguana birth glyph is used here whereas GI's tablet uses the "touched the earth" version of birth, but the difference is negated by the *alfarda* text on GIII's temple, which lists GIII's birth with the latter verb. Therefore, they are both referring to the same type of event.

CHAPTER SEVEN

ZUYUATHAN: SECRET KNOWLEDGE AND THE MAINTENANCE OF POWER

I have noted that this book constitutes an elite history of a short time period at Classic Maya Palenque. The attempt has not been to retrieve life as it was experienced by all inhabitants of the ancient city. Rather, the goal has been to retrieve a noble perspective in order to gain a view of the world they aimed to construct both physically and intellectually.

Although it closes some doors, such an approach opens others. For example, we may now focus on the fact that the astronumerology recorded in the Triad Group was maintained in a highly private ritual space. This focus leads to the observation that in other places at Palenque, such as in Temple XIV, dates were recorded that anchored events in the mythic past, but the texts in which they were embedded did not contain the pieces of the puzzle necessary to reveal the astronomical knowledge lying underneath. A similar lack of astronumerological subtext also occurs at other cities, such as Naranjo and Tikal. At these cities, mythic dates were included in texts, but they were not cast in the types of puzzles that yielded telling mythological or sacred knowledge (Aldana 2001b:184–185; Naranjo Altar 1; Tikal Lintel).

If we accept the soundness of the recovery of astronumerology at Palenque and take into account the lack of corroborating practices at other Maya cities, we are forced to consider the possibility that through our mathematical portal, we have stumbled upon a single *ajaw*'s construct that really does not tell us much about royal society beyond his reign or outside of his kingdom. It is possible that Kan B'ahlam commissioned these inscriptions purely for his own intellectual amusement.

Floyd Lounsbury suggested that the mathematical puzzles were not meant for a great mortal audience; he proposed that they were intended solely for the gods. Since the texts were sequestered in temples far from virtually everyone's eyes, he reasoned, and since they took some work to find and then solve, perhaps they were not meant for human minds but for appreciation by the divine (Schele and Mathews 1991). This interpretation is not so farfetched, as it finds cross-cultural parallel in the Gothic cathedrals of Medieval Europe. At Notre Dame, for example, the highest quality stained-glass windows were placed at the very top in locations inaccessible to mortal visitors (Gingerich, personal communication 1997). This placement was intentional as they were meant only for examination by the Christian god.

Lounsbury's hypothesis is therefore perfectly consistent with the interpretation we have reconstructed so far considering the various levels on which the message of Re-Creation was intended to operate. We have already seen separate but consistent messages for commoners and nobility. At the textual level, we are intercepting a message that was only available to those who could enter the sacred temples of the Triad Group: the *ajawtahk*, possibly their families, and the gods who "owned" the temples. The riddles were appropriately reserved only for the properly initiated.

We have also seen in the last two chapters that K'an Joy Chitam, Kan B'ahlam's brother, picked up the same overall metaphor for his artistic patronage, but this similarity does not specify anything about his interest in the 819-day count. Here, then, we will step back to consider the place of astronumerology in the social world of the ancient Maya nobility. In doing so, we will find resonance with a practice maintained by Maya people well into the sixteenth century that perpetuates a "secret knowledge" available only to select nobility.

Key here is the recognition that a structure just to the south of the Triad Group contains evidence for an astronumerology maintained beyond Kan B'ahlam's reign. Therein, Ahkal Mo' Naab', the twelfth ruler of Palenque and successor to Kan B'ahlam's brother, commissioned a smaller temple some thirty years after the construction of Kan B'ahlam's Triad Group. This temple housed a large rectangular altar.[1] On the sides of the altar, Ahkal Mo' Naab' commissioned images of himself and his court framed by a series of texts. Following the format of the inscriptions of the Triad Group, these texts recorded mythological events juxtaposed with historical events. This format proved amenable to astronumerology, and in fact here again do we find it in substantial amounts. Before we tackle the numerology, though, we should review a few of this twelfth ruler's credentials.

AFTER RE-CREATION

Kan B'ahlam II's reign was quite successful, and he was able to prevent attacks on Palenque while he served as *ajaw* (Grube 1996). K'an Joy Chitam, however, was not so lucky. His reign started off well and he had the opportunity to commission Temple XIV. Janaab' Pakal's second son, who took the throne on 9.13.10.6.8 5 Lamat 6 Xul, held it for only nine years though before meeting military defeat. Perhaps seeking revenge for Kan B'ahlam's early battle, the ruler of Tonina attacked Palenque and captured K'an Joy Chitam on 9.13.19.13.3 13 Ak'bal 16 Yax (Martin and Grube 2000:171, 183). Afterward Palenque fell on dark times for a period of about ten years.

Fortunately for the Palenque citizenry, a grandson of Janaab' Pakal — though not a child of either Kan B'ahlam or K'an Joy Chitam — successfully took over the highest office in the land (Martin and Grube

2000:172). Ahkal Mo' Naab' acceded to the throne and commissioned a temple to the west of Kan B'ahlam's Triad Group—the recently excavated Temple XIX. From this structure, archaeologists have recovered the abovementioned altar. And it is here that we find that astronumerology was not restricted to the recreation of a single ruler's tenure.

Ahkal Mo' Naab's altar was carved on all four vertical sides. In the two main scenes, the ruler is portrayed flanked by members of his royal court. The interesting scene for us is the one in which Ahkal Mo' Naab' is carrying a rope bundle. Stuart (2000b) has connected the event recorded to a pre-accession ritual evidenced elsewhere at Palenque, but our interest here concerns the text framing the scene and not the event itself.

The text begins with the accession in ancient times of the first GI and continues with the hieroglyphic record of the myth referenced in Chapter 3. Here, we read of the "chopping" (*ch'ak u b'aah*) of the Celestial Dragon, officiated by GI$_{father}$.

1 Etz'nab 6 Yax k'in he chops the body of the [Black Hole] Celestial Dragon, the Tz'ibal Celestial Dragon. . . . He drilled fire. He formed it. It is officiated by GI$_{father}$.

This text provides a number of interesting points. First, the accession record for GI$_{father}$ opening the inscription makes clear that Lounsbury's reconstruction of GI$_{father}$'s deer hoof event must be in error. As we saw in Chapter 1, Lounsbury's reconstruction required that GI$_{father}$ be born on 12.19.11.13.0, but here GI$_{father}$ accedes over 180 years before then. Clearly, therefore, the deer hoof event belongs to Ix Muwaan Mat as argued in Chapter 5. Second, the inscription records the formation of the cosmos in the presence of GI$_{father}$ after the Celestial Dragon was chopped. Moving from mythic to historic times, the rest of the text jumps forward over 3,000 years to capture Ahkal Mo' Naab's accession to the throne owned by the Celestial Dragon, who was chopped in the previous passage.

TABLE 7.1: Astronumerology in Temple XIX

Date 1	Date 2	Interval	Significant factors
–0.9.18.4.18	1.18.5.3.2	346,840	260, 116, 2,392
1.18.5.3.2	2.0.0.10.2	12,740	260, 364
2.0.0.10.2	9.14.10.4.2	1,112,280	260, 780, 2,392

It is his first k'altun. He takes the ajaw throne of the [Celestial Dragon] in the presence of GI$_{son}$, Unen K'awiil, and GIII.

It is within these passages that we confront an example of the astronumerology patronized by Ahkal Mo' Naab'. Here, two of the events that concern the Celestial Dragon were linked with a third event to form a legitimizing puzzle (see Table 7.1). The accession of the first GI was tied to the birth of the second GI by K'awiil (Mercury) and the Moon (2,392).[2] The birth of the second GI was connected to the recorded accession of Ix Muwaan Mat as we have already seen in GI's temple within the Triad Group. Next, though, Ix Muwaan Mat's accession was tied to Ahkal Mo' Naab's taking of the Celestial Dragon throne by Martian periods (780) and again the grand lunar period (2,392).

The first part of the puzzle is relatively straightforward if we recall the connection between Ix Muwaan Mat and the moon. Here, Ahkal Mo' Naab' connected the two GIs through the moon because she was the wife of one and the mother of the other. Both were also connected by K'awiil (Mercury, 116) since they both carried the blood of the ajawtahk. The next link was borrowed from Kan B'ahlam's numerology, and it set up the connection between Ahkal Mo' Naab' and the Creation-era "family." Through the numbers, Ix Muwaan Mat as the moon presided over Ahkal Mo' Naab's taking of the Celestial Dragon's throne; this relationship constitutes a numerological analogue to Temple XIV's description of the Moon Goddess passing the k'awiil to Kan B'ahlam.

The astronumerology of this relationship is also interesting since, unlike that of Kan B'ahlam, the astronumerology patronized by Ahkal Mo' Naab' was not flagged by incongruities in the 819-day count.

Although he still recorded an 819-day count with the Initial Series date, Ahkal Mo' Naab' used the "erroneous" 2.0.0.10.2 9 Ik' 0 Sak date recorded in GI's temple as the accession date of Ix Muwaan Mat for the base of his projection. This point is critical. Had Ahkal Mo' Naab' been uninitiated in the inscriptions of the Triad Group or had the original record really been a mistake, he would have used 2.1.0.14.2 9 Ik' 0 Yax—the date that fits other data in GI's inscriptions. Furthermore, the scribe used this date as the base for a projection implementing the approximation to the lunar synodic period recovered by Teeple in 1931, that is, 2,392 days or 81 moons. Ahkal Mo' Naab's astronumerology thus demonstrated a familiarity with the methods and results of Kan B'ahlam's esoteric language.

Ahkal Mo' Naab's work also provides new information regarding the identity of the mythological affiliate of Mars, which is not unequivocally determinable from the Triad Group texts.[3] If we appeal to the observational character of the planet, however, we find one very suggestive possibility. Looking to the night sky, we recognize that when considering synodic periods, Mars is the slowest of the planets, taking 780 days to complete a cycle.[4] Because of its relative orbit in the solar system, Mars can also be the brightest object in the night sky (with the exception of the moon, of course). Thus, Mars appears as the slowest yet most potent of the celestial bodies. As seen previously, when we consider that the mythological identities of the planets most likely originated in the qualitative rather than quantitative characters of the celestial bodies, Mars becomes a suitable celestial realization of Itzamnaaj.

During Postclassic and Postcontact times, Itzamnaaj was considered the first and greatest priest among the gods (Coe 2005:216; Schele and Miller 1986; Thompson 1960:11). He is also always depicted as being quite old. Both of these representations are consistent with an association with Mars. Corroboration possibly comes from the inclusion of Mars in Ahkal Mo' Naab's numerology, here associated with the text that describes GI_{father}'s accession to the *ajawlel* under Itzamnaaj's authority. This interpretation, keeping in mind our caveat of Chapter 2 that astronomical patterns themselves not be the main source of identifications, argues for a mythological identification of Mars and a coherence to Ahkal Mo' Naab's astronumerology.

There are other examples of astronumerological puzzles in the text of the altar, but these puzzles will remain until archaeologists have recovered more evidence concerning the political, scientific, and religious scenarios driving Ahkal Mo' Naab's royal interests. Here, though, we must address the one apparent incongruity between the tradition created by Kan B'ahlam and the version preserved in Ahkal Mo' Naab's inscription. Ahkal Mo' Naab' did not commission Temple XIX to fit into the same architectural category as the structures of the Triad Group, whose temples were dedicated to the gods and seemed to hold only private ritual functions. Temple XIX, on the other hand, is compartmentalized in a manner suggesting that it may have served a larger audience. Furthermore, the inscription's location on an altar implies that the text would have been visible to at least some members of the royal court — an audience greater than the one that had access to Kan B'ahlam's astronumerology.

The architecture of the room, though, presents one possibility to explain this problem. Namely, a number of postholes were uncovered during the latest excavation, the utility of which has gone undetected. These postholes were spaced strategically around the base of the altar. Assuming the inscription was intended only for a select few, we may argue conservatively that the postholes were meant to anchor a removable covering for the text or the altar itself. A curtain, for example, may have hung from a frame allowing for a "public" view of the imagery and a restricted view of the inscription. Such curtains are commonly represented in images of court scenes and seem to have been used extensively in House E of the Palace Complex (Robertson 1985a:36–40). Regardless, whether the texts were thusly maintained as "private" or if the circle of nobility with access to the text was larger here, the overall number of readers of the text would have remained quite small.

The important point here, however, is that with Ahkal Mo' Naab's addition to this form of knowledge, we are forced to recognize that astronumerology was not simply the frivolous entertainment of a single ruler but something shared by at least one of his successors. Ahkal Mo' Naab' and at least one of his scribes were sufficiently familiar with the esoteric knowledge in Kan B'ahlam's ritual inscriptions to have created new puzzles using the same methods.

If astronumerology was not an oddity of one ruler's esoterism but part of a ritual language restricted to members of the highest echelons of the nobility, it resonates with a tradition maintained into the Colonial period by the Yucatec Maya. This tradition we encounter in a manuscript known as the *Book of Chilam Balam of Chumayel*. Before treating the "language of Zuyua" found therein, however, we will review the context of this manuscript as it bears directly on the interpretation of astronumerology during the Classic period.

POSTCLASSIC AND COLONIAL MAYA AUTHORITY

During the sixteenth century, Maya priests in and around the major cities of northern Yucatán strove to preserve indigenous knowledge in the face of Christian persecution (Aldana 2001b:273–312; Collins 1977; Farriss 1984:286–300). Early within this period, many Maya priests or sons of priests took on the roles of the choirmasters (*maestros cantores*) within the new Christian churches being built in each pueblo (Collins 1977). The Franciscans taught these choirmasters to read and write in the Latin script so that they could in turn instruct their own communities in Christian songs and doctrine. As sons of indigenous nobility, however, the choirmasters were also learned in native traditions. One example of the intellectual mestizaje that resulted was contained in the *Books of Chilam Balam.*[5]

These books contain compendia of records initiated by a translation of a hieroglyphic codex into the Latin script and augmented by the many Maya choirmasters who kept the book over the ensuing generations (Collins 1977; Roys 1973). The earliest recorded material provides the modern reader with a window into Postclassic Yucatec Maya culture. Here do we encounter the prophecies of *k'atun* counts, including the foretelling of the Spaniards' coming. Here also do we confront a section known as the "Interrogation of the Chiefs."

Within this section we find a series of questions that appear rather "strange." As translated by David Bolles and Alejandra Bolles, the passage in question reads:

> The language and understanding of Zuyua for our lord the military governor. Here on the fourth day of the month of September in the

year 1628, the unusual Mayan language was composed so that it appeared written in the heaven known to the men whoever will see it in the written book of the Language and Understanding of Zuyua. It will be understood by the chiefs of the towns and the head chiefs, passed on to the mayors and aldermen.

Here is the Language of Zuyua. Thus will be the word, thus will be the interrogation of the head chiefs of the towns. . . . The examination which comes in the katun ends today. The time has arrived for the chiefs of the towns to be asked about their knowledge, if they know how the ruling men came, whether or not it is true that all come from lineages, whether it is said that they come from chiefs, from head chiefs whether they are from lineages of kings or lineages of captains; to this they speak the truth.

Riddles from the First List

1:1 Here is the first word which will be asked of them. They will be asked for his food. Earnestly will the head chief say to them; thus will be spoken to the captains: "Child, bring me the sun in my plate, carry it in your hand. A lance with a lofty cross is planted in the middle of its heart. There is a green jaguar seated on top, it is bleeding its blood." Zuyua Language is being understood. Here is what is being asked of them, that is a regal (large) fried egg. Here is the lance and the lofty cross which is stuck in its heart, that of which he speaks, it is the benediction. Here is the green jaguar seated on top, bleeding its blood, it is green chile, it is very hot. Zuyua language.

1:2 This is the second difficult word which will be asked, which will be told to them: that they go to take the heaven's brains so that the head chief can see how much there is of it. "I desire to see it, it has been a long time since I have seen it." It is graciously told to them. Here is the heaven's brains, it is copal resin. Zuyua language.

The text makes clear that only those of the lineage of chiefs will have the knowledge to pass the tests of Zuyua language. Moreover, such knowledge is not highly technical and does not require special training. Rather, it is held secret in order to restrict access to the leadership. As historian Nancy Farriss (1984:247) puts it, these were "riddles based on an esoteric knowledge that was handed down within the 'lineage of rulers' and which, like the pea under the princess's mattress, was considered an infallible test of royal or at least noble origins." The relevant point here is that even in the smaller cities and dynastic houses of the late Postclassic period, the nobility maintained relatively tight control over local governance. Rulers or chiefs could not be appointed unless they were able to pass a test of knowledge, yet that knowledge was accessible only to members of the noble families.

During the early Colonial period, this knowledge was maintained as the "language of Zuyua" (Roys 1967:192), a language with some interesting properties. In particular, from evidence recovered thus far, it seems to have been flexible enough to reflect the changing experiences of the Maya elite over time. Early on, for example, as demonstrated in Part IV of the *Popol Vuh*, Zuyua appears to reflect the Postclassic dominance of Central Mexico such that inclusions of Nahuatl words were common (D. Tedlock 1985). Indeed, the K'iche place of origin was called Tulan Zuyua, reflecting an elite interest in affiliation with Central Mexican Tula or Tollan. Later, as preserved in the *Books of Chilam Balam*, riddles incorporated references to animals brought over by Europeans. The point, therefore, was not necessarily to preserve a specific message but rather to preserve a specific community with access to power.

Herein do we notice a direct parallel to the astronumerology of Late Classic Palenque. In the 819-day count, Kan B'ahlam found a tool to ensure the intellectual aptitude, historical knowledge base, and appropriate bloodlines of his successors. Housed within the sweatbaths of the gods, the history of Kan B'ahlam's polity may be considered a great test. Subsequent rulers-elect would have to be well versed in the mechanics of the 819-day count. They also would have had to be alerted to the types of riddles possible with calendric manipulations. And finally, they would have to have known their city's history well enough to understand the meaning of the puzzles recovered.

Ahkal Mo' Naab', the successor to K'an Joy Chitam, appears to have been the first to go through and pass this test. That he did so is well attested by his adding to the corpus of astronumerology at Palenque in a very familiar manner several decades after it was invented.

CONCLUDING THOUGHTS

We are now in a position to see that the astronumerology of Palenque grew out of a grand vision. Not only was Kan B'ahlam attempting to re-create his kingdom in the eyes of the commoners and his noble colleagues, but Kan B'ahlam also sought to ensure that an understanding of that Re-Creation would be essential knowledge for any later pretenders to the throne. His vision would have to have been powerful enough to capture the effect his father had on the fate of the kingdom but also complex enough to intellectually challenge his successors.

It may appear a bit farfetched to attribute such a feat to one person and, indeed, we have seen that Kan B'ahlam appears to have been assisted by the *aj k'ujuntahk* Chak Chan and Mut and the sajal Yuhk Makab'te. On the other hand, the conceptualization of the project would not have been unreasonable considering the life that Kan B'ahlam led. As noted earlier, his father firmly guided the city until Kan B'ahlam was over forty-eight years old. During this time, Kan B'ahlam would have had ample opportunity to travel and meet with colleagues throughout the Maya world. His would have been a cosmopolitan lifestyle, with sufficient experiences to inspire such an ambitious project.[6] With a vision of Re-Creation in the back of his mind, he would have needed only a perceptive astronomer and a keen historian to realize this project.

The presence of these learned scholars in the maintenance of the astronumerological language speaks to a continuity with the tradition recovered from the *Books of Chilam Balam* and maintained by the Yucatec choirmasters. Of course we do not have to propose that the idea of a secret knowledge or a secret language was invented at Palenque or even that it was unique to the Maya. It may be that the tradition was used throughout Mesoamerica and accompanied the first writings of the Epi-Olmec or Zapotec.

As for a K'awiilil Zuyua, we have a clue as to how widespread it may have been within Classic Maya civilization. We can link the recording of the 819-day count in hieroglyphic inscriptions with the practice of using it within a specialized language. Then, the presence of the 819-day count in the inscriptions of a given Classic Maya city may well implicate their nobility as having maintained a form of K'awiilil Zuyua. Given this assumption, we have only four known cities whose inscriptions contain 819-day counts: Palenque, Yaxchilan, Quirigua, and Copán. Given the time span of its use at Palenque, we might then estimate conservatively that approximately fifteen rulers acceded through a test of K'awiilil Zuyua, perhaps instructed or assisted by another fifteen *aj k'ujuntahk*. Although this number represents a relatively small scientific community, it provides us with a window into what was very likely a much larger tradition of maintaining power among specific lineages in greater Mesoamerica.

From the standpoint of recovering such traditions, however, the Maya have become unique. In the *Books of Chilam Balam* and the texts of Palenque we have access to essentially private documents. There is no question that the content of the inscriptions from the Temple of Inscriptions and Triad Group differs from the more public texts carved into stelae in the plazas of other cities. This difference along with a unique historical context and a new perspective brought from the history of science permits us to retrieve not only a Maya application of astronomical knowledge but also the social function it held within Classic Maya culture. It is my hope that this work will serve to complicate considerations of politics, science, and religion in a way that respects the choices of and pressures on the individuals in Classic Maya communities.

NOTES

1. The altar is in the recently excavated Temple XIX.

2. The number 2,392 corresponds to the lunar formula recovered by John Teeple (see Chapter 3).

3. But see Aldana (2001b:56) for one speculation that corroborates the Mars affiliation here.

4. Naturally this observation is an artifact of the proximity of Mars with Earth in the solar system, but as far as observation is concerned, this characterization holds.

5. There were actually several of these books, each named after the town that kept them. There is enough redundancy among them that scholars have been led to believe that they came from the same source (Roys 1967).

6. Mary Miller (personal communication, 2002) shares this view of Kan B'ahlam's life, comparing it to that of Cosimo Medici during the European Renaissance (see also Robertson 1991:9–10).

EPILOGUE

As noted at the end of the last chapter, Kan B'ahlam II was able to patronize a calendric invention and convert it into a tool that served the state as a demonstration of the intellectual resources available to the ancient Maya *ajaw-tahk* in their quests for political legitimation. We have also seen that the project built with the 819-day count served in a much larger agenda. Partially, it preserved the memory of Janaab' Pakal's ritual recovery of the religious charter of Palenque. But the 819-day count also facilitated the preservation of a Nal-k'awiil-based Zuyua within an architectural group that brought Palenque aesthetically into the Maya fold.

Such treatment has demonstrated that the message contained a number of levels. Kan B'ahlam II constructed

197

messages for each audience composing his society: for the common-ers, Re-Creation was hewn of stone; for the nobility, Re-Creation was depicted in artwork; and for the would-be *ajawtahk*, Re-Creation uti-lized a mathematical re-creation to yield secret knowledge in the form of a series of puzzles. Having now solved several of these puzzles, we enter deeper into the intellectual world of the ancient Maya.

In the process of recognizing and solving some of these puzzles, though, we have also witnessed something about the history of science as a discipline. In particular, we have recognized here that it may be valuable to take into account the agency of science itself. Before defin-ing what an *agency of science* might mean, it is necessary to provide a definition of *science* as it is used in this work.

When considering premodern cultures, *science* generally has referred to areas of knowledge that maintain historical trajectories with bodies of contemporary "scientific" knowledge. Healing traditions, for exam-ple, can be considered pre-medical sciences, natural philosophy as pre-physical science, and even alchemy as early/pre-chemistry. For non-cMd cultures, then, *sciences* are those analogues to these pre-modern sciences. This definition is perfectly functional, but it is entirely teleo-logical. A more interesting alternative is to appeal to recent studies of modern science. In many of these studies, it is not the specific sub-ject matter that defines *science* but rather the approach (Biagioli 1999; Latour 1987). *Science* is thus defined by the combination of a commu-nity of practitioners, a common specialized language with a quantita-tive basis, a collectively maintained and produced repository of knowl-edge, and a collectively agreed upon quantifiable phenomenon (or set of phenomena) suitable for investigation. Subgroups — or the different modern sciences — may be defined by placing restrictions on one or more of these aspects. Notice that this definition is more liberal as it allows for practices that modern cMd culture does not typically rec-ognize as "science." The "pseudo-sciences," for instance, are no longer defined relative to some ideal or "true" science; rather, the validity or legitimacy of a science is left to be determined sociologically.

As soon as we introduce the qualification of quantification, though, we bring along the intellectual constraints of logic. Mathematics works by maintaining structured relationships among language elements. The structures themselves must be consistent regardless of referent.

The interesting part—the utility—comes from the variety of available structures. For example, a geometer and an algebraist can address the same kinematic problem but come away with different insights based on the structures peculiar to the sub-languages they use. In other words, within science, quantifying languages are localized.

By the same token, each local region of mathematics carries with it an idiosyncratic set of algorithms or "tricks" that facilitate application, such that along with the specialized quantitative language comes the social factor of training. Use of a specialized language requires the adoption of methodological conventions. As the apprentice works through various training "problems," she acquires mental habits in the application of the language. These habits eventually constitute a "structuring structure" (Bourdieu 1995) particular to the local mathematical language being used. This "scientific habitus," then, guides the scientist as she approaches new problems. It is this process of guidance by the language itself that I refer to as the *agency of science*. In science, discovery and creation are essentially identical, and they are in part the product of the scientist's attention to the hints provided by the languages in which she works.

Kan B'ahlam Chak Chan, Mut, and Yuhk Makab'te took part in the science maintained by the Maya nobility utilizing the 819-day count to investigate the relationship between celestial bodies and historical figures and produce ritual texts. The sixteenth-century Maya nobility would have had a specific name associated with this science: Zuyua. As we saw in the last chapter, the size of the K'awiilil Zuyua community during the Classic period appears to have included around fifteen *ajawtahk* and so possibly thirty contributing scholars.

In the history of Late Classic Palenque, we recognize an agency of mathematics within Kan B'ahlam's political agenda. Here an astronomer followed a suggestion generated by the numerology tying together the individual periods of the planets to discover/create a construct that would bring them all together. This construct became a new tool, the 819-day count, which in turn perpetuated its own scientific habitus. Thus, we have seen vestiges of the agency of science in the texts of Kan B'ahlam's Triad Group.

We have seen, for instance, that Zuyua scientists leaned on the ability of the 819-day count to capture Saturn's and Jupiter's periods in order to place an ambiguous event in K'uk' B'ahlam's life in a historical-astronomical-political space. This placement led to an "error" according to modern epigraphers' readings of these hieroglyphic texts; but with an understanding informed by the approach to the construction of these texts, we see a window into a concerted effort guided by *ajaw,* astronomer, historian, and the 819-day count itself.

Attributing agency to science may seem odd when considering twentieth-century genetics or particle physics, but for the Maya it may have been very sensible. If we look closely, we see within the astronumerological puzzles, for example, a philosophy of time vastly different from that subscribed to east of the Atlantic. This content leads us to the long-recognized but little-treated fact that from the Maya perspective, the mathematics of time existed in a different language from other forms of mathematics (Aldana 2003a). Specifically, the numbers that represented time periods were not reducible to pure symbols but retained personality along with computational functionality. Such a concept is plain to all eyes in Kan B'ahlam's own inscriptions. In the Triad Group tablets, period coefficients in the Initial Series Long Count dates were represented by human (or humanlike) faces (see Figures 4.1, 6.1, 6.3). The beginning of a month in the *haab'* was not denoted by zero or one but was considered with animate agency. Each new month was registered as the seating of that month into office.

This conceptualization of time was not unique to the intelligentsia of Palenque. At Copán and Quirigua, cities where we also find this 819-day count, a number of inscriptions reveal the same perspective. Just as with K'an Joy Chitam's Palace Tablet, the example shown in Figure E.1 gives a complete Maya date represented as living entities interacting with one another. The most straightforward to interpret is the first, wherein the personified number carries the period—the *bak'tun* bird—with a tumpline strapped to his forehead.[1] In this image, the *bak'tun* becomes the burden of the coefficient, and the scribe captured this relationship in his inscription.

In looking to the sky and using their calendrical mathematics, then, Maya astronomers sought foremost a meter counted out by the beings wandering about in the sky. In contrast to those of his cross-Atlantic counterparts, Kan B'ahlam's universe and mathematics were populated by personalities about whom the deepest knowledge attainable would

FIGURE E.1: *Full-figure hieroglyphic date from Copán Stela D*

be that pertaining to negotiation. There was no need to seek an underlying language (mathematical or otherwise) of the spiritual; it was already known. Theology was politics. Certainly mathematical characterization of a god would be useful in dealing with that god, but equally certain was that not all deities could be characterized by mathematics. The lack of universality ascribed to mathematics thus made a difference. Epistemologically, mathematics did not contribute a more fundamental form of knowledge about the universe because personalities determined the workings of the cosmos, not mechanical regularity.

Viewed in this light, an attribution of agency to Maya mathematics does not appear unreasonable. Time was the product of a negotiation among a supernatural society, and the language used to describe it and discourse with its members started with the basic parts of Maya calendrics (the Long Count, the *chol qiij,* and the *haab'*) and was further elaborated at Palenque using the 819-day count.

With this perspective, the deep value in K'inich Kan B'ahlam's 819-day count is obvious. Just as K'awiil opened oracular portals to royal ancestors, so did the count perform an oracular function on Palenque's history. Through it, the *aj k'ujuntahk* of Palenque were able to reconstruct their own sacred history. For this specific case, the agency of science may be considered a conceptual translation of the agency of K'awiil himself. Namely, K'awiil was the entity who made it possible for the dynasty to function in its sacred role—K'awiil was the essence of royal blood. The 819-day count—the mathematics behind the count—made the computations possible but at the same time constrained the possible outcomes via its associated scientific habitus. Modern scholarship might try to see the count as a computationally efficient algorithm; but ancient scholars may well have seen it as an oracular tool revealing the sacred history of a living Time.

An acceptance of the agency of mathematics and the agency of science, then, might allow for new perspectives on histories of science in other cultures.[2] Scholars might then grapple with the structures of scientific languages and how they, along with sociological, historical, and environmental influences, have suggested novel approaches to old problems. In doing so, they might develop profound insights into the relationship between the researcher and the researched. They might just as well revel in the idea that they may be viewing "science" in the same way that Kan B'ahlam once did.

NOTES

1. The tumpline constituted the primary means by which Maya commoners carried bundles of firewood or other heavy objects.

2. To some extent, this result is what we see in modern scientific textbooks. Herein, the science seems to move by itself in order to train the novitiate—the individuals and histories behind the science are regarded as tangential. The recognition of the agency of science, then, avoids characterization as a banal hypothesis when we consider that such a portrayal has precedents.

GLOSSARY

aj tz'iib. Person of the writing/painting

ajaw. Lord, ruler; plural is *ajawtahk.* See also *ajawlel*

ajawlel. Rulership

aj k'in. Keeper of the ritual calendar and its various uses (also spelled *ah kin*)

aj k'ujuun. Title for a learned member of the royal court; may translate as "worshipper"

astronumerology. A mathematically based discourse utilizing astronomical periods to add layers of meaning to the dates of a historical text

b'ahlam. Jaguar

bak'tun. Period of 144,000 days, or 20 *k'atuns*

ch'ajom. Person who offers incense

ch'ak. To chop

ch'en. Cenote, well, cave

chak. Red; great

Chak Ek'. Literally, "red/great star"; the name for Venus in the Dresden Codex and at Copán Structure 10L-11

chan. Sky

chitin. Oven

chol qiij. Ritual count of 260 days

chumtun. Literally "stone seating," but since *tun* was also used to refer to a period of time, *chumtuns* occur at the end of any *tun, k'atun,* and *bak'tun;* an event required of a *k'ujul ajaw* in the maintenance of the polity's ritual life. See also *k'altun*

ek'. Star, celestial object

ek'emey. To descend

El Mirador. Archaeological site name for a large Preclassic polity, apparently associated with Kalak'mul during the Early Classic

GI, GII, GIII. Original designations for the Palenque Triad; GII has now been read as Unen K'awiil

haab'. Tropical year count of 365 days

Ik'. Wind; breath; also a day name in the *chol qiij*

ikatz. Charge, burden

itz'aat. A learned person

Itzamnaaj. Priestly deity; he authorized GI's pre-Creation accession to the *ajawlel*

jubuy. To descend; to go down

Junajpu. Literally "hunter"; name of the older Hero Twin in the *Popol Vuh*

Jun Junajpu. "One Hunter," name of the father of the Hero Twins (Junajpu and Xbalamke) in the *Popol Vuh*

Jun Kame. "One Death," name of one of the lords of the Underworld in the *Popol Vuh*

juntan. Precious one; signifier of the relationship between mother and child as well as between *ajaw* and deities

k'ak'. Fire

k'altun. Binding of the tun; synonym for chumtun

k'atun. Period of 7,200 days, or 20 tun

K'awiil. Personification of royal blood

K'awiilil Zuyua. Version of Zuyua produced at Palenque that used the 819-day count

k'in. Sun; day

k'inich. Brilliant; this term is often attached to a ruler's name but can also be integral to a ruler's name

k'uj. Deity

k'ujul ajaw. Ruling lord for a polity

k'uk'. Quetzal

kab'. Earth

kab'al. Earthly

kalab'tun. Period of 57,600,000 days, or 20 *pik'tuns*

kalomte. Occasionally accompanies the title of *k'ujul ajaw*; used most frequently at Tikal and Copán

Lakam Ja'. Literally, "Big Water"; toponym for the center of Palenque

milpa. Maize field

milpero. Person working a milpa

muwaan. Hawk

Paddler Gods. Deities who transported the Maize God to the place of his ritual dressing after his rebirth

pakal. Shield

pib naah. Sweatbath

pik'tun. Period of 2,880,000 days, or 20 *bak'tuns*

sajal. Literally, "feared"; usually used as a title for a member of the royal court; possible association with war

Sak Juun. Literally, "white paper"; refers to the headband tied onto a ruler at his/her accession

Teotihuacan. Metropolis in the Basin of Mexico that flourished slightly prior to the Classic Maya period

Tok'. Flint; stone used for spearheads

Tun. Literally, "stone"; period of 360 days, or 20 *winal*

tz'aak. To set in order; to place in sequence

tzak. To conjure

u kab'ijiiy. Under the authority of

Vukub Junajpu. "Seven Hunter," younger brother of Jun Junajpu and uncle to the Hero Twins in the *Popol Vuh*

Vukub Kame. "Seven Death," name of the Lord of the Underworld in the *Popol Vuh*

winal. Period of 20 days

Xbalamke. Name of the younger Hero Twin in the *Popol Vuh*

Xkik'. Name of the mother of the Hero Twins in the *Popol Vuh*

Zuyua. Ritual language used in Postclassic (through sixteenth century) Yucatán to restrict access to positions of authority

REFERENCES

Aldana, Gerardo

2001a   "K'in in the Hieroglyphic Record: Implications of a Pattern of Dates at Copán, Honduras." *Mesoweb,* www.mesoweb.com/features/aldana/implications.html.

2001b   Oracular Science: Uncertainty in the History of Maya Astronomy. Ph.D. Dissertation, History of Science Department, Harvard University.

2002   "Solar Stelae and a Venus Window: Science and Royal Personality in Late Classic Copán." *Archaeoastronomy Supplement to the Journal for the History of Astronomy* 27(xxxiii):S30–S50.

2003a   "Ancient Communities of Time." In *Religion and American Cultures: An Encyclopedia of Traditions, Diversity, and Popular Expressions,* ed. Gary Laderman and Luis León, 2:599–601. ABC-CLIO, Santa Barbara.

2003b   "K'uk'ulkan at Mayapán: Venus and Postclassic Maya Statecraft," *Journal for the History of Astronomy* 24:33–51.

2004a   "El trabajo del alma de Janahb Pakal: La cuenta de 819 días y la politica de Kan Balam." In *Culto Funerario en la Sociedad Maya: Memoria de la Cuarta Mesa Redonda de Palenque,* Rafael Cobos, 283–307. INAH, Mexico.

2004b   "Lunar Alliances: Conflicting Classic Maya Hegemonies." Paper given at the 7th Oxford Conference on Archaeoastronomy and Astronomy in Culture. Flagstaff, AZ.

2005a   "Agency and the 'Star War' Glyph: An Historical Reassessment of Classic Maya Astrology and Warfare." *Ancient Mesoamerica* 16 (2): 305–320.

2005b   "Cosmology: Indigenous North and Central American Cosmologies." In *Encyclopedia of Religion,* 2nd ed., vol. 3, ed. Lindsay Jones. Macmillan Reference USA, Detroit.

2006a   "Lunar Alliances: Conflicting Classic Maya Hegemonies." In *Proceedings of the VIIth Oxford Conference on Archaeoastronomy and Astronomy in Culture.* Arizona State Museum, Tucson.

2006b   "Violence against Indigenous People." In *Encyclopedia of Race and Racism.* Macmillan, New York.

Aldana, Gerardo, Nathan Henne, and Amara Solari

n.d.   "The World Embodied: Celestial Dragon Imagery and Violence in Maya Creation Accounts." Manuscript in possession of the authors.

Anderson, Neal, and Moises Morales

1981   "Solstitial Alignments of the Temple of Inscriptions at Palenque." *Archaeoastronomy Bulletin* 4(3):30–33

Andrews, E. Wyllys, IV

1938   "Glyphs Z and Y of the Maya Supplementary Series." *American Antiquity* 4:30–35.

Ardren, Traci

2002   *Ancient Maya Women.* AltaMira Press, Walnut Creek, CA.

Arellano Hernández, Alfonso

1995   "El Monstruo de la Tierra: Una Revisión." *Religión y Sociedad en el Area Maya.* Publicaciones de la S.E.E.M. Núm. 3, Mexico City.

Aveni, Anthony

1980   *Skywatchers of Ancient Mexico.* University of Texas Press, Austin.

1992   "Nobody asked, but I couldn't resist: A response to Keith Kintigh on archaeoastronomy and archaeology." *Archaeoastronomy and Ethnoastronomy News* 6(1):4.

2001   *Skywatchers: A Revised and Updated Version of Skywatchers of Ancient Mexico.* University of Texas Press, Austin.

Aveni, Anthony, and Horst Hartung

1986   "Uaxactun, Guatemala, Group E and Similar Assemblages: An Archaeoastronomical Reconsideration." In "Maya City Planning and the Calendar," *Transactions of the American Philosophical Society* 76:7 (1986):441–461.

Aveni, Anthony, Horst Hartung, and J. Charles Kelley

1982   "Alta Vista (Chalchihuites): Astronomical Implications of a Mesoamerican Ceremonial Outpost at the Tropic of Cancer." *American Antiquity* 47:316–335.

Aveni, Anthony, and Lorren Hotaling

1994   "Monumental Inscriptions and the Observational Basis of Maya Planetary Astronomy." *Archaeoastronomy* 19/*JHA* 25:S21–S54.

Barrera Vásquez, Alfredo

1995   *Diccionario Maya, Terceda Edición.* Editorial Porrúa, S. A., México D.F.

Baudez, Claude F.

1996   "Cross group at Palenque." In *Eighth Palenque Round Table, 1993,* ed. Martha J. Macri and Jan McHargue, 121–128. Pre-Columbian Art Research Institute, San Francisco.

Berlin, Heinrich

1958   "El glifo 'emblema' en las inscripciones Mayas." *Journal de la Société des Américanistes* 47:111–119.

Biagioli, Mario (editor)

1999   *The Science Studies Reader.* New York, Routledge.

Boone, Elizabeth Hill

1998   "Pictorial Documents and Visual Thinking in Postconquest Mexico." In *Native Traditions in the Postconquest World,* ed. Elizabeth H. Boone and Tom Cummins, 149–199. Dumbarton Oaks, Washington, DC.

2000   *Stories in Red and Black: Pictorial Histories of the Aztecs and Mixtecs.* University of Texas Press, Austin.

Boot, Erik

    2002   "The Dos Pilas–Tikal Wars from the Perspective of Dos Pilas HS4." http://www.mesoweb.com.

Bourdieu, Pierre

    1977   *Outline of a Theory of Practice.* Trans. Richard Nice. Cambridge University Press, Cambridge, UK.

    1995   "Structure, *Habitus*, Practices." In *Rethinking the Subject: An Anthology of Contemporary European Social Thought,* ed. James D. Faubion, 31–45. Westview Press, Boulder.

Bourdieu, Pierre, and Loïc Wacquant

    1992   *An Invitation to Reflexive Sociology.* University of Chicago Press, Chicago.

Braswell, Geoffrey

    2003   *The Maya and Teotihuacan: Reinterpreting Early Classic Interaction.* University of Texas Press, Austin.

Bricker, Harvey M., Anthony F. Aveni, and Victoria R. Bricker

    2001   "Ancient Maya Documents Concerning the Movements of Mars." *Proceedings of the National Academy of Sciences* 98(4):2107–2110.

Brinton, Daniel G.

    1890   Ancient Nahuatl Poetry: Containing the Nahuatl Text of XXVII Ancient Mexican Poems with a Translation, Introduction, Notes, and Vocabulary. Dumbarton Oaks, Library of Aboriginal American Literature, No. 7, Philadelphia.

Brotherston, Gordon

    1995   *Painted Books from Mexico: Codices in UK Collections and the World They Represent.* British Museum Press, London.

Calderón, Hector

    1966   *La ciencia matematica de los Mayas.* Editorial Orion, México D.F.

Calhoun, Craig, Edward LiPuma, and Moishe Postone (editors)

    1993   *Bourdieu: Critical Perspectives.* Polity Press, Cambridge, UK.

Carlson, John B.

    1976   "Astronomical Investigations and Site Orientation Influences at Palenque." In *Art, Iconography and Dynastic History of Palenque,* ed. Merle Greene Robertson, 3:107–122. PARI, Pebble Beach, CA.

    1977   "Copan Altar Q: The Maya Astronomical Congress of A.D. 763?" In *Native American Astronomy,* ed. Anthony F. Aveni, 100–109. University of Texas Press, Austin.

1981   "Numerology and the Astronomy of the Maya." In *Archaeoastronomy in the Americas: Ballena Press Anthropological Papers*, ed. Ray A. Williamson, 22:205–213.

1993   "Venus Regulated Warfare and Ritual Sacrifice in Mesoamerica." In *Astronomies and Cultures*, ed. Clive Ruggles and Nicholas Saunders, 202–252. University Press of Colorado, Boulder.

Chakrabarty, Dipesh

1992   "Postcoloniality and the Artifacts of History: Who Speaks for 'Indian' Pasts?" *Representations* 37(Winter):1–26.

Chase, Diane

1985   "Between Earth and Sky: Idols, Images, and Postclassic Cosmology." In *Fifth Palenque Round Table, 1983*, ed. Merle Greene Robertson and Virginia M. Fields, 223–233. Pre-Columbian Art Research Institute, San Francisco.

Chase, Diane Z., and Arlen F. Chase (editors)

1992   *Mesoamerican Elites: An Archaeological Assessment*. University of Oklahoma Press, Norman.

Ciudad Real, Antonio de

1873   *Relación breve y verdadera de algunas cosas de las muchas que sucedieron al padre fray Alonso Ponce en las provincias de la Nueva España, siendo comisario general de aquellas partes. Trátanse algunas particularidudes de aquella tierra, y dícese su ida á ella y vuelta á España, con algo de lo que en el viaje le aconteció hasta volver á su provincia de Castilla. Escrita por dos religiosos, sus compañeros, el uno de los cuales le acompaño desde España á México, y el otro en todos los demás caminos que hizo y trabajos que pasó*. Impresa de la Viuda de Calero, Madrid.

Clendinnen, Inga

1987   *Ambivalent Conquests: Maya and Spaniard in Yucatan, 1517–1570*. Cambridge University Press, Cambridge, UK.

Clifford, James

1988   *The Predicament of Culture: Twentieth-Century Ethnography, Literature, and Art*. Harvard University Press, Cambridge, MA.

Closs, Michael

1994   "A Glyph for Venus as Evening Star." In *Seventh Palenque Round Table, 1989*, ed. Merle Greene Robertson, 229–236. Pre-Columbian Art Research Institute, San Francisco.

Closs, Michael P., Anthony F. Aveni, and Bruce Crowley
  1984 "The Planet Venus and Temple 22 at Copan." *Indiana: Gedenkschrift Gerdt Kutscher Teil* 1.

Coe, Michael
  1992 *Breaking the Maya Code.* Thames and Hudson, London.
  1993 *The Maya.* Thames and Hudson, London.
  1999 *The Maya.* 6th ed. Thames and Hudson, London.
  2005 *The Maya,* 7th ed. Thames & Hudson, New York.

Coe, Michael D., and Justin Kerr
  1998 *The Art of the Maya Scribe.* Harry N. Abrams, New York.

Coe, Michael D., and Mark Van Stone
  2001 *Reading the Maya Glyphs.* Thames & Hudson, New York.

Coggins, Clemency Chase
  1975 Painting and Drawing Styles at Tikal: An Historical and Icono-graphic Reconstruction. Ph.D. Dissertation, Harvard University, Cambridge, MA.
  1983 "An Instrument of Expansion: Monte Alban, Teotihucán, and Tikal." In *Highland-Lowland Interaction in Mesoamerica: Interdisci-plinary Approaches,* ed. Arthur G. Miller, 49–68. Dumbarton Oaks Research Library and Collection, Washington, D.C.
  1993 "Age of Teotihuacan and Its Mission Abroad." In *Teotihuacan: Art from the City of the Gods,* ed. Kathleen Berrin and Esther Pasztory, 140–155. Thames and Hudson, New York.

Collins, Anne
  1977 "The Maestros Cantores in Yucatan." In *Anthropology and History in Yucatan,* ed. Grant D. Jones, 233–247. University of Texas Press, Austin.

Cowgill, George
  1993 "What We Still Don't Know about Teotihuacan." In *Teotihuacan: Art from the City of the Gods,* ed. Kathleen Berrin and Esther Pasz-tory, 116–125. Thames and Hudson, New York.

Culbert, T. Patrick
  1991 "Maya Political History and Elite Interaction: A Summary View." In *Classic Maya Political History: Hieroglyphic and Archaeological Evidence,* ed. T. Patrick Culbert, 311–346. Cambridge University Press, Cambridge, UK.

Daston, Lorraine, and Katherine Park
  1998   *Wonder and the Order of Nature, 1150–1750*. Zone Books, New York.

De Jonghe, Edouard
  1905   "Histoyre du Mechique." *Journal de la Société des Américanistes* 2: 1–45.

de la Parra, Francisco
  1547   Archivo General de Indias, AHN/DIVERSOS, 23, Doc. 8.

Derrida, Jacques
  1997   *Of Grammatology*. John Hopkins University Press, Baltimore.

Duret, Claude
  1613   *Thresor de l'histoire des langues de cest univers: Contenant les origines, beautés, perfections, decadences, mutations, changemens, conversions et ruines des langues hebraique, chananeenne, samaritaine . . .* Imprimé par M. Berjon pour la Societé caldoriene, Cologny (Microfiche. France Expansion, Paris, 1973).

Dütting, Dieter
  1985   "Lunar Periods and the Quest for Rebirth in the Mayan Hieroglyphic Inscriptions." *Estudios de Cultura Maya* 16:113–147.

Dütting, Dieter, and Anthony F. Aveni
  1982   "The 2 Cib 14 Mol Event in the Palenque Inscriptions." *Zeitschrift für Ethnologie* 107:233–258.

Erickson, Martin J.
  1996   *Introduction to Combinatorics*. John Wiley & Sons, New York.

Farriss, Nancy
  1984   *Maya Society Under Colonial Rule: The Collective Enterprise of Survival*. Princeton University Press, Princeton, NJ.

Fash, Barbara, William Fash, Sheree Lane, Rudy Larios, Linda Schele, Jeffrey Stomper, and David Stuart
  1992   "Investigations of a Classic Maya Council House at Copán, Honduras." *Journal of Field Archaeology* 19(4):419–442.

Fash, William
  1991   *Scribes, Warriors, and Kings: The City of Copán and the Ancient Maya*. Thames and Hudson, London.

Fleck, Ludwig
  1981   *Genesis and Development of a Scientific Fact*. University of Chicago Press, Chicago.

Folan, William J., Joyce Marcus, Sophia Pincemin, María del Rosario Domín-
guez Carrasco, Laraine Fletcher, and Abel Morales López
    1995   "Calakmul: New Data from an Ancient Maya Capital in Campeche,
            Mexico." *Latin American Antiquity* 6(4):310–334.

Förstemann, Ernst Wilhelm
    1906   *Commentary on the Dresden Codex,* trans. Selma Wesselheoft and
            A. M. Parker. Reprint of English translation. Aegean Park Press,
            Laguna Hills, CA. Originally published as *Commentary on the
            Maya Manuscript in the Royal Public Library of Dresden.* Papers of
            the Peabody Museum of American Archaeology and Ethnology,
            Harvard University, 4:2, Peabody Museum of American Archae-
            ology and Ethnology, Cambridge, MA.

Fowler, Bridget
    1997   *Pierre Bourdieu and Cultural Theory: Critical Investigations.* Sage Pub-
            lications, London.

Freidel, David, Linda Schele, and Joy Parker
    1993   *Maya Cosmos: Three Thousand Years on the Shaman's Path.* William
            Morrow, New York.

Furst, Peter T.
    1974   "Morning Glory and Mother Goddess at Tepantitla, Teotihuacan:
            Iconography and Analogy in Pre-Columbian Art." In *Mesoamerican
            Archaeology: New Approaches,* ed. Norman Hammond, 187–215.
            University of Texas Press, Austin.

Galison, Peter
    1997   *Image and Logic: A Material Culture of Microphysics.* University of
            Chicago Press, Chicago.

Gillespie, Susan D.
    2001   "Agency, Personhood, and Mortuary Ritual: A Case Study for the
            Ancient Maya." *Journal of Anthropological Archaeology* 20:73–112.

Gillespie, Susan D., and Rosemary A. Joyce
    1998   "Deity Relationships in Mesoamerican Cosmologies: The Case of
            the Maya God L." *Ancient Mesoamerica* 9(2):279–296.

Griffin, Gillett G.
    1974   "Early Travelers to Palenque." In *Primera Mesa Redonda de Palen-
            que,* ed. Merle Greene Robertson, 1:9–34. Robert Louis Stevenson
            School, Pebble Beach, CA.

Grube, Nikolai

1996   "Palenque in the Maya World." In *Eighth Palenque Round Table, 1993*, ed. Martha J. Macri and Jan McHargue, 1–13. Pre-Columbian Art Research Institute, San Francisco.

Hall, Robert L.

1998   "A Comparison of Some North American and Mesoamerican Cosmologies and Their Ritual Expressions." In *Explorations in American Archaeology: Essays in Honor of Wesley R. Hurt*, ed. Mark G. Plew, 55–88. University Press of America, Lanham, MD.

Harner, Michael

1977   "The Ecological Basis for Aztec Sacrifice." *American Ethnologist* 4(1): 117–135.

Harrison, Peter D.

1999   *The Lords of Tikal: Rulers of an Ancient Maya City*. Thames & Hudson, London.

Hawkins, Gerald

1965   *Stonehenge Decoded*. Doubleday, Garden City, NY.

Houston, Stephen

1993   *Hieroglyphs and History at Dos Pilas: Dynastic Politics of the Classic Maya*. University of Texas Press, Austin.

1996   "Symbolic Sweatbaths of the Maya: Architectural Meaning in the Cross Group at Palenque, Mexico." *Latin American Antiquity* 7(2): 132–151.

Houston, Stephen, John Robertson, and David Stuart

2000   "The Language of Classic Maya Inscriptions." *Current Anthropology* 41(3):321–356.

Houston, Stephen, and David Stuart

1992   "On Maya Hieroglyphic Literacy." *Current Anthropology* 33(5):589–593.

1996   "Of Gods, Glyphs and Kings: Divinity and Rulership among the Classic Maya." *Antiquity* 70(268):289–312.

Houston, Stephen D., Oswaldo Chinchilla Mazariegos, and David S. Stuart

2000   *The Decipherment of Ancient Maya Writing*. University of Oklahoma Press, Norman.

Hunn, Eugene

1982   "Did the Aztecs Lack Potential Animal Domesticates?" *American Ethnologist* 9(3):578–579.

Inomata, Takeshi, and Stephen Houston (editors)

2001   *Royal Courts of the Ancient Maya.* Westview Press, Boulder.

Jackson, Sarah, and David Stuart

2001   "The *aj k'uhun* Title: Deciphering a Classic Maya Term of Rank." *Ancient Mesoamerica* 12(2):217–228.

Jones, Christopher

1991   "Cycles of Growth at Tikal." In *Classic Maya Political History: Hieroglyphic and Archaeological Evidence,* ed. T. Patrick Culbert, 102–127. Cambridge University Press, Cambridge, UK.

Jones, Grant D.

1998   *The Conquest of the Last Maya Kingdom.* Stanford University Press, Stanford, CA.

Justeson, John, and James Fox

1978   "A Mayan Planetary Observation." *UC Berkeley Archaeological Reports Facility, Department of Archaeology Contributions* 36:55–59.

Justeson, John, and Terrence Kaufman

1992   "Desciframiento de la escritura jeroglífica epi-Olmeca: Métodos y resultados." *Arqueología* 8:15–25.

1993   "A Decipherment of Epi-Olmec Hieroglyphic Writing." *Science* 259: 1703–1711.

Justeson, John S., and Peter Mathews

1983   "Seating of the Tun: Further Evidence Concerning a Late Preclassic Lowland Maya Stela Cult." *American Antiquity* 48(3):586–593.

Kelley, David H.

1980   "Astronomical Identities of Mesoamerican Gods." *Archaeoastronomy* 11(2):S1–S54.

1983   "The Maya Calendar Correlation Problem." In *Civilization in the Ancient Americas: Essays in the Honor of Gordon R. Willey,* ed. Richard Leventhal and Alan Kolata, 157–208. University of New Mexico Press, Albuquerque.

Kerr Maya vase database. www.famsi.org.

Kidder, Alfred V., Jesse D. Jennings, and Edwin M. Shook

1946   *Excavations at Kaminaljuyu, Guatemala.* Carnegie Institution of Washington, Publication 561, Washington, DC.

Kintigh, Keith

1992   "I Wasn't Going to Say Anything, but Since You Asked: Archaeoastronomy and Archaeology." *Archaeoastronomy and Ethnoastronomy News* 5(1):4

Klein, Cecelia F., Eulogio Guzmán, Elisa C. Mandell, and Maya Stanfield-Mazzi

2002   "The Role of Shamanism in Mesoamerican Art: A Reassessment." *Current Anthropology* 43(3):383–419.

Laporte, Juan Pedro, and Vilma Fialko

1995   "Reencuentro con Mundo Perdido, Tikal, Guatemala." *Ancient Mesoamerica* 6(1):41–94.

Latour, Bruno

1987   *Science in Action.* Harvard University Press, Cambridge, MA.

Linden, John H.

1986   "Glyph X of the Maya Lunar Series: An Eighteen-Month Lunar Synodic Calendar." *American Antiquity* 51(1):122–136.

1996   "The Deity Head Variants of Glyph C." In *Eighth Palenque Round Table, 1993,* ed. Martha J. Macri and Jan McHargue, 343–356. Pre-Columbian Art Research Institute, San Francisco.

Looper, Matthew

2003   *Lightning Warrior: Maya Art and Kingship at Quirigua.* University of Texas Press, Austin.

Lounsbury, Floyd

1976   "A Rationale for the Initial Date of the Temple of the Cross at Palenque." In *The Art, Iconography and Dynastic History of Palenque,* ed. Merle Greene Robertson, 3:211–224. Pre-Columbian Art Research Institute, Pebble Beach, CA.

1978   "Maya Numeration, Computation, and Calendrical Astronomy." *Dictionary of Scientific Biography,* ed. Charles Coulson Gillispie, 15:759–818. Charles Scribner's Sons, New York.

1980   "The Identities of the Mythological Figures in the Cross Group Inscriptions of Palenque." In *Fourth Palenque Round Table,* ed. Elizabeth P. Benson, 45–58. Pre-Columbian Art Research Institute, San Francisco.

1992   "Derivation of the Mayan-to-Julian Calendar Correlation from the Dresden Codex Venus Chronology." In *The Sky in Mayan Literature,* ed. Anthony F. Aveni, 184–206. Oxford University Press, New York.

Lyotard, Jean-Francois

1993   *The Postmodern Condition: A Report on Knowledge.* University of Minnesota Press, Minneapolis.

Macri, Martha, and Matthew Looper

2003   *Catalog of Maya Hieroglyphs.* University of Texas Press, Austin.

Maler, Teobert

1908   *Explorations in the Department of Petén, Guatemala, and Adjacent Region: Topoxte, Yaxha, Benque Viejo, Naranjo: Reports of Explorations for the Museum.* Memoirs of the Peabody Museum of American Archaeology and Ethnology, 4:2. Harvard University, Cambridge, MA.

Marcus, Joyce

1983   "Teotihuacán Visitors on Monte Albán Monuments and Murals." In *The Cloud People,* ed. Kent Flannery and Joyce Marcus, 175–181. Academic Press, New York.

1993   *Mesoamerican Writing Systems: Propaganda, Myth, and History in Four Ancient Civilizations.* Princeton University Press, Princeton, NJ.

Martin, Simon

1996   "Tikal's Star War Against Naranjo." In *Eighth Palenque Round Table, 1993,* ed. Martha J. Macri and Jan McHargue, 223–236. Pre-Columbian Art Research Institute, San Francisco.

Martin, Simon, and Nikolai Grube

1995   "Maya Superstates." *Archaeology* 48(6):41–45.

2000   *Chronicle of the Maya Kings and Queens: Deciphering the Dynasties of the Ancient Maya.* Thames & Hudson, London.

Mathews, Peter, and Gordon R. Willey

1991   "Prehistoric Polities of the Pasion Region: Hieroglyphic Texts and Their Archaeological Settings." In *Classic Maya Political History: Hieroglyphic and Archaeological Evidence,* ed. T. Patrick Culbert, 30–72. School of American Research Book. Cambridge University Press, Cambridge.

Maudslay, Alfred Percival

1974   *Biologia Centrali-Americana or, Contributions to the Knowledge of the*
[1889] *Fauna and Flora of Mexico and Central America.* Facsimile edition prepared and introduction written by Dr. Francis Robicsek. Milpatron Publishing Corp., New York.

1974   *Archæology.* Facsimile edition with introduction by Dr. Francis Robicsek. Milpatron Publishing Corp., New York.

McAnany, Patricia
  1995   *Living with the Ancestors: Kinship and Kingship in Ancient Maya Society.* University of Texas Press, Austin.

Mignolo, Walter D.
  2003   *The Darker Side of the Renaissance: Literacy, Territoriality, and Colonization.* University of Michigan Press, Ann Arbor.

Milbrath, Susan
  2002   "The Planet of Kings: Jupiter in Maya Cosmology." In *Heart of Creation: The Mesoamerican World and the Legacy of Linda Schele,* ed. Andrea Stone, 118–142. University of Alabama Press, Tuscaloosa.

Miller, Arthur
  1986   *Maya Rulers of Time: A Study of Architectural Sculpture at Tikal, Guatemala.* University Museum, Philadelphia.

Miller, Mary Ellen
  1999   *Maya Art and Architecture.* Thames and Hudson, New York.

Millon, René
  1993   "Place Where Time Began: An Archaeologists's View of What Happened in Teotihuacan History." In *Teotihuacan: Art from the City of the Gods,* ed. Kathleen Berrin and Esther Pasztory, 16–43. Thames and Hudson, New York.

Morley, Sylvanus
  1920   *The Inscriptions at Copán.* Carnegie Publication 219, Washington, DC.

Neugebauer, Otto
  1952   *The Exact Sciences in Antiquity.* Princeton University Press, Princeton, NJ.

Newsome, Elizabeth
  2001   *Trees of Paradise and Pillars of the World: The Serial Stela Cycle of "18-Rabbit-God K," King of Copan.* University of Texas Press, Austin.

Novick, Peter
  1988   *That Noble Dream: The "Objectivity Question" and the American Historical Profession.* Cambridge University Press, Cambridge, UK.

Ortiz de Montellano, Bernardo R.
  1978   "Aztec Cannibalism: An Ecological Necessity?" *Science* 200(4342): 611–617.

REFERENCES

Pasztory, Esther
1993   "Teotihuacan Unmasked: A View through Art in Teotihuacan." In *Art from the City of the Gods,* ed. Kathleen Berrin and Esther Pasztory, 44–63. Thames and Hudson, New York.

Paulos, John Allen
1988   *Innumeracy: Mathematical Illiteracy and Its Consequences.* Hill & Wang, New York.

Plank, Shannon
2003   "Monumental Maya Dwellings in the Hieroglyphic and Archaeological Records: A Cognitive-Anthropological Approach to Classic Maya Architecture." Ph.D. Dissertation, Boston University, MA.

Powell, Christopher
1998   "A New View on Maya Astronomy." M.A. Thesis, University of Texas, Austin.

Price, B. J.
1978   "Demystification, Enriddlement, and Aztec Cannibalism: A Materialist Rejoinder to Harner." *American Ethnologist* 5(1):98–115.

Proskouriakoff, Tatiana
1960   "Historical Implications of a Pattern of Dates at Piedras Negras, Guatemala." *American Antiquity* 25:454–475.
1993   *Maya History,* ed. Rosemary A. Joyce. Austin, University of Texas Press.

Proyecto Lingüístico Francisco Marroquín
1996   *Diccionario del Idioma Ch'orti'.* P.L.F.M. Antigua, Guatemala.

Rands, Robert L.
1974   "A Chronological Framework for Palenque." In *Primera Mesa Redonda de Palenque,* ed. Merle Greene Robertson, 1:35–41. Robert Louis Stevenson School, Pebble Beach, CA.

Reents-Budet, Dorie
1994   *Painting the Maya Universe: Royal Ceramics of the Classic Period.* Duke University Press, Durham, NC.

Restall, Matthew
1998   *Maya Conquistador.* Beacon Press, Boston.

Rice, Prudence M.
2004   *Maya Political Science: Time, Astronomy, and the Cosmos.* University of Texas Press, Austin.

Robbins, Derek

1991   *The Work of Pierre Bourdieu.* Open University Press, Buckingham, UK.

Robertson, Merle Greene

1983   *The Sculpture of Palenque.* Vol. 1: *The Temple of Inscriptions.* Princeton University Press, Princeton, NJ.

1985a   *The Sculpture of Palenque.* Vol. 2: *The Early Buildings of the Palace and the Wall Paintings.* Princeton University Press, Princeton, NJ.

1985b   *The Sculpture of Palenque.* Vol. 3: *The Late Buildings of the Palace.* Princeton University Press, Princeton, NJ.

1991   *The Sculpture of Palenque.* Vol. 4: *The Cross Group, the North Group, the Olvidado, and Other Pieces.* Princeton University Press, Princeton, NJ.

Roys, Ralph L.

1943   *The Indian Background to Colonial Yucatán.* Carnegie Institution of Washington, Washington, DC.

1967   *The Book of Chilam Balam of Chumayel.* University of Oklahoma Press, Norman.

1973   *The Book of Chilam Balam of Chumayel.* Rev. ed. University of Oklahoma Press, Norman.

Ruggles, Clive L.N.

1988   *Records in Stone: Papers in Memory of Alexander Thom.* Cambridge University Press, New York.

1999   *Astronomy in Prehistoric Britain and Ireland.* Yale University Press, New Haven, CT.

Sahagún, Bernardino de

1953   *General History of the Things of New Spain: Florentine Codex.* School of American Research 14:7, Santa Fe, NM.

Sandoval, Chela

2000   *Methodology of the Oppressed.* University of Minnesota Press, Minneapolis.

Satterthwaite, Linton

1951   "Moon Ages of the Maya Inscriptions: The Problem of Their Seven-Day Range of Deviation from Calculated Mean Ages." In *Civilizations of Ancient America: Selected Papers of the 29th International Congress of Americanists,* ed. Sol Tax, 1:142–154. Cooper Square Publishers, New York.

1959   "Early 'Uniformity' Maya Moon Numbers at Tikal and Elsewhere." *International Congress of Americanists* 2(33):200–210.

1965   "Calendrics of the Maya Lowlands." In *Handbook of Middle American Indians,* vol. 3, ed. Gordon Randolph Willey, 2:603–631. Archaeology of Southern Mesoamerica, Austin.

Schele, Linda

1981   "Sacred Site and World-View at Palenque." *Mesoamerican Sites and World-Views,* ed. Elizabeth P. Benson, 87–117. Dumbarton Oaks, Washington, DC.

1990   "Lounsbury's Contrived Numbers and Two 8 Eb Dates at Copán." In *Copan Note 81.* The Copan Mosaics Project, dir. William L. Fash and the Instituto Hondureño de Antropologia y Historia.

1991   "Venus in the Monuments of Smoke-Imix-God K and the Great Plaza." In *Copan Note 101.* The Copan Mosaics Project, dir. William L. Fash and the Instituto Hondureño de Antropologia y Historia.

1992   *Notebook for the XVIth Maya Hieroglyphic Workshop at Texas,* March 14–15. Institute of Latin American Studies, Austin.

Schele, Linda, and Barbara Fash

1991   "Venus and the Reign of Smoke-Monkey." In *Copan Note 100.* The Copan Mosaics Project, dir. William L. Fash and the Instituto Hondureño de Antropologia y Historia.

Schele, Linda, and David Freidel

1990   *A Forest of Kings: The Untold Story of the Ancient Maya.* William Morrow, New York.

Schele, Linda, and Nikolai Grube

1994   *Notebook for the 18th Maya Hieroglyphic Weekend at Texas. Tlaloc-Venus Warfare: The Peten Wars 8.17.0.0.0–9.15.13.0.0,* ed. Timothy Albright. Department of Art and Art History, College of Fine Arts, and the Institute of Latin American Studies, University of Texas at Austin.

Schele, Linda, Nikolai Grube, and Federico Fahsen

1992   "The Lunar Series in Classic Maya Inscriptions: New Observation and Interpretations." *Texas Notes on Precolumbian Art, Writing, and Culture,* No. 29. CHAAC, University of Texas, Austin.

Schele, Linda, and Rudi Larios

1991   "Some Venus Dates on the Hieroglyphic Stair at Copan." In *Copan Note 99.* The Copan Mosaics Project, dir. William L. Fash and the Instituto Hondureño de Antropologia y Historia.

Schele, Linda, and Peter Mathews

1991   *Notebook for the 15th Workshop on Maya Hieroglyphics at Texas.* March 9–10. Art Department, University of Texas, Austin.

1998   *The Code of Kings: The Language of Seven Sacred Maya Temples and Tombs.* Simon and Schuster, New York.

Schele, Linda, and Mary Miller

1986   *The Blood of Kings.* George Braziller, New York.

Schellhas, Paul

1904   "Representation of Deities of the Maya Manuscripts." In *Papers of the Peabody Museum of American Archaeology and Ethnology,* 4:1. Harvard University, Cambridge, MA.

Schlak, Arthur

1996   "Venus, Mercury, and the Sun: GI, GII, and GIII of the Palenque Triad." *RES* 29/30:180–202.

Shapin, Steven, and Simon Schaffer

1985   *Leviathan and the Air-Pump: Hobbes, Boyle, and the Experimental Life.* Princeton University Press, Princeton, NJ.

Smith, Linda Tuhiwai

1999   *De-Colonizing Methodology.* Zed Books, London.

Sprajc, Ivan

1996   *Venus, lluvia y maíz: Simbolismo y astronomía en la cosmovisión mesoamericana.* Colección Científica 318. Instituto Nacional de Antropología e Historia, México.

Stephens, John Lloyd

1996   *Incidents of Travel in Yucatan,* ed. Karl Ackerman. Smithsonian Institution Press, Washington, DC.

Stone, Andrea

1985   "Variety and Transformation in the Cosmic Monster Theme at Quirigua, Guatemala." In *Fifth Palenque Round Table,* ed. Merle Greene Robertson, 39–48. Pre-Columbian Art Research Institute, San Francisco.

Stuart, David

1995a   "Blood Symbolism in Maya Iconography." *Res* 7/8:6–20.

1995b   "A Study of Maya Inscriptions." Ph.D. Dissertation, Department of Archaeology, Vanderbilt University, Nashville, TN.

223

1996   "Kings of Stone: A Consideration of Stelae in Ancient Maya Ritual and Representation." *Res* 29/30:148–171.

1998   "'The Fire Enters this House': Architecture and Ritual in Classic Maya Texts." In *Function and Meaning in Classic Maya Architecture,* ed. Stephen D. Houston, 373–425. Dumbarton Oaks Research Library and Collection, Washington, DC.

2000a   "'The Arrival of Strangers': Teotihuacan and Tollan in Classic Maya History." In *Mesoamerica's Classic Heritage: From Teotihuacan to the Aztecs,* ed. Davíd Carrasco, Lindsay Jones, and Scott Sessions, 465–513. University Press of Colorado, Boulder.

2000b   "Ritual and History in the Stucco Inscription from Temple XIX at Palenque." *PARI Journal* l(1):1–7.

2003   "A Cosmological Throne at Palenque." In *Mesoweb,* www.mesoweb.com/stuart/notes/Throne.pdf.

Tambiah, Stanley Jeyaraja

1990   *Magic, Science, Religion, and the Scope of Rationality.* Cambridge University Press, Cambridge, UK.

Tate, Carolyn

1985   "Summer Solstice Ceremonies Performed by Bird Jaguar III of Yaxchilan, Chiapas, Mexico." *Estudios de Cultura Maya* 16:85–112.

1992   *Yaxchilan: The Design of a Maya Ceremonial City.* University of Texas Press, Austin.

Taube, Karl

1993   *Aztec and Maya Myths.* University of Texas Press, Austin.

Taussig, Michael

1987   *Shamanism, Colonialism, and the Wild Man: A Study in Terror and Healing.* University of Chicago Press, Chicago.

Tedlock, Barbara

1982   *Time and the Highland Maya.* University of New Mexico Press, Albuquerque.

Tedlock, Dennis

1992   "Math, Myth, and the Problem of Correlation in Mayan Books." In *The Sky in Maya Literature,* ed. Anthony F. Aveni, 247–273. Oxford University Press, Oxford, UK.

Tedlock, Dennis (translator)

1985   *Popol Vuh: The Definitive Edition of the Mayan Book of the Dawn of Life and the Glories of Gods and Kings.* Simon and Schuster, New York.

Teeple, John
    1931   *Maya Astronomy*. Carnegie Institution of Washington, Washington, DC.

Thom, Alexander S.
    1967   *Megalithic Sites in Britain*. Clarendon Press, Oxford.

Thompson, J.E.S.
    1943   "Maya Epigraphy: A Cycle of 819 Days." *Carnegie Institution of Washington Notes on Middle American Archaeology and Ethnology* 1:137–151.
    1960   *Maya Hieroglyphic Writing: An Introduction*. University of Oklahoma Press, Norman.
    1972   *A Commentary on the Dresden Codex: A Maya Hieroglyphic Book*. American Philosophical Society, Philadelphia.

Van der Waerden, Bartel L.
    1974   *Science Awakening II: The Birth of Astronomy*. Noordhoff, Leyden.

Velásquez, Primo Feliciano (translator)
    1975   *Códice Chimalpopoca: Traducción directa del náhuatl, segundo edición*. Universidad Nacional Autónoma de México, Instituto de Investigaciones Históricas, México D.F.

Villagutierre Soto-Mayor, Juan de
    1983   *History of the conquest of the province of the Itza: Subjugation and events of the Lacandon and other nations of uncivilized Indians in the lands from the kingdom of Guatemala to the provinces of Yucatan in North America*. Trans. Robert Wood. Labyrinthos, Culver City, CA.

Vogt, Evon
    1976   *Tortillas for the Gods: A Symbolic Analysis of Zinacanteco Rituals*. Harvard University Press, Cambridge, MA.

Watanabe, John M.
    1983   "In the World of the Sun: A Cognitive Model of Mayan Cosmology." *Man* n.s. 18(4):710–728.

Wells, Bryan, and Andreas Fuls
    2000   *The Correlation of the Modern Western and Ancient Maya Calendars*. ESRS (West), Monograph no. 6, Berlin.

Whorf, Benjamin
    1956   "An American Indian Model of the Universe." In *Language, Thought, and Reality: Selected Writings of Benjamin Lee Whorf*, ed. John B. Carroll, 57–64. Massachusetts Institute of Technology Press, Cambridge.

REFERENCES

Wichmann, Soren
   2004   *The Linguistics of Maya Writing.* University of Utah Press, Salt Lake City.

Zender, Mark
   2004   "A Study of the Classic Maya Priesthood." Ph.D. Dissertation, Department of Archaeology, University of Calgary, Canada.

INDEX

LaVergne, TN USA
30 October 2010
202882LV00004B/4/P